James N. Howbern
May 1970
U of M

Arthur Miller

Portrait of a Playwright

BENJAMIN NELSON

Arthur Miller

Portrait of a Playwright

DAVID McKAY COMPANY, INC.
NEW YORK

For Miriam, Sharon, Rachel, and
Jennifer—Blue Roses

ACKNOWLEDGEMENTS

I would like to thank the following publications and publishers for permission to reproduce extracts:

Ashley Famous Agency: *Focus* and *Situation Normal* by Arthur Miller

Citadel: *Arthur Miller: The Burning Glass* by Sheila Huftel

Commentary: 'Arthur Miller Out West' by Henry Popkin

The Cresset Press: From 'On Social Plays' *A View from the Bridge* (Copyright © 1955, 1957 by Arthur Miller)

The Emory University Quarterly: 'Arthur Miller and the Loss of Conscience' by William B. Dillingham

Encounter: 'A Conversation with Arthur Miller' by Kenneth Alsop

Esquire: 'The Creative Agony of Arthur Miller' by Allan Seager; 'Making *The Misfits* or Waiting for Monroe or Notes from Olympus' by Alice T. McIntyre; 'Bridge to a Savage World' by Arthur Miller

Estate of Robert Warshow: *Commentary* by Robert Warshow

Grove Press: *Arthur Miller* by Dennis Welland

Harper's: 'The Shadows of the Gods' and 'The State of the Theater' by Arthur Miller

Holiday: 'A Boy Grew In Brooklyn' by Arthur Miller (Copyright © 1955 by Curtis Publishing Company); 'The American Theater' by Arthur Miller (Copyright © 1955 by Curtis Publishing Company); 'University of Michigan' by Arthur Miller (Copyright © 1953 by Curtis Publishing Company)

Alfred A. Knopf, Inc.: *In Search of Theater* by Eric Bentley (Copyright © 1947, 1953, by Eric Bentley); *The Spirit of Tragedy* by Herbert J. Muller (Copyright © 1956 by Herbert J. Muller)

Look Magazine: by courtesy of the editors, 'Marilyn's New Life' by Jack Hamilton (Copyright © by Cowles Communications, Inc.)

The Nation: 'A Modest Proposal for Pacifying the Public Temper' by Arthur Miller

The New Republic: *After the Fall* reviewed by Robert Brustein; 'How Not to Produce a Film' by Walter Goodman (Copyright © 1955 by Harrison-Blaine of New Jersey, Inc.)

New York Herald Tribune Book Review: *After the Fall* reviewed by Richard Gilman

New York Post: *After the Fall* reviewed by Richard Watts

The New York Review of Books: 'Arthur Miller and the Fallacy of Profundity' by Philip Rahv

New York Times: 'Arthur Miller Ponders "The Price"' by Joan Barthel (Copyright © 1968 by The New York Times Company); 'Mr Miller Has a Change of Luck' by John K. Hutchens (Copyright © 1947–1964 by The New York Times Company); 'Tragedy and the Comman Man' by

CONTENTS

Introduction

In a recent review of two rather esoteric one-act plays by a prominent American dramatist, a fascinated but puzzled critic compared them momentarily with the dramas of Arthur Miller by contrasting their obfuscation to the lucidity of Miller's works. In an age of frantic experimentation and iconoclasm, the critic commented, one could always return to Miller's plays with a sense of certainty and reassurance.

The statement was intended neither to praise nor to denigrate. It was simply an observation that Miller's dramas have a sureness and solidarity that is unique in a period in the theater marked by uncertainty and flux. In the last two decades a veritable parade of playwrights has marched, strutted, danced, and crawled to oblivion, while Arthur Miller, stepping firmly and boldly, has remained on the high road of American drama. As time goes by, his plays continue to endure, many of them in fact gaining in strength and impact.

The purpose of this book is to examine and evaluate this impact by studying the theater of Arthur Miller in depth, observing it in the context of his life and times, and analyzing his relationship to the world to which he has addressed himself and which he has dramatized in a dozen plays.

A few years ago, in a prefatory note to a study of Tennessee Williams, I declined to pretend that I had written a definitive work, on the grounds that any such claim would be presumptuous in the light of a career that was still developing. With respect to the following study, this denial still holds. Since I began this project, two new Miller plays were produced, and this is the clearest deterrent to any definitive statement about him.

At this point let me also decline objectivity, since I am not at all certain that there is such an animal in the critic's menagerie. I am sure it will be clear that although my opinion of his plays varies greatly, on the whole I am impressed with Arthur Miller's work. Certainly I have not spent the past three years indulging in a quaint form of literary masochism.

This is not to imply that I have written a valentine to Arthur Miller. If in all conscience I cannot claim unadulterated objectivity in my treatment of his work, I can and do claim fairness and as balanced a subjective approach as I can maintain. Hopefully, the result is a clear, cool look at one of the most powerful and important dramatists in the contemporary theater, an attempt to evaluate his strengths and weaknesses, and an effort to explain why he has captured a worldwide audience that has returned again and again to his plays, not only with a sense of reassurance, but with wonder and appreciation and joy.

Finally, two words of thanks: to my wife, Miriam, without whose encouragement, faith, and generally gentle prodding this book may never have been completed, and to Arthur Miller, without whose plays it would unquestionably never have been started.

B. N.
Englewood, New Jersey
October 13, 1968

1

*'It'll be all out of mind
as soon as you turn the corner'*

Arthur Miller came of age the way a goodly number of individuals did in the 1930s: with the sudden and painful revelation that the Fall of Man could be as much an economic reality as a theological postulate. But until the bleak November of 1929, the young man was not particularly preoccupied with either economics or theology. Miller was born October 17, 1915, on East 112 Street in New York City to a middle-class Jewish family of Germanic stock. He was the second of three children, preceded by a brother, Kermit, and followed by a sister, Joan. His father, Isadore, a large, square-headed man whose look of steady severity concealed an often impish sense of humour, was a successful manufacturer of ladies' coats. His mother, Augusta, who had taught public school in Manhattan, was an intelligent woman whose devotion to her children was concomitant with her ambitions for them.

Although they were not strictly Orthodox, the Millers observed Jewish customs and holidays and provided their family with a fairly sound background in Judaism. But the boy's principal interest in the ethics of his fathers was confined to the preparation for his bar mitzvah. The rest of the time he was much more concerned with hauling in a thirty-yard pass as an end on the sandlot football team. He attended Public School 29 in Harlem and played havoc with his mother's great expectations by managing to become a particularly undistinguished student, albeit a rather competent athlete.

In 1928, when Miller was thirteen years old, his father's business slackened off, and the family moved to the Midwood section of Brooklyn, near Coney Island. The shift was not arbitrary since a veritable host of relatives had moved to the area since the end of the First World War, and the new arrivals were warmly welcomed.

Although the Millers were now living in what the playwright has
since termed 'middle-class poor' surroundings, for the boy life was
rather serene and insouciant. The section was almost rural with its
great elm trees and flat grassland. The elevated subway nearby
ran to Coney Island, only a couple of miles away.

Miller's neighborhood was just a few blocks long, and essentially Jewish, though a sprinkling of Irish and Italian families
helped it retain a deceptive semblance of ethnic heterogeneity.
Socializing between different neighborhoods was limited, but within each area everyone knew his neighbor, and the resultant relationships formed the societal pattern, acting even as deterrents
against petty crimes.

'I don't recall any time when the cops had to be called,' Miller
commented in retrospect. 'Everyone was so well and thoroughly
known that the frown of his neighbor was enough law to keep
things in line. When we stole from the candy store, when we
played handball against the druggist's window and broke it, it was
enough for the offended proprietor to let it be known to the
parents.'[1]

For the youngster the days passed simply and leisurely. At James
Madison High School he diligently managed to substitute action for
thought at every possible opportunity, indulging particularly in
football and track. In the summer he and his friends challenged
the surf at Coney Island, and all through the year fished off the
rocks for sea bass and flounder. Perhaps the single element of responsibility in this casual existence was provided by the job he
held with the local bakery, delivering bread and rolls each morning
before school. Miller would load the warm, bulging bags into the
basket of his bicycle, and at about five o'clock start off on his
daily rounds. It was during one of these dawn patrols that the
young man gained an early inkling into the meaning of tragedy.

To set the following drama in its proper perspective, one particular point must be emphasized. Unlike the delivery of mail, milk,
or the morning paper, the distribution of hot rolls, fresh bread, and
bagels to Jewish families for breakfast ranged somewhere in urgency and import between Paul Revere's Ride and the Message
to Garcia. Not only did the mission require strict punctuality, but
also the utmost precision in delivering the right bag to the proper

[1] Arthur Miller, 'A Boy Grew In Brooklyn,' *Holiday*, 17 (March 1955),
p.119.

house. A bagel man expected his bagel on time. Give him his prize late and his outlook for the day would be soured. Give him an onion roll when he'd been anticipating a bagel and no one, least of all his wife, could vouch for his subsequent behavior.

Thus, on a particularly cold winter morning, as the young man piloted his bicycle through the sleepy grey streets, its basket jammed with overloaded bags marked in crayon with addresses, he might have been pondering the sacred calling to which he had been entrusted. Whatever the reason, he failed to notice a patch of ice in front of him, and by the time he applied the brakes he was too late. Sprawled on the snowy pavement, the stunned rider watched with mounting horror as bagels, rolls, rye breads, and pumpernickels skidded in every direction on the deserted street.

The mature and sophisticated dramatist has since recalled that until that moment he had never realized how incredibly far a bagel could slide on glazed asphalt. But his ruminations on distance and time rapidly gave way to more practical considerations, and he quickly decided to gather up as many items as he could and replace them as efficiently as possible. Collecting every piece he could find, he piled them in a heap and began stuffing the bags. Realizing the hopelessness of accuracy, he settled for equality, filling each bag with a ryebread, a pumpernickel, a few rolls, and a liberal sprinkling of bagels. The few bagels left over, he ate.

By the time he made his deliveries and returned to the bakery the catastrophic results were pouring in. The baker, already plagued with gallstones, was now about to add apoplexy to his medical history. Mrs Levine had called, frantically inquiring about the missing onion rolls; Mrs Roth could not understand why she had six onion rolls and only one bagel; and Mrs Goldstein sarcastically reminded him that she had not ordered seeded rye for the past eight years. By the time Miller was able to explain, his stammered apology was useless. His employer was obviously in a state of shock.

Thus the artist, as a young delivery boy, came face to face with the catastrophic potential in the human condition, and with the inexplicable buffetings which man can expect from an essentially alien universe.

He not only survived; he progressed. He passed from James Madison to Abraham Lincoln High School, and managed, by sheer will power, to remain as placidly anonymous in the new establishment as in the old. 'Because the idea all of us subscribed to, was to get out onto the football field with the least possible scholastic interference,' he remembered, 'I can fairly say we were none of us encumbered by anything resembling a thought.'[2] In fact, the youngster's main encumbrance was a knee injury he sustained in one of the games, and although it would eventually exempt him from military duty, for the present it proved no significant hindrance to his easy going existence.

The hindrance took quite a different form. It came late in 1929 when a few million Americans suddenly found themselves unexpectedly and crudely banished from the Garden of Eden. Some departed by way of open windows; others less theatrically bent began again by the sweat of their brows. Young Miller's initial awareness of the situation began when he noticed a crowd milling in front of the Bank of the United States, about five blocks from his home. The fact that the bank had closed did not particularly disturb the boy since he had only recently withdrawn his entire deposit of twelve dollars and spent it on a bicycle. But his aloofness from the national calamity lasted only about twenty-four hours. The next day he left the bike outside his house while he went in for a snack, and when he returned it was gone. With the sudden pang of emptiness, he was introduced to the age of the Depression, a time when the postman became the most envied individual in the neighborhood because his job was secure.

Changes came about, not suddenly or violently, but slowly, almost imperceptibly, and yet with a bruising kind of finality. The Government gradually took over most of the mortgages on Miller's block, an event which he recalled led to the intriguing tangential result that the housewives started making more and better coffee.

'When the man came to our house to collect the payments, my mother, for one, got out the coffeepot and her wonderful coffeecake, and he would sit down and before he could say a number she was stuffing him, and for about a year or so this collector always left our block bloated, and not with the money either. It got so he would never mention the mortgage, but just sit there and wait to be served.'[3]

But many things could not be postponed by dangling coffee and cake in the face of fate. Increasingly the young man noticed that

[2] *Ibid.*, p.120.
[3] *Ibid.*, p.122

more and more stores closed down. He could see the desolate counters and hollow shelves as he walked by on his way to school. He became aware of the diminishing number of classmates as one after another was forced to seek work. And on his way home he could see many of the older men sitting on their front porches, their faces passive and sombre masks. At home a spilled cup of milk became a serious incident, and a carelessly torn short was a minor catastrophe. Often in the middle of the night the boy would be awakened by the loud voices of his mother and father, arguing with and berating each other, blaming and rationalizing, and dying out on anguished whines of frustration.

But although the domestic situation became increasingly painful, it was punctuated by humorous interludes, such as the time when Miller's maternal grandfather almost became a Communist. A blunt, Germanic individualist, the old man had once been a successful factory owner whose concept of labor-management relations consisted of lifting up two striking workers and using their heads as flints. Politically a staunch Republican, he was ideologically a monarchist who believed that an enlightened despot, working responsibly with big business, would provide the most stable, efficient, and productive government. Now, with his savings dissipated by the Depression, he lived at the home of his daughter, one of several sisters who took turns housing him.

One evening, after dinner, he put down his paper, gazed somberly at his grandson, and gave him a piece of advice: 'You know what you ought to do?' he proclaimed. 'You ought to go to Russia.'

Miller recalled that the silence that followed this unexpected travel direction could best be described as 'a vacuum so powerful it threatened to suck the walls in. Even my father woke up on the couch.'

When his grandson asked him for the reasons behind his startling proposal, the old man replied that 'in Russia they haven't got anything. Here they got too much. You can't sell anything here any more.' And then he boomed out his prophetic vision: 'You go to Russia and open a chain of clothing stores; you could do a big business. That's a new country, Russia!'

But the boy's reply rapidly snuffed out his grandfather's incipient enthusiasm for the new Red frontier. 'You can't do that there,' Miller explained, proving that he had absorbed at least a smattering of contemporary history. 'The government owns the stores there.'

Arthur Miller

The old man stared balefully at him for a moment, a crimson flush of anger suddenly mottling his rugged features. 'Them bastards,' he muttered, and returned to his paper, forever lost to the Cause.

In 1930 and 1931 the neighborhood began to change radically. As greater numbers of people poured out of the city into Brooklyn, the rural atmosphere vanished. Trees and grassy fields gave way to houses. Many of the empty stores reopened as bars, and neon glitter and noise reverberated familiarly through the neighborhood. The last empty lot used by the boys as a football field was converted into a junkyard, and the star halfback in Miller's class became a shipping clerk and was elated to get the job. If he had been wrenched out of his cocoon in 1929, by 1932 Arthur Miller was beginning to realize that there would be no return to it.

That June he graduated from high school and applied to Cornell University ('they offered a free course in biology, although I had not the slightest interest in the subject') and to the University of Michigan. For the first time in his life he regretted the unenviable scholastic record he had compiled over the past four years. When both schools unceremoniously rejected him, he made a second effort for Michigan, and, surprisingly, was offered reconsideration if he could furnish statements from four of his teachers indicating that he had shown some kind of progress in his senior year that would offset the dreary record of the previous terms.

As he thought of the teachers he would petition, the student again felt like the delivery boy who helplessly watched the rolls and bread slide blithely away on the icy pavement. One instructor had just failed him in Algebra for the third time; another had expelled him from his class; and three others considered him at best a highly dubious intellectual specimen. Imagining the letters they would write about him, he finally decided to forgo the whole sticky business and begin seeking a job.

He did not have far to look: he went to work for his father. However his first taste of the garment industry soon became acrid. The job was claustrophobic, the people loud, and the tasks routinized. He particularly loathed the vulgarity and aggressiveness of the buyers who treated his father and the salesmen with arrogant contempt, and he became acutely aware of the meaning of self-respect when he saw how cruelly it was abused. So upset was he with this facet of the business that he wrote his first story, an angry and awkward character study of an aging salesman, titled 'In Memoriam.' Written only to express his wrath, the story was obviously the initial record of a situation and idea that would blossom some seventeen years later.

Torn between his commitment to his father and his increasing distaste for his job, the young man stuck it out for a few months before finally striking out on his own. Trudging from one employment agency to another, he learned two bruising lessons in rapid order: jobs were scarce, and jobs for Jews even more so. Anti-Semitism, which was an abstract and distant concept in his comfortably clannish neighborhood, now emerged as a personal and particular fact of life.

In the next few months he held a number of jobs, running the gamut from truck driver to crooner on a local radio station. Finally he settled down to a relatively stable position as a shipping clerk in an automobile parts warehouse on Tenth Avenue in Manhattan, where he worked for more than a year for fifteen dollars a week. The routine was simple, but stultifying, and as he punched in and out day after day, and picked up his paycheck week after week, he began to realize more than ever how desperately he wanted to make something of his life, and how casually it could erode into automated oblivion.

It was at this time that he turned to literature, not just as an escape from his daily existence, but as a new means of understanding and coping with it. He was particularly impressed by the complexity and depth of Dostoyevsky's *Brothers Karamazov*, and although much of it left him bewildered, he was nonetheless dazzled by its drama, particularly by the conflict between father and sons, and brother and brother. Even more encompassingly, the sheer sense of wonder he felt at exploring the book's world overwhelmed him as he compared the story's literalness with its continual probing into the deepest complexities of human life.

The Brothers Karamazov kindled his imagination and transformed literature from just another word—and a rather distasteful one at that—into a joyous and challenging experience. He read more in a year than in all his previous life. And with his reading came the first sense that writing could be a way of communicating, of defining experience, shaping chaos, making some kind of sense out of apparent senselessness. But if he felt the desire to write, he lacked the opportunity; the warehouse saw to that. He knew he would have to make a move soon or be trapped.

Living at home, he managed to save an average of thirteen dollars out of the weekly fifteen, and after a year he reapplied for admission to the University of Michigan. He wrote two unabashedly pleading letters in which he claimed new maturity and seriousness of purpose, along with a desire to become a journalist. In the light of his high school record he was too embarrassed to admit that he was really interested in serious creative writing. To his surprise and elation, he was accepted on the condition that he achieve proper grades by the end of the first semester.

Arthur Miller said goodbye to his friends at the warehouse with mixed feelings. He tried to conceal his exuberance but the effort was difficult. He had made it; he was on his way. The occasion was momentous. Except that none of them seemed to think so. For all their affection for him, his departure only meant another boy to break in. College, journalism, literature were words that meant very little to them. A man left, another arrived, the work droned on. Why should they take any special notice of his departure? Would he remember them? Perhaps one of them made the rueful comment to him that Kenneth makes to Bert in the semiautobiographical play, *A Memory of Two Mondays*, when Bert halfheartedly promises to return—sometime: 'Oh, not likely; it'll be out of mind as soon as you turn the corner.'

But it would never be out of mind, as *A Memory of Two Mondays* attests. Miller had learned too much in that warehouse and in the couple of years that enclosed it. He had learned about emptiness and despair, and about hope and its fulfilment. And from those he left behind he had learned 'the heroism of those who know, at least, how to endure (hope's) absence.'[4] He had gained his first awareness of man and his world, and in so doing began to notice 'how things connected. How the native personality of man was changed by his world, and the harder question, how he could in turn change his world.'[5] He learned to feel 'beyond the edges of things.' In the following years his new knowledge would be broadened, deepened, and above all—tested.

[4] Arthur Miller, 'Introduction,' *Collected Plays* (New York: Viking, 1957. London: 1958, The Cresset Press), p.49. The page references are the same for the American and English editions.

[5] Arthur Miller, 'The Shadows of the Gods,' *Harper's Magazine*, 217 (August, 1958), p.36.

2

'I fell in love with the place'

The bus trip had been long and tiring, and he felt grimy and stiff from cramming his tall and lean frame into the inadequate space allotted to it. But as he stood on the sprawling green campus on a crisp, sun-spattered day he forgot his discomfort and weariness.

Compared to the warehouse, the University of Michigan was a reincarnation of Paradise, and through a reversal of the Adamic procedure, Arthur Miller, late of Abraham Lincoln High School, was being allowed entry.

'I fell in love with the place,' he recalled, and 'I resolved to make good.'

He did, although not easily. He had never been much of a scholar, and a two-year absence from academic life made self-discipline all the more difficult. The nights before examinations he crammed theories and facts into his mind, and went forth the next day, groggy but prepared to do battle. If his method lacked classical purity, it nevertheless showed results. He did well in his subjects, although once his mind went blank during a history exam and he had to be rescued by a compassionate professor who, noticing his glazed look, led him out of the room, urged him to get a good night's sleep, and allowed him to take the test the following morning.

With each passing day, Miller grew more attached to Michigan. Its basic difference from the depression world he had come to know so intimately in Brooklyn and New York was its vibrancy and hope. Though linked to the economic and political realities of the thirties, the atmosphere was one of challenge rather than despairing finality. The school was not so large that he became a statistic lost in an avalanche of numbers and not so small that it lulled him into cozy security.

It was not a time for allegiances to fraternities and football teams. It was a time of sit-down strikes and protests, of debates and political agitation, a time of searing anger over the labor unrest in Flint and Detroit, and of cool admiration at President Roosevelt's daring with the TVA. It was a time when sitting in the library and trying to concentrate on the ramification of the Triple Entente was almost an impossibility because the lawn outside was boisterous with students stridently arguing the merits and flaws of the New Deal.

The campus was alive with speeches, meetings, leaflets, and issues. On the walks, in dormitories, in meeting halls, and in fraternities, impromptu courses in political education were being hurled at anyone who wanted to listen or debate.

His fellow students at Michigan were no less exciting to Miller than the ideas and causes they espoused and attacked. In glaring contrast to the homogeneity of his previous social life, his classmates came from just about everywhere. Sons of bankers, lawyers, doctors, farmers, laborers, and even unemployed recipients of relief, they were from all parts of the country and brought with them their particular beliefs, wisdoms, and prejudices. And they voiced them, loudly, heatedly, not always rationally, but with passion and fervor. Arthur Miller's education at the University of Michigan was a ceaseless, churning process, and he loved every minute of it.

He also enjoyed some of the extracurricular activities. He found that when it was cold enough during the winter, he could ice-skate along the streets of Ann Arbor, provided he did so late at night after they had been stealthily hosed down. He learned the places he could swim without the encumbrance (and cost) of a bathing suit. And most importantly, he discovered that the Arboretum, a grassy tract of land where botany students examined the local flora, was also an ideal setting for the study of fauna, with specific emphasis on comparative anatomy. Life was not wholly political at the University of Michigan.

To support himself, Miller washed dishes in the cafeteria for his meals, and earned a small salary as night editor of the *Michigan Daily*. He also earned fifteen dollars a month from the National Youth Administration for tending to hundreds of mice in one of the university laboratories, a job which proved to be a special triumph for him, since he had feared and detested them ever since his childhood. Now, he was not only playing den mother to the furry creatures, but whenever one escaped he was responsible for retrieving it and ensuring that it was still in good shape for further experiments. It was not long before he began to look upon his tiny charges with something akin to benevolence, and even affection. When a couple of his professors suggested that he design a mouse trap that could catch strays without hurting them, he eagerly accepted the challenge, and by the time he graduated, he had 'almost' solved the problem. 'If they had given me a post-graduate scholarship, I would have licked it,' he commented recently, his tongue fixed rather firmly in his cheek.

Out of his earnings he paid $7 a month for his room and nursed the remainder for his books, laundry, and current vice, Granger pipe tobacco (at the going rate of two packs for thirteen cents). The campus health service supplied his glasses and fixed his teeth for the cost of materials, and if he was still solvent, he took in an occasional movie. Equally occasional dates paid their own way.

Although he began as a journalism major, he quickly gravitated toward the English Department, which provided him with a double incentive for creative writing. The first came from Professor Kenneth Rowe, who taught playwriting and who impressed his student not only with his knowledge and ability, but with his dedication and interest in his pupils' projects.

'He may never have created a playwright, no teacher ever did,' Miller commented in retrospect, 'but he surely read what we wrote with the urgency of one who actually had the power to produce the play.'[1]

While the young man's interest in playwriting was ignited by the tutelage and consideration of Professor Rowe, it was fanned into a flame by the legacy of a man Miller had never met.

In 1922, Avery Hopwood, a highly successful author of comedies and bedroom farces, sporting such subtle titles as *Getting Gertie's Garter* and *Up In Mabel's Room*, made out his will. When it was read six years later, after he had drowned on the Riviera, his alma mater, the University of Michigan, suddenly

[1] Arthur Miller, 'University of Michigan,' *Holiday*, 14 (December, 1953), p.70.

found itself the recipient of one-fifth of his substantial estate, or approximately $300,000, which was to be invested so that the subsequent income could be awarded annually to students who produced the finest achievements in playwriting, fiction, poetry, and the essay.

Since 1931, these awards, named after Hopwood and his mother, had been bestowed by the regents of the university in amounts ranging from $250 to more than $1,000. Although the regents fixed the sums, the winners of the prizes were chosen by independent judges, usually critics in the specified categories. In playwriting, awards of $250 went to most undergraduate winners, while $1,250 prizes were granted to seniors and graduate students. Not only did the Avery Hopwood Award invoke a rather awesome prestige on its recipient, but in Miller's case the money would handsomely implement his income. So he decided to write plays.

The trouble lay in finding the time to do so. Between schoolwork and jobs his schedule at the university extended from 6 A.M. to approximately midnight, leaving very little time for the practice of this newly chosen profession, much less for the emotion-remembered-in-tranquility from which the artist's inspiration is often expected to bloom. Not until spring vacation of his sophomore year did the opportunity afford itself. Although he had only a week to write a play and submit it to the judges, he was breezily unperturbed, not so much because of his confidence in his skills, but because the thought that the creation of a play might possibly take longer than the time it took the Lord to create the world never occurred to him. In fact, when he learned that Ibsen had spent two years on a single drama, he could not understand what the procrastinating Norseman was doing all that time.

Having seen only one play in his life—*Tobacco Road*, to which his mother had treated him shortly after his graduation from high school—Miller had no idea of what writing a play entailed. So he just wrote. With the idea, plot, and characters firmly fixed in mind, he labored steadily for the better part of four days and nights. When the opus was completed, he ambled across the dormitory hall to a friend's room.

'About how long does an act run?' he asked.

Informed that the average playing time was about thirty-five to forty minutes, he returned to his room and read the script aloud, timing himself with a watch he propped up on his bureau. Every thirty-five minutes he looked for a place to ring down the curtain, and each time, giving or taking a minute, he found it. To his delight, the play fit perfectly into a three-act form, each act building to an appropriate climax, with each succeeding act slightly shorter than the preceding one.

Miller put the finishing touches on his drama, titled it *Honors at Dawn*, and submitted it to the judges, Alexander Dean, Edith J. R. Isaacs, and Alfred Kreymborg. Then, on a stifling day in June of 1936, he waited among a crowd of hopefuls to hear the announcement of the awards. After fidgeting through a series of speeches by assorted luminaries ('How I hated those speakers for holding up the awards! . . . I have never sweated on an opening night the way I did at Hopwood time.') he heard his name called: Arthur Miller, for *Honors at Dawn*, two hundred and fifty dollars! Suddenly, and with disarming simplicity, he had achieved recognition, cash, and most significantly, the realization that a promising vocation lay before him. His hopes were bolstered the following year when judges Allardyce Nicoll, Percival Wilde, and Susan Glaspell awarded him a second Avery Hopwood prize of $250 for his drama, *No Villain*.

Honors at Dawn and *No Villain* are unpublished and unproduced plays which Miller refers to, along with a half-dozen others he wrote in the late 1930s and early forties, as 'trunk plays,' dramas that belong to his youth, and that he has no intention of resurrecting. However, their essential value today lies not in their inherent worth as plays, but in their seminal characters and situations, and in the thematic directions toward which they pointed the young dramatist.

Honors at Dawn tells the story of a young man named Max Zabriskie, who has reluctantly participated in a strike at his factory. Ironically, he is blacklisted for his part in the venture, although he understands very little of the cause for which his co-workers have been struggling. With scant prospects for finding any work in the near future, he is influenced by his older brother, and goes to college. Max initially views the university where his brother is already enrolled, as a citadel of idealism. But his optimism is short-lived, and disillusionment soon sets in. He sees corruption in many areas of university life, but none more personally shattering than the revelation that his brother is being subsidized by the administration to spy and inform on young radicals. Heartsick over his brother's betrayal, and disgusted with the college, Max leaves and rejoins the union, but with a new sense of commitment. He participates in another strike, but this time with a full understanding of its meaning. The play closes with Max taking a bad beating, but knowing that he has finally gained at a new 'dawn' the 'honors'—the personal integrity and social responsibility—he had falsely sought at the university.

Honors at Dawn is about as good as a play written in five days by a young man in the first flush of rebellion against a social system can be expected to be. It is melodramatic, didactic, and wonderfully naïve. Flashing the Odets fire and fury, but lacking his perception, *Honors at Dawn* is clearly influenced by protest literature of the Depression era. Yet, for all its adherence to a particular mold, the play also has themes its author would dramatize and develop in greater depth in ensuing works.

Set against a negative mirror image of the University of Michigan, the conflict between the Zabriskie brothers is the first of a number of struggles involving sibling rivalry that form a typical Miller pattern of familial strife within the more encompassing conflict between the individual and his society. The broader struggle in *Honors at Dawn* is clearly the Marxist battle between the ogre of capitalism and the emerging proletariat hero. It is a duel rigidly fixed in the leftist cast of its time, and its resolution is as predictable as a *Daily Worker* editorial on H. L. Hunt.

However, beneath the blatant philosophical conflict is the more profound clash between the individual and his conscience, a struggle involving self-knowledge and the attempt to find a meaningful place in the world. Max Zabriskie finds it on the figurative barricades with a group of strikers.

Like many later protagonists, this early Miller hero is a confused man who is out of focus with the world around him. His bewilderment manifests itself in a blurred moral vision which creates reality-distorting illusions. In *Honors at Dawn*, these deceptive illusions are centered in Max's overinflated concept of the university, and it is up to him to gain clarity. Max's self-awareness begins with a situation that suddenly compels him to reevaluate his previous beliefs. Like a pair of spectacles in the novel, *Focus*, a letter in *All My Sons*, an accusation of witchcraft in *The Crucible*, and a mistaken identity in *Incident at Vichy*, the revelation that his brother is an informer hardens into the rock that shatters the complacent waters of Max's ignorance and initiates the flow toward awareness.

But although Max is forced into a reexamination of his life because of a specific situation, the role of his will is not negated. As in Miller's subsequent plays, the situation does not impel action, but rather presents the individual with the alternatives of either facing the new turn of events or of backing off. Max Zabriskie simply cannot back off. Although Miller probably was not thinking of this early protagonist when in the Introduction to his *Collected Plays* he defined the kind of hero who interested him, the image of Max Zabriskie moves impressively through the definition:

> I understand the symbolic meaning of a character . . . to consist of the kind of commitment he makes to life or refuses to make, the kind of challenge he accepts and the kind he can pass by. . . . Time, characterizations, and other elements are treated differently from play to play, but all to the end that *the moment of commitment* be brought forth, that moment when, in my eyes, a man differentiates himself from every other man, that moment when out of a sky full of stars he fixes on one star. I take it, as well, that the less capable a man is of walking away from the central conflict of the play, the closer he approaches a tragic existence.[2]

Max ultimately submerges himself in the Movement, but he has initially *differentiated* himself by his commitment to a highly personal sense of integrity.

Clifford Odets called one of his plays *Paradise Lost*; the title could also apply to *Honors at Dawn*. Or perhaps *After the Fall* would be even more apropos, for in Miller's initial drama, just as in the controversial play he wrote almost three decades later, the stress is not only on the loss of innocence, but more significantly on the events following the painful but providential fall.

Honors at Dawn obviously cannot be compared critically with any of Miller's mature dramas, much less *After the Fall*. In fact, from the comparative safety of a thirty-year point of perspective, the reader can at once note the unintended irony of Max Zabriskie's moral development. His return to the union after his

[2] Miller, 'Introduction,' *Collected Plays*, p.7.

disillusionment at college is not so much a movement toward reality as it is an exchange of illusions. But although the play's resolution is reflected through the prism of a class conflict, the evolution of the protagonist's awareness is strikingly similar to the pattern of many of Miller's subsequent dramas.

I am certainly not claiming that the novice playwright had satisfactorily worked out in one effort the dramatic structure and thematic considerations which he would pursue for the next thirty years. But I am suggesting that although Miller's growth as a dramatist has shown a profound development and has embraced some striking changes in outlook, it is nevertheless rooted in his experiences of the Depression years and in the plays born of these experiences. The Marxism would fade, but the personal conflicts which are so readily and stridently resolved in *Honors at Dawn* would remain and become central to the playwright's thought and art.

3

A preview of coming attractions

They Too Arise, an expanded and revised version of Miller's second Avery Hopwood Award winning play, *No Villain,* continues the pattern established in *Honors at Dawn* of integrally linking familial conflicts to broader problems beyond but impinging upon the family.

The first act opens in the parlor of Abe Simon's home in a New York City suburb in the 1930s. Although it is late, the family, consisting of Abe, a manufacturer of women's coats, his son Ben, who works with him, his wife Esther, and his young daughter Maxine, are awaiting the arrival of the younger son Arnie, who is hitchhiking home from the University of Michigan where he has just completed his freshman year.

The tensions in the family become increasingly evident. Although they are facing a strike by their shipping clerks which could bankrupt them, the Simons are unable to show any solidarity. Esther, who feels isolated from her husband and son, can only reach out to them with remonstrations, berating Ben for not marrying the daughter of a wealthy manufacturer, and badgering Abe for his ineffectuality. Increasingly alienated from his wife, Abe has built a wall of indifference between them, spending most of his time at the shop and lavishing his greatest affection on his daughter. Caught in the middle of this antagonism at home, and frustrated with his job, Ben is growing steadily bitter and morose. His bitterness emerges when Esther's eighty-year-old father enters the parlor and immediately touches off a long-standing argument between Abe and her. They have been alternating with Esther's sister in caring for him, and although Abe does not dislike the old man, he resents the burden foisted upon him by his affluent sister-in-law.

The only pleasant topic of conversation is Arnie, and even he becomes a bone of contention when Ben counters his father's intention to offer Arnie a position in the shop with the observation that his younger brother has always hated the work. When his parents protest, Ben reminds them that it would be unfair to make Arnie, who has become increasingly radical at college, defy the strikers' picket lines to work for his father. Implicit in his argument is Ben's fervent hope that Arnie will not be trapped as he is.

At this point Arnie enters and is warmly greeted. He is sincerely touched by his family's affection, and in turn his presence softens the acrimony in the house. The act closes with Abe delicately asking his intentions for the summer, and Arnie's reply that he wants to work on a small newspaper.

The second act begins in the Simon Coat and Suit Company. Despite Ben's protests, Arnie, who knows nothing of the strike, agrees to help his father temporarily. As the day wears on, business pressures and tension increase. Finally Arnie is beaten up when he unknowingly tries to cross a picket line to make a delivery. He berates his father for duping him, then proclaims his allegiance to the strikers. Abandoned by one son, and facing financial ruin, Abe now begs Ben to make the marriage which will save the family from bankruptcy. Reluctant and ashamed, Ben accedes to his father's wishes.

The second scene of the act takes place at a meeting of the Manufacturers' Association, where a proposal is made that all the manufacturers enlist the aid of strikebreakers to combat the union. Despite the assertions of Abe and Ben that they will have no part of it, the resolution is passed.

The final scene is set in the Simon home that evening, and finds Arnie trying to persuade his parents to sympathize with the strikers. As the others go to supper, he asks Ben to break off his impending marriage, abandon the shop, which will eventually be squeezed out of business by the large firms anyway, and join the right side of the struggle. But when Ben overhears their grandfather volunteer to help Abe, he is ashamed, and orders his younger brother to forget about his grand ideals and come to his father's aid.

Torn between family loyalty and principles, Arnie refuses, and is berated for his cowardice. Just as the brothers are at each other's throats, Esther cries out that her father is having a heart attack.

Immediately quelling their animosity, Arnie and Ben rush into the dining-room together.

The third act opens in the shop. Abe is besieged by creditors and unable to get merchandise through the picket lines. In despair, he realizes the business is finished.

The concluding scene is again in the Simon home, later in the evening. The first signs of tenderness between Abe and Esther emerge as he tries to comfort her for the death of her father. Having experienced defeat and death, the family has begun to come to terms with life, and for the first time the gnawing tension is gone and the mood is calm, almost serene. As the mother and father look at their sons in wonder, Ben cancels the prearranged marriage and declares his intention to make his own way in the world. He is more confident than he has been for years, and Arnie is exuberant over his brother's newly discovered independence.

After the two young men go up to bed, Abe says gently to Esther: 'We gotta learn how to laugh again, we gotta learn how to laugh.'

Her reply closes the play and delineates the effect the crisis has had on the whole family. 'Yeh, we gotta learn,' she says softly, 'a lotta things we gotta learn.'[1]

In its didacticism, melodrama, hypersensitive social consciousness, blatantly youthful exuberance, and glowing panaceas for the rather simple problems of a world split between noble commoners and ogreish capitalists, *They Too Arise* multiplies the weaknesses of *Honors at Dawn*. But like the previous play, its importance to a critical consideration of Miller's subsequent work lies not so much in its ideology, but in its dramatization of character and situation.

To a great extent the characters of *They Too Arise* are based upon Miller's family. The shopowning father who was once a salesman and is now struggling to keep his family from financial ruin; the mother whose compassion and tenderness have been eroded by frustrations; the older brother who worked for his father; the younger who went on to college; the daughter; the aged grandfather who became a burden to his family; and the Depression, with the crushing pressures it put upon everyone—all are partially autobiographical.

In fact, some of the situations are taken literally from Miller's

[1] Arthur Miller, *They Too Arise*, typescript, 1938, p.63.

life and inserted unembellished into the play. Like the dramatist, Arnie is a student at the University of Michigan, Abe's shop is a re-creation of Isadore Miller's and the grandfather, like Miller's grandfather, is passed from one daughter to another. Indeed, one of the exchanges between Arnie and the old man about economic opportunity in Russia is a verbatim transcript of the conversation between the young Miller and his grandfather, already cited in an earlier chapter.

But although the characters of *They Too Arise* shed some light on their author's life, they are primarily significant within the context of their play. Essentially superficial, and blatantly manipulated by the playwright, they nevertheless form the nucleus of a dramatic family, which will develop in depth and complexity with each successive Miller drama.

Abe Simon has staked his life on the coin of success and cannot understand why it has evolved so differently from his expectations. And even though success is measured in terms of material benefits, it ultimately takes on a mystique of its own, signifying a father's legacy to his children, as both a proof of his love and a guarantee of his immortality, an assurance that he will live on through them.

Thus the paradoxical drives that motivate this father: the apparently selfless desire to sacrifice himself for his sons, intermingled with the subconsciously egocentric hope of perpetuating himself in them. Although these motives do not comprise an overt consideration in Abe Simon's story, they are unmistakably manifested in his anguished cry to Ben when he finally realizes the business has collapsed.

'We're finished. Through,' he exclaims. 'But Ben, some day I want you should—I wanna see you on top. You can do it Ben, without me. You gotta do it, Ben. It ain't fair that I should give my life like this and go out with—with nothing Ben! You hear me Ben? It ain't fair!'[2]

Abe's cry will be echoed by Patterson Beeves in *The Man Who Had All the Luck*; it will be contained in Joe Keller's tortured justification of his life in *All My Sons*; in *Death of a Salesman* it will be interwoven into Willy Loman's garishly inflated dreams for Biff and Happy; and it will reverberate again in *After the Fall* in the Father's helpless rage at the discovery of his ruination. 'It ain't fair,' complain these men who have committed themselves

[2] *Ibid.*, p.57.

too intensely and blindly to their children and their dreams. And the sons, torn between love and disillusionment, can only voice Ben's anguished reply: 'No Dad, it ain't fair.'

Abe Simon precedes subsequent Miller protagonists in yet another way. Much as he loves his children, he cannot communicate with them because he does not understand them. Although his way of life is obviously insufficient for his sons, Abe does not know why and cannot comprehend their rebellion. He is a bewildered man in a world that is rapidly losing all the familiar boundaries that once ordered and defined it:

In my day when a father needed help all he had to do was open his mouth and like that!—he got it, no questions asked. Nowadays they go to college . . . they learn . . . they get *so* smart, they don't know how to work no more. But they ain't lazy. . . . Years ago, they called it lazy. . . . *Now* they call it principles. The elevator boys got em. The truckmen's got em, the shipping clerks got em. Only *I* ain't got em.[3]

Simon's pride in his son's education, coupled with his feeling of inferiority in the face of it, his reliance on tangible facts of life, and his bewilderment when confronted by anything too abstract for him to comprehend, all point unerringly to the dilemmas of Joe Keller and Willy Loman. Abe's defensive pride and growing sense of dislocation will be echoed in Keller's perplexity at the realization that the apparently invincible 'building line' which had defined and protected his family is crumbling. It will resound again in Loman's terror-etched confusion with a family and a world that have incomprehensibly slipped out of his grasp.

Finally, Abe Simon embodies the sense of commitment to a dream, and the intense determination to infuse his sons with his personal vision of grandeur. A small, battered man who refuses to give up in the face of overwhelming odds, who must have his stature even when that seems an impossibility, he calls out his promise to his son:

What the hell do you mean, we'll never be big? You can still do it. . . . You gotta' be big. It ain't right it should end like this. . . . It ain't gonna. If we close up, Benny—if we close up I'm finished. . . . But as long as we got something—as long as

[3] *Ibid.,* p.33.

we got what's left—whatever it is—Benny we gotta hold on to
it. Ben, ya understand? We gotta fight for what we got.[4]

This same determination, fear, and hope will be concentrated
into another father's angry reply to his son's desire to capitulate
to reality.

'I am not a dime a dozen!' exclaims Willy Loman in a rejoinder
to his son's attempt to make him abandon his dream. 'I am Willy
Loman, and you are Biff Loman!'

This fanatic refusal to submit to necessity is tangential to the
story of Abe Simon. It is an element in his character which is
suggested rather than developed, and in fact is ultimately subverted by his acceptance of the inevitable and his willingness to
change. But it is nonetheless a trait which will increasingly define
Miller protagonists from Willy Loman to Count Von Berg of
Incident at Vichy.

Just as her husband embodies many characteristics which Miller
will develop in ensuing father figures, Esther Simon possesses some
of the features which will distinguish the mothers of the playwright's dramatic family. The woman she most clearly antedates
is Quentin's mother in *After the Fall.* Intelligent, devoted to their
families, and frustrated in their marriages, both women cannot
control the rancor they feel toward their husbands, a bitterness
that is not without some justification, but that nevertheless turns
their homes into simmering kettles of recriminations. Nor is the
abrasive relationship of the Simons mirrored only in *After the
Fall*; it recurs with variations and qualifications in the marriages
of Elizabeth and John Proctor in *The Crucible* and Beatrice and
Eddie Carbone in *A View from the Bridge.*

At first glance the similarity between Esther Simon and the
wives of *All My Sons* and *Death of a Salesman* seems to be
negligible. While Esther's conflicts with Abe manifest a basic antagonism between them, Kate Keller and Linda Loman are
epitomes of the dutiful, protective wife who submerges her entire
identity into her husband's. But although they veer sharply from
her in their ironclad commitments to their husbands, Kate and
Linda share Esther's frustrations and anxieties, particularly her
inability to communicate meaningfully with the man she married.
Consequently, their differences are not so much inherent in char-

[4] *Ibid.*, p.33.

acter as in the situations in which they are involved. And significantly, the three women hold complementary attitudes toward their sons, and more abstractedly toward their concepts of family. Although sometimes disastrously misunderstanding their children, these mothers display a fierce, maternal loyalty, which is simultaneously protective and stifling. They provide their sons with the best possible homes, and yet, because of their inability to see clearly beyond the confines of living room and kitchen, they help to erect and maintain the barriers of narrow allegiances which these young men must hurdle if they are to realize their destinies.

As the younger brother, Arnie Simon is part of a pattern that Miller will develop in succeeding dramas, whereby two brothers, blinded by the glare of their father's burning insistence on success, are propelled toward potential catastrophe unless they can achieve a self-awareness that will free them from the deceptive and destructive glitter of their father's vision. In *They Too Arise*, this motif hovers in the shadows of the overt drama, subordinate to its more strident and superficial demands. In later plays it will emerge into a central dramatic consideration.

Like Max Zabriskie, Arnie also functions as his play's raisonneur, a character who in finally orienting himself in the world becomes Miller's spokesman in his attempt to communicate his knowledge to those whom he loves. This is precisely what Arnie tries to do when he explains why he cannot help his family if his aid means undermining the cause of the strikers:

> You think that because you close your door in the front of the house then anything that happens outside doesn't have anything to do with you. That's the way you've always been ... because you don't want to understand causes. You only want things to 'get better.' Well the time has come when things don't get better unless you make them better.[5]

The exhortation is strikingly similar to Chris Keller's denunciation of his father in *All My Sons*: 'Is that as far as your mind can see, the business? . . . What the hell do you mean, you did it for me? Don't you have a country? Don't you live in the world?'

Although Miller's blanket approval of Arnie is replaced by a

[5] *Ibid.*, p.47

highly qualified acceptance of Chris, who is a much more complex figure than his youthful and exuberant predecessor, the idea
inherent in both speeches, of responsibility to a world beyond the
family, is crucial to the meaning of both plays.

Arnie touches still another thematic motif that will be orches-
trated in Miller's subsequent dramas, but he brushes it so obliquely
that I want only to point to it, without unduly stressing its pertinence. When the young man is asked by his mother why he
would rather hitchhike home when he could have the trainfare
by simply writing for it, Arnie replies:

> Gosh, you see the white highways and then along the sides
> out West farther there's waving wheat. It's not bad. Outside
> of a little town in Ohio I just lay down and listened to the
> sshhh of the wind through the leaves and grass. You can't do
> that on a train.[6]

The reply is a fairly innocuous and self-conscious bit of lyricism,
and he never speaks this way again. Nevertheless, this casual comment strikes a chord that will be heard in a few succeeding plays.
Arnie's reverie will be faintly echoed in Joe Keller's pride in his
Midwest climate. It will resound more clearly in Biff Loman's
reminiscences about the West. And it will permeate *The Misfits*,
which contrasts the tinseled falsity of Reno with the awesome
serenity and rugged truth of the Nevada countryside around it. In
They Too Arise, there is no more than a hint at this motif, but
in many of his subsequent works, Miller will dramatize the characteristically American theme of the conflict between the values of
the natural world and the chimeras of civilization.

Unlike the other members of his family, Ben Simon, the older
brother, is relevant to Miller's subsequent writings by the fact that
his role will be increasingly diminished, rather than developed.
With the exception of *The Price, They Too Arise* marks the only
time that two brothers carry equal dramatic weight in a Miller
play. As the son who is most clearly sacrificed to his father's
dream, Ben is the prototype for Amos Beeves of *The Man Who
Had All the Luck*, Larry Keller of *All My Sons*, Happy Loman of
Death of a Salesman, and Dan of *After the Fall*. But in these
dramas the Ben figure recedes as the Arnie figure gains promin-

ence; he is essentially a minor character in three of the plays, and is dead before the action of *All My Sons* even begins.

There are two basic reasons for the reduced importance of the second brother. In *They Too Arise*, Arnie is little more than a catalyst, while Ben is the man who undergoes the deep emotional crisis of being torn between loyalty to his father and commitment to his personal hopes and ambitions. In succeeding dramas, the Arnie figure will become a more fully realized character and will consequently absorb much of Ben's dramatic identity and purpose.

In *All My Sons*, Chris comes home, but then like Ben works with his father and is finally caught between his antagonism and devotion to the older man. In *Death of a Salesman*, Biff also traces Arnie's catalytic return but, like Ben, is hopelessly enmeshed in his father's vision, and must experience his parent's degradation as the prerequisite to his possible salvation. Thus, with Ben's ambivalent relationship to his father transferred to the Arnie character, Ben's prototype is shorn of his intensity and purpose, and eventually evolves into a foil for the dominant brother. What often remains is a Happy Loman, whose situation is similar to Ben's, but who lacks his sensitivity, awareness, and depth.

The second reason for the diminished importance of one of the brothers is the growing dominance of the father, and the corresponding shift from sibling rivalry to the conflict between father and son. In *Honors at Dawn*, the crux of the drama is the antagonism between two brothers; in *They Too Arise*, the father is drawn into it. In the following plays, the father-son struggle will provide the strongest dramatic tension. Only in *The Price* do the two brothers have equal dramatic stature, and one obvious reason is that in this family conflict, although his memory is crucial to their relationship, their father is dead before the current action of the play begins. Consequently the rivalry between these evenly matched antagonists emerges as the dramatic hub of the play.

They Too Arise suggests one more theme that will prove significant to Miller's drama. It is sounded by Abe Simon when he learns of the Manufacturers' Association's intent to hire thugs to disperse the strikers:

> I want you to know . . . that *I* will not vote to hire gangsters . . . because someway I—I *feel*—I don't know why—but someway it seems to me that this ain't the way an honest man or

honest men do business. . . . I can't see that it's the way for
Jewish men to act—. . . . That's all I got to say. But I hope
so that I can keep my respect for all of you—hope you will
not act like this—like—like—beasts.[7]

What Abe gropingly tries to express to the men around the table
is basically the same thing John Proctor eloquently voices in *The
Crucible* when he cries out against surrendering his name. It is the
cry of individual conscience for its self-respect.

Significantly, Abe's personal integrity is meaningfully linked with
his Jewishness. The play is saturated with the Jewish atmosphere
of the Simon home and business.

But Miller's Jewishness does not consist solely of ethnic traits;
it is humanistic, exhibiting a profound faith in man's capacity for
suffering for his ideals and integrity; and nowhere in *They Too
Arise* is this Jewishness more pervasive than in Abe's comment
that he 'can't see that it's the way for Jewish men to act.' The
thought is simple, but it is firmly entrenched in a two-thousand-
year foundation of history and morality. It abounds with memories
of persecution and suffering, ethics and law, righteousness and purpose, and it reverberates with the voice of a people who historically
never coveted the hero's role, who were forced into concessions
to survive, but who always stopped short of surrendering conscience.

In future Miller works, with the notable exceptions of *Focus,
Incident at Vichy*, and *The Price*, Jewish settings and characterizations disappear. But the implications in that single line of dialogue help to give substance and definition to much of the drama
of Arthur Miller.

[7] *Ibid.*, p.38.

4

Of pussycats and plumbers

In 1938, with two Avery Hopwood awards tucked comfortably in his pocket, the young playwright made an all-out assault on the big prize of $1,250 for the best drama for a senior, but for the first time in his brief writing career he tasted defeat. He submitted *They Too Arise*, the ambitious revision of his earlier play, *No Villain*, but the judges found it 'heavy' and 'turgid.' However, Miller's disappointment did not last long, since the following year the drama won a thousand-dollar award from the Hollywood-financed Bureau of New Plays, under the aegis of Theresa Helburn and John Gassner of the Theatre Guild.

His disappointment was also tempered by another factor: he was in love. Her name was Mary Slattery, she was the daughter of an insurance salesman, and like Miller, she was working her way through college. He met her during his sophomore year, at a basement party. Spotting her across the room, the tall, rangy young man ducked overhead heating pipes as he approached to strike up a casual conversation. A couple of weeks later they again met accidentally at another party. He asked for a date, she suggested a local movie, he frankly admitted he had no money, and she treated. It was the beginning of a romance. A few dates later, he was sufficiently entranced to ask the loan of her radio, and their unofficial engagement was formalized. Two years after graduation, they were married.

Two days after graduation, Arthur Miller was unemployed. He left the university in the spring of 1938 with a Bachelor of Arts degree, two playwriting awards, another in the offing, a fiancée, and a lot of high hopes. And then the Depression world caught up with him again. But in the interim he had equipped himself to face it. The Michigan years proved to be a crucial and positive time in his life; they enabled him to get his bearings and find out a few things about himself and his relationship to the world around him.

'I felt I had accomplished something there. I knew at least how much I did not know. . . . It had been a small world, gentler than the real one, but tough enough.'[1]

The real world did not knuckle him under for very long. He got a job with the Federal Theatre's WPA writing project, and under its auspices, co-authored with Norman Rosten a comedy called *Listen My Children*. But the WPA undertaking was financially reeling when he joined it, and in four months it collapsed. For the next couple of years he tried various occupations, from truckdriver to steamfitter in the Brooklyn Navy Yard. After his marriage he managed to squeeze his way into radio writing, while his wife did secretarial work for publishing houses. Because of his old football injury, he was deferred from military service. Consequently, after the outbreak of the Second World War, Miller divided his time between radio scriptwriting and working on ships at the Navy Yard. His first year's efforts at turning out radio scripts garnered him the less-than-dazzling sum of $300; in his second year he brought home $1,200; but after the third year radio writing proved lucrative enough to become his primary source of income.

Nevertheless, he was not enraptured with his career. Radio simply imposed too many strictures on a writer who felt he had a number of important and exciting things to say. He had to contend with the censors, and deadlines, and he had to cram each story into a thirty-minute format which allowed him little time to develop character or idea. Worst of all, he was continually pressured to keep everything simple, and above all, non-controversial. Even though he became so adept at his craft that he could hammer out a half-hour show in less than a day, he grew constantly more frustrated with his efforts.

'I despise radio,' he remarked vehemently to an interviewer, shortly after the success of *All My Sons* had liberated him from the medium forever. 'Every emotion in a radio script has to have a tag. It's like playing a scene in a dark closet.'[2]

---

[1] Arthur Miller, 'University of Michigan,' *Holiday*, p.70.
[2] Miller, quoted in 'Mr Miller Has a Change of Luck,' by John K. Hutchens, *New York Times* (Feb 23, 1947), Theatre Section, p.3.

But although his recollections of radio writing are colored by the artist's self-righteousness, the economic stability the position offered enabled him to temper his indignation for at least a couple of years. Five hundred dollars to a thousand dollars per script may not have brightened his murky closet, but the sums certainly helped his eyes grow accustomed to the dark. Also, as he has readily acknowledged, his particular situation was much less stultifying than those of many other writers. He was not on a treadmill of soap operas and situation comedies. Most of his writing was done for two of the more experimental and exciting radio shows of the early 1940s, the Columbia Workshop and the Cavalcade of America, which gave him the opportunity to create some original and stimulating scripts. These are noteworthy for a couple of reasons: they display a light touch and whimsical sense of humor, and in a few situations and comments they reinforce some of the themes in his college plays and point to important underlying premises in his later works.

Both the charm and seriousness are apparent in Miller's 1941 fantasy, 'The Pussycat and the Expert Plumber Who Was a Man.' In this delightful comedy about a talking cat named Tom (what else?) who blackmails some politicians into running him for governor, before he is finally exposed by an honest and stalwart plumber, Miller dramatizes political chicanery and demagoguery meeting their match in the common man. In a roundabout way, the script echoes the theory in *They Too Arise* that through an exercise of will, a man of the people can block the cynical corruptors of democracy. Arnie and Ben have now become Sam the plumber, and that whole nasty crew of the Manufacturers' Association have been reincarnated into a Machiavellian tabby.

From the conflict between these two, Miller reiterates a familiar theme, in a comment by Tom about the nature of man:

> The one thing a man fears most next to death is the loss of his good name. Man is evil in his own eyes, my friends, worthless, and the only way he can find respect for himself is by getting other people to say he's a nice fellow.[3]

In another radio play 'Grandpa and the Statue,' the protagonist,

[3] Miller, 'The Pussycat and the Expert Plumber Who Was a Man,' *100 Non-Royalty Radio Plays*, compiled by William Kozlenko (New York, 1941), p.26.

who initially balks at donating money for the pedestal of the Statue of Liberty, finally realizes that he is wrong in remaining aloof from his society and makes his donation. As the play concludes, the Statue stands as the symbol of the integral relationship which must exist between the individual and the world in which he lives.

It is interesting, though, that while stressing man's need for the respect of others as a prerequisite for self-respect, Tom's speech does so cynically and condescendingly. It links man's social needs to negative aspects of his character, namely his lack of belief in himself, and his willingness to accept anyone who will feed his voracious ego. Our little pussycat is not a very nice fellow. With one sly purr, he asserts the need of harmony between the individual and society, while with the next he demonstrates how this requirement is an outgrowth of man's weakness and renders him easy prey for a demagogue.

It is the plumber's reply to Tom which cuts through the feline cynicism and touches the core of Miller's preoccupation with the human being and his world:

A cat will do anything, the worst things, to fill his stomach, but a man . . . will actually prefer to stay poor because of an ideal. That's why I could never be president; because some men are not like cats. Because some men, some useful men, like expert plumbers, are so proud of their usefulness that they don't need the respect of their neighbors and so they aren't afraid to speak the truth.[4]

Let's put aside the intriguing equation of presidents with predatory tomcats, and the rather less fascinating parallel of usefulness and manual labor. The important point in Sam's speech is the elaboration of the difference between one kind of man and another —the person who can never bear to stand alone, and the man who realizes that he must sometimes stand alone if he is to stand at all.

Miller does not deny the individual's need for society, but in none of his plays, whimsical radio scripts included, does he view this need as wholly essential. Our expert plumber is suggesting that even the respect of peers sometimes comes at too high a price,

[4] *Ibid.*, p.29.

that society may occasionally ask too much for the benefits it is
ready to bestow upon the individual, and in such situations some
men simply cannot barter their integrity. Sam is reminding his
audience that the respect of others is not always the prerequisite
for self-respect, but in some instances may even be inimical to it,
and at those times a man must make a choice.

Miller wrote numerous radio plays. Many celebrate the honesty
and potential of the common man. Some, like 'The Story of Gus,'
about the wartime merchant marine, are blatantly and understandably patriotic, and one, 'That They May Win,' written for a war
bond drive, urges good citizens to turn in OPA price ceiling
violators. It is the only time that Miller advocates informing. Subsequently it became for him a primary threat to societal relationships.

Aside from thematic interest, his radio scripts are also noteworthy for what they show of Miller's dramatic technique. Because
the medium for which they were written catered to an audience's
imagination, his plays manifest a wide range of nonrealistic experimentation. Fantasy situations, the use of a narrator, rapid and
plastic shifts of scene, and the breakdown of conventional time
barriers—all these elements which are refined in *Death of a Salesman*, *A Memory of Two Mondays*, *A View from the Bridge*, and
After the Fall—are used boldly and interestingly in his radio
dramas. And they completely invalidate the popularly held notion
that until he wrote the structurally iconoclastic *Death of a Salesman*, Miller was a rockbound practitioner of the cinder-block-and-
cement realism ascribed to Ibsen.

Despite his success in radio, Miller was dissatisfied. His first love
was playwriting; to him his radio scripts were extracurricular, albeit monetarily rewarding, activities. Although he could have made
a great deal more money by devoting more of his time to his
radio efforts, he spent no more than three months a year writing
for that medium. The rest of his time he devoted to plays.

After *Listen My Children*, he wrote a drama about the tribulations of a prison psychologist. Another play, *The Half-Bridge*,
dealt with piracy on the high seas, conducted by a man with an
uncontrollable death wish. And still another, *Montezuma*, focused
on the duel between Cortez and the Aztec chieftain. Miller was dissatisfied with all these efforts and never tried to produce or publish
any of them. The basic problem facing him in these dramas was

his inability to find an idea that he could develop dramatically.

'I had picked themes at random,' he reflected later, 'which is to say that I had no awareness of any inner continuity running from one of these plays to the next, and I did not perceive myself in what I had written. . . . I was writing about what lay outside me.'[5]

This dilemma continued to plague him as he began a new play early in 1943. He had heard the story of a young midwesterner who had become quite wealthy and respected in his town, but who suddenly and unreasonably began to suspect everyone of wanting to rob him, a suspicion that so obsessed him that within a year he committed suicide. The image of a man fearing good fortune to the incredible extent that he ultimately destroys himself caught Miller's imagination.

However, as he labored on the first draft of the play, he ran into one dead end after another. Where he had never spent more than three months on a single manuscript, this one rambled on into six, with no resolution in sight. The young playwright who had wondered how Ibsen could possibly have spent two years on a play was now beginning to find out. Even after the drama was optioned to producer Herbert H. Harris for Miller's first Broadway production, its author could not satisfactorily come to terms with his material, and as the deadline approached he was still wrestling with it, doggedly and unsuccessfully trying to make the play coalesce.

It was not until a couple of weeks before the drama's premiere that a crucial shift of relationships involving the change of two friends into brothers tightened the structure enough to allay some of Miller's anxieties. Still vaguely disturbed, he could only hope that the play's title would apply to its author as well. It was called *The Man Who Had All the Luck*, an ironic name for a project that had fought its creator scene by scene and character by character all the way to opening night.

The Man Who Had All the Luck premiered at the Forrest Theatre on the evening of November 23, 1944. The following day, Burton Rascoe, drama critic of the *New York World-Telegram*, glowingly reported that he had witnessed a play that was 'a challenge to defeatism . . . an attack on the idea that man is ruled by fate.' Finding 'nothing pretentious, arty or preachy' about it,

[5] Miller, 'Introduction,' *Collected Plays*, p.14.

Rascoe concluded that the drama was 'touching, realistic, and challenging.' Unfortunately for Arthur Miller, none of the other New York critics shared Mr Rascoe's buoyant opinion.

While they accepted the validity of the play's theme, both Louis Kronenberger of *PM* ('the treatment is too overt and didactic') and Ward Morehouse of the *New York Sun* ('inexpert writing') noted the wide gulf between intent and execution. The other reviewers dismissed the drama entirely. Howard Barnes of the *Herald Tribune* called it 'incredibly turgid and stuttering,' John Chapman of the *Daily News* found it 'too Saroyanesque . . . and confused,' and the *New York Post's* Wilella Waldorf hammered the final nail in the coffin with her terse summation: 'Three addled acts.'

The Man Who Had All the Luck had very little. It closed after four performances and left its author somewhat sadder but wiser, and its backers approximately $55,000 poorer. For Arthur Miller, overnight success was still a couple of years around the corner.

5

'Far from being a waste and a failure'

The protagonist of *The Man Who Had All the Luck* is a young man of twenty named David Frieber who works as a mechanic in a small midwestern town. Content with his job, he is frustrated in his personal life. Although he has made enough money to provide a home for his childhood sweetheart, Hester, he cannot marry her because she is afraid to disobey her father, a dour, neurotic man who burns with an intense and irrational hatred for David.

With this situation rapidly established in the opening scene, the rest of the play dramatizes David's rise to fortune through a series of incredible twists of fate. Pressured into buying an unnecessarily large amount of antifreeze alcohol, which seems destined to go to waste in the warm spring weather, David is suddenly benefited by a providential cold wave that enables him to sell his product at a handsome profit. But this is only a mild preview of the astounding luck that awaits him.

Just as David is seriously considering giving up Hester, he learns that her father has been killed in an automobile accident, and with this obstacle erased the young people are free to marry. Immediately, fate deals David still another hand. A wealthy, eccentric farmer named Dan Dibble brings an expensive but temperamental car to his shop and promises the young man his patronage and that of his affluent friends if David can fix it. But although he works on the automobile through most of the night, David is stymied. At this moment a stranger appears, introduces himself as Gustav Eberson, and informs him of his plans to open a garage in the town. Despite the fact that they will be competitors, the two men become friendly, and the newcomer offers to help David with the car. Though he tries to continue working, David is so exhausted that he falls asleep, and Eberson completes the repairs alone. The following day, the young man tries to credit him with the success, but Eberson demurs and David gains the admiration and financial benefits promised by Dibble.

The second act is set three years later. David is now a man of substantial means. Married to Hester, he has seen his business prosper tremendously and is currently considering expanding his holdings into new ventures, most notably, mink ranching. However, the fortuitousness of his good fortune continually overwhelms and frightens him, particularly when he contrasts it to the adversities that have plagued many of his friends.

One is a crippled victim of a boiler explosion; another has lost a wife and baby in childbirth; a third sees his lifelong dream explode when he is rejected by a major league baseball scout; and most ironically, because of David's success, Eberson has been unable to maintain his own shop and is now in the younger man's employ.

Morbidly assured by these examples that good fortune must inevitably be balanced out by bad, David awaits the return swing of the pendulum and is even masochistically pleased with his wife's childlessness, viewing their barrenness as a kind of appeasement to the fates. But at the close of the act, when Hester happily informs him of her pregnancy, he is thrown into panic, and in a desperate effort to convince himself that skill counts more than luck, he signs over his entire business to Eberson and mortgages all his subsidiary holdings to start anew in mink ranching.

However, in the final act, which takes place almost a year later, David's scheme to prove his worth and will has backfired completely. His lot is better than ever, and it still seems wholly gratuitous. Having mesmerized himself into believing that his baby would be stillborn, he ambivalently views the child's robust health. And his expectations that mink ranching would be a hazardous test of his mettle have dissolved in the simple and singular success of the project.

Certain that his efforts to prove that skill and initiative supersede blind luck have proved vain, David has grown so obsessed with the fear of divine retribution that Hester is afraid he may even kill their son as a sacrifice to the powers he feels dominate his life. She is so distraught that when she learns that a batch of fish for feeding the mink is diseased, she resolves not to inform her husband of the lethal provender in the hope that the subsequent destruction will convince him that the fates have finally evened the score. But when Eberson assures her that the apparently accidental death of the mink will only verify David's diseased belief in the ineffectuality of his will and the fortuitousness of his life, she tells him about the poisoned fish.

Then, even though all their material belongings are staked on the success of the venture, she persuades David to let the animals die, not as an act of chance but as proof that he has made a choice and exercised a responsibility.

'It's not that they *must* die,' she reasons. 'It's that *you've got* to kill them. . . . I want you to know once and for all that it was you who did it.'

David complies, and the drama concludes with his new awareness of his personal responsibility for his life.

Although it is usually proper to qualify a synopsis with the reminder that a summary rarely does a play justice, I am unable to make this apology. The preceding résumé not only does *The Man Who Had All the Luck* justice, it even tempers it with mercy by omitting a number of characters, situations, and speeches that render the drama even more incredible than the synopsis suggests.

The greatest problem in the play is inherent in its basic idea. How does a writer create a situation which is overwhelmingly dependent upon the most extraordinary coincidence and simultaneously elicit from his audience that crucial suspension of disbelief? Shakespeare is still chided for dropping handkerchiefs and Thomas Hardy for losing letters, but Miller makes the well-made plays of Eugene Scribe look like trenchant examples of naturalism by the way he multiplies coincidences in *The Man Who Had All the Luck*.

Not only is Hester's father eliminated at the providential moment, but he is killed while pushing his broken-down car, which just minutes earlier he had angrily refused to let David repair. And the automobile that runs him down is (yes, you've probably guessed) none other than the one which will be responsible for the upsurge in David's career. Then, just when David has vainly spent half the night attempting to fix Dibble's car, out of the darkness emerges a stranger, and in the next few minutes the audience is asked to believe that a new mechanic in town would choose three in the morning to make a get-acquainted call on his competitor, that by immediately locating the source of trouble he proves to be the one man in the territory whom David has needed, and that he would then spend the ensuing three hours repairing his competitor's merchandise like some providential elf, while the competitor gently slept nearby. Compared to these shenanigans, Hester's perfectly timed announcement of her pregnancy and the coincidental batch of poisoned fish seem like casual slices of life.

Miller was not so much trapped by an inability to create believable situations and relationships as he was by a premise that required him to catwalk a tenuous and treacherous line between the credible and the incredible. This movement might have worked in a fantasy, but bounded by the four oaken walls of realism, it proved highly erratic at best and downright ludicrous at worst. These are not the coincidences of life but of artifice, and a rather clumsy artifice at that.

Unfortunately the strained coincidences are not idiosyncratic, but rather comprise one facet of a generally chaotic arrangement by which the play is cluttered with glaringly incidental situations and characters.

'I had struck upon what seemed a bottomless pit of mutually cancelling meanings and implications,' Miller subsequently explained. 'In the past I had had less difficulty with forming a "story" and more with the exploration of its meanings. Now, in contrast, I was working with an overwhelming sense of meaning, but however I tried I could not make the drama continuous and of a piece; it persisted with the beginning of each scene, in starting afresh as though each scene were the beginning of a new play.'[1]

This painful lack of cohesion between idea and story is apparent throughout *The Man Who Had All the Luck*, but most blatantly in the final act, where a situation involving nothing less than individual choice in conflict with the fatalistic determinism of the universe is resolved by feeding a few mink some spoiled fish. The hanger is simply too flimsy for the apparel the dramatist wants it to support.

As his preceding comment suggests, Miller sensed this weakness almost from the moment he began the play, and his refusal to include it in his *Collected Plays* was final proof of his dissatisfaction with it. But if he felt that *The Man Who Had All the Luck* was not a success, he was still not ready to dismiss it as an unqualified

[1] Arthur Miller, 'Introduction,' *Collected Plays*, p.14.

disaster. In his own words, 'far from being a waste and a failure,' the drama was a 'preparation'—a connecting link between the earlier plays and those yet to come.

One manifestation of that link is clearly seen in an important change he made prior to the play's Broadway premiere. One of the glaring weaknesses of *The Man Who Had All the Luck* is David Frieber's poorly motivated relationships with most of the other characters. As an orphan, he has a rather inordinate amount of friends who seem wonderfully predisposed to doing good things for him. In the eleventh-hour revision of the play (which is not in print), this glibly altruistic situation was rendered more plausible when Miller changed two of these friends into members of David's family.

'What I saw,' said the playwright, 'without laboring the details, was that two of the characters, who had been friends in previous drafts, were logically brothers and had the same father.'[2]

The men who deliver David from orphanhood are Amos and Patterson Beeves, a son and father who enact one of the instances of ill fortune which David feels must soon strike him. Patterson has devoted a good part of his life to grooming his son to be a major league pitcher, and when he arranges for a scout from the Detroit Tigers to watch Amos play, Patterson is sure that all the years of intensive training are finally about to be gloriously justified. But in one of the drama's better scenes, the scout sadly tells the father that his boy has been ruined by the rigorous schedule Patterson had set for him winter after winter in the cellar of their home. Accustomed to pitching in solitude, Amos simply cannot function under normal game pressures, with men on base, in front of a noisy crowd, and undoing the pattern into which the young man has fallen would be too long and tentative a process.

To Patterson's puzzled declaration that his training program was established to utilize every moment of free time, Augie Belfast, the scout, replies, 'Yeh, that's just where you made your mistake, Mr Beeves.' And when Patterson agonizingly confesses that Amos will be lost because he had never been prepared for any other vocation, Belfast can only repeat his answer: 'I guess that was another mistake.' After the scout leaves, Amos turns on his father in rage, shame, and despair.

'You liar,' he cries. 'I'll kill you, you little fake, *you liar!*'

[2] *Ibid.*, p.15.

This wail of rebuke is the chilling predecessor of Chris Keller's denunciation of his father, and of Biff Loman's condemnation of Willy ('You fake! You phoney little fake!') and shows that in a subplot of this poorly structured drama, Miller again uncomprehendingly fashioned a conflict that he had stumbled upon in *They Too Arise* and that would become pivotal in his next two plays: the struggle between a father who has tried too hard to propel his child to success and a son whose life has been damaged by the older man's blind zeal.

Not until Miller changed Amos and Patterson Beeves into David's brother and father (he was David Beeves in the stage production) did the pattern which lay buried beneath the strident social protest of *They Too Arise* and the metaphysical confusion of the original version of *The Man Who Had All the Luck* begin to clarify itself.

With the inclusion of David into the Beeves' family, Miller returned to the seminal relationship in *They Too Arise* and gave it renewed definition. Patterson Beeves now has two sons: one who, anticipatory of Larry Keller and Happy Loman, is destroyed by his father's misguided thinking, while the other, heralding Chris Keller and Biff Loman, manages to survive through a painful exertion of will which enables him to tear away from his father's frenzied devotion. Finally, in its treatment of the father-son relationship, *The Man Who Had All the Luck* is the last of Miller's dramas until *The Price* in which the son is the protagonist. In the following plays the father moves out of the shadows into the glare of center stage and brings with him all the strengths and weaknesses that will define him.

However, in 1944 Miller would still have to wait a few years before he could grasp the significance of this emerging design. Only later would he realize that much of his dissatisfaction with *The Man Who Had All the Luck* was due to the fact that:

> the overt story was only tangential to the secret drama its author was quite unconsciously trying to write. But in writing of the father-son relationship and of the son's search for relatedness there was a fullness of feeling I had never known before; a crescendo was struck with a force I could almost touch. The crux of *All My Sons* . . . was formed; and the roots of *Death of a Salesman* were sprouted.[3]

[3] *Ibid.*, p.15.

Interestingly, Miller's omission of *They Too Arise* in his description of the genesis of this father-son relationship shows just how deeply this 'secret drama' was buried beneath the 'overt story' of that early and angry young play.

Although the playwright came to view the 'secret drama' of *The Man Who Had All the Luck* as its outstanding feature, the 'overt story' also rests upon a premise that would continue to be crucial to his outlook, namely, the idea of individual responsibility. Too simply and noisily heralded in *They Too Arise*, this theme is not successfully dramatized in *The Man Who Had All the Luck* either; but two aspects of it do emerge in this play: the relationship between materialism and morality—here neatly resolved, as the loss of material well being becomes a prerequisite for spiritual regeneration*—and the more complex union of actions and consequences.

David is a semirealized composite of Chris and Joe Keller. Like Chris, he is an idealist who simply cannot accept the nihilism of one of his friends. Simultaneously, he anticipates the elder Keller in his inability to relate himself to the consequences of his actions. The marked difference between David and the antagonists of *All My Sons* is that David works out his destiny in a social vacuum. Despite Miller's awkwardly earnest attempts to provide *The Man Who Had All the Luck* with an authentic communal life, the play remains essentially what one critic aptly called 'a disengaged moral fable about a particular individual.'[4] In his later works this fabulistic quality never quite vanishes, but as the dramas are set in firmer social contexts, the disengagement does. Henceforth the connection between individual responsibility and social relatedness will personally and deeply involve the author of *The Man Who Had All the Luck*.

---

* Some of David's guilt seems to stem from his suspicion that his prosperity is divorced from manual labour. The salutary quality of this industry (Hester finally convinces David that he is good with his hands) is a leitmotif in much of Miller's work, most notably in *Death of a Salesman*. Although it is a concept inherent in the colonial agrarianism and frontier spirit of early America, Miller undeniably owes his allegiance to it to the romanticized proletarianism of the Depression era.

4 Robert Hogan, *Arthur Miller*, University of Minnesota Pamphlets on American Writers (Minneapolis: University of Minnesota Press, 1964), pp.13-14.

6

'It doesn't matter anyway. Does it?'

Miller's old football injury kept him out of the armed forces during the Second World War, and although he wrote scripts in behalf of bond drives and worked in the Brooklyn Navy Yard, he could not help feeling dissatisfied and even somewhat guilty as he played the unwilling part of sideline observer to the greatest drama of his time. So it was with great eagerness that he accepted an offer by film producer Lester Cowan to gather material for a motion picture about the war. Cowan had been told about the young writer by Broadway producer Herman Shumlin, who had heard some of Miller's radio scripts and read a couple of his unproduced plays, and when they met he told the playwright of his plans to make a movie based on war correspondent Ernie Pyle's *This Is Your War*, a compilation of battlefield reports and newspaper columns.

Miller was to visit various army bases and installations around the country to absorb atmosphere which Cowan hoped would imbue the film with an authenticity that was noticeably lacking in most of the glossy Hollywood products churned out by the ream since 1941. The producer wanted a movie that would tell as honestly and graphically as possible what its title promised: *The Story of G.I. Joe.*

Miller was immediately enthusiastic about the project. He wanted to capture the life at the camps, emphasize the training and discipline, and portray as frankly as possible the tough and gritty process of molding civilians into soldiers. Most of all, he hoped to hammer out a scenario that would eliminate the stereotyped Hollywood G.I.s and replace these pasteboard replicas with some recognizable human beings.

He spent two months visiting placement centers, infantry bases, officer candidate schools, and tank and parachute installations. He talked with thousands of men, ate with them, and accompanied them on maneuvers. He rode atop the tanks and crouched in a foxhole as one of the steel rhinos lurched and roared over him. He interviewed generals and privates, patients hospitalized for injuries suffered in jump school and on obstacle courses, and malcontents in the stockades. In the evening, in barracks and on trains, he jotted down impressions, snatches of dialogue, and descriptions of the men and situations he had encountered. At the end of his tour he spent a couple of days with Ernie Pyle, checking out his observations against those of the correspondent who had lived with these soldiers at the other end of the route, in the flame and mud of real combat. Miller then submitted his material to Cowan for absorption into what became perhaps the finest motion picture about the infantryman in World War II.

Once the producer received his reports, Miller's role in the project was over, and since the film, under the impressive direction of William Wellman, dealt exclusively with the soldier in combat, the writer's contributions were at best tangential. But so involved had Miller become with his efforts that he fashioned them into a project of his own. Compiling all the material he had accumulated, he shaped it into a book of reportage and personal impressions that he published in 1944 under the title *Situation Normal*. Implied in the name, and in the basic motif of the book, were the three remaining words of the United States Army's most famous descriptive phrase about its efficiency: All Fouled Up.

Reviewers were almost unanimous in their receptions of the book: they found the objective reportage first-rate, but were disappointed with the stretches of impressions and ideas which the author interpolated. In the *New York Herald Tribune* of December 17, 1944, Herbert Kufferberg reported that 'Miller was an excellent reporter . . . with an eye for the little things that give meaning to the big ones,' but that his narrative was marred by his continual 'wondering just how this incident or that soldier can best be worked into the film.'

This preference for more clear-eyed and tight-lipped observation was echoed by Russell Maloney in the *New York Times* a week later.

'Miller is at his best when he is describing actual happenings,' wrote the critic, 'and poorest stalking ideas and impressions and trying to come up with the philosophy of the soldier.'

Continuing an assessment that would anticipate scores of sub-sequent commentaries on Miller's drama in general, Maloney com-pared the strengths and weaknesses of *Situation Normal* to the virtues and faults of the war films Miller had tried to improve upon and rendered the ironic judgement that like most of them the book was trapped between its photographic realism and its didac-ticism.

'When they show us somebody actually doing something, they're fine,' Maloney concluded. 'When they're just talking, they're not so impressive.'

Now, more than twenty years after its publication, *Situation Normal* is still an interesting work, but for reasons opposite to those given by its initial reviewers. The reportage, which comprises the bulk of the volume, has the accuracy and depth of a competent newsreel; it is tight, objective, and hard-hitting, but it is no better and no worse than thousands of articles about American fighting men during the war. However, the book's particular interest is not provided by the reportorial skill of its author but by precisely those 'ideas and impressions' that discomfited the critics in 1944.

The philosophy of *Situation Normal* is not tangential to the book; it is its core.

'You cannot make a true picture of this war,' he stated in his preface, 'until you make up your mind as to what this war is about'.

Situation Normal is *not* a record of Miller's attempt to make up his mind; almost every word in the book proves that he did that before he ever began the assignment. Rather, it is a chronicle of his efforts to see his beliefs substantiated by the men who were going out to put their lives on the line. Miller was sure of what the war was about. It was a struggle between the right of each individual to determine his freedom and the tyrannic corporate control of the minds and wills of men. And he knew 'not only that America must win, but that Fascism must be destroyed.'

This was of course the idealism of the young radical of the 1930s, but now it embraced a cause and conflict infinitely wider and deeper in scope than the labor unrest of that previous decade. America had entered a struggle that was marked—for all its horror and destruction—by a moral simplicity, and like the overwhelm-ing majority of his countrymen, Arthur Miller found himself rally-ing round the flag.

Ironically, *Situation Normal* is less a validation of a faith than a catalog of disillusionment exhibiting its author's increasing bewilderment. Never doubting his idealistic premise about the war, Miller questioned soldier after soldier in a vain attempt to find the awareness he had taken so blithely for granted at the beginning of his tour.

'It was obvious that the men are not impressed with the connection of their intimate fates with those of other peoples fighting the war,' he exclaimed with a bitter new realization. 'I am beginning to understand why so many men in the Army regard the war as a kind of personal calamity, like an auto accident or something.'[1]

At first Miller tried to rationalize his findings with a forced optimism about the subliminal beliefs of the American soldier: 'I couldn't help believing, though, as I watched those men sprawled on the floor (in the barracks) that somewhere in their subconscious they knew. . . . It is just a hope on my part, but the awareness, must be in them somewhere.'[2]

He reached out avidly for any manifestation of this awareness, citing a Czech immigrant who had recently been granted citizenship and knew exactly for what he was fighting ('For my country, yes. . . . I am a citizen here now. And so I have two countries and I feel like fighting twice as hard').

But Miller was too honest to allow himself to take any smug comfort from exceptions like this. With every succeeding interview he grew more disillusioned as he was forced to face the fact that most of the trainees simply did not view the war in terms of principles.

'I can't seem to find men who betray a social responsibility as a reason for doing or not doing anything,' he wearily acknowledged. 'Maybe it was always so. Maybe that's why Tom Paine got drunk all the time.'[3]

There is something grimly humorous in the young writer's frustration and chagrin at swallowing the bitter but obvious truth that in the midst of soul-stirring causes, the majority is motivated by self-preservation and little else. To the glorious and spiritually exalting cry of 'Charge!' the khaki-clad Light Brigade was reply-

---

[1] Arthur Miller, *Situation Normal* (New York: Reynal & Hitchcock, 1944), pp.39–40.

[2] *Ibid.*, p.40.

[3] *Ibid.*, p.44.

ing with a raised eyebrow and a tentative and grudging step forward.

The pivotal point in *Situation Normal* is Miller's interview of a
soldier named Watson. In the light of his subsequent work, it is
perhaps one of the most significant conversations in the writer's life.

While touring an officers candidate school, Miller was asked by
the commanding officer to speak with one of the candidates, a
veteran with an above-average I.Q. who nevertheless was failing
the program. It was midmorning as the tall, lean writer strode over
to the wooden barracks where he found the soldier alone, lying
listlessly on his bunk smoking a cigarette.

From the moment they began to speak, Miller noticed that the
other man was nervous, almost distraught, and 'seemed a million
miles away.' Unlike most of the candidates, Watson was a combat
veteran who was being sent through the program as part of his
promotion for heroism in battle. He had joined the army just prior
to the attack on Pearl Harbor and, after America was plunged into
the conflict, was sent to the Pacific where he was immediately
hurled into the sweltering fury of hand-to-hand jungle combat.
His description of the ferocious and gruesome close-quarter fighting stunned Miller, but when Watson tried to describe his feelings
about these experiences, the writer knew he had struck upon something crucial.

'It got so, after being in the line for almost two months, that I
forgot I had ever lived any place else,' the soldier recalled. And
then, speaking more to himself than to his companion, he continued:

> You find out all about yourself out there, as if all the excuses
> you've always made for yourself were suddenly very silly.
> Friendship is the greatest thing out there. I mean real friend-
> ship, not because a guy can give you something you want. I
> tell you the truth: I would die for any one of thirty or forty
> men out there just as easy as I'd flick out this match. I swear
> that's the truth. I don't expect you to understand it, but I
> swear it. It never seemed a terrible thing or a sacrifice after
> a while. I would die for them. I love them with everything in
> my heart.[4]

Listening to him, Miller knew that no matter how uncompre-

⁴ *Ibid.*, p.145.

hendingly he had entered the war, Watson had found some meaning in its horrible maw. Terms like friendship, love, and responsibility that had never meant much to him before, suddenly took on profound significance as their implications were tested in the midst of a terrible nativity.

When questioned about his apparent failure at the officers candidate school, Watson admitted to the writer that he simply could not fit into the program. The entire experience was strangely superficial to him, and he felt about the school pretty much the way he felt when he returned home on furlough to be treated like a conquering hero, with brass bands, parades, and star-spangled oratory. Nothing was real; it was all a bizarre dream. No one at home really existed for him anymore.

'I feel now like every friend I ever had in the world is either dead or fighting over there,' he confessed. 'Everything I know about is over there.'

He explained to Miller that he felt guilty for being safely back in the United States while his remaining friends were still fighting and dying in enemy jungles. And the knowledge that not only did they not resent his good fortune but were actually counting on him to succeed in OCS as their surrogate, dug like a bayonet into his heart. Almost wholly incapacitated by his guilt, he even found himself sexually impotent.

' I just can't imagine myself doing anything like that,' he admitted, 'till they're finished fighting out there and on their way home.'

He concluded the conversation by reiterating his fervent hope of returning to his old outfit.

After Miller head Watson's story, he related it to the company commander in the hope that something could be arranged to enable the soldier to receive the commission he wanted so badly. But the officer surprised the writer by suggesting that the veteran did not really want to receive the commission at all. Noting the quizzical look on Miller's face, the captain exclaimed that Watson knew that the chances of a reunion with his original unit were less than 100 to 1. When Miller protested that the soldier could have been referring to frontline fighting men in general, rather than to his specific company, the officer expounded his interpretation of Watson's plight.

Explaining to the writer that the main thing the army tried to instill in trainees was Unit Pride—the intense belief in and commitment of each soldier to his company—the captain suggested that Watson's current dilemma rose out of his feeling of alienation from his outfit.

'Through no fault of his own, he had been cut away from them. And the company pride that made him do the great things he did do is gone now and he is left unattached, an individual.'

The company commander leaned forward, quietly driving his words home.

'And he may regard a return to the front with all the horror that any individual regards it with—any individual like yourself, who is not spurred on by company pride, who has to go through hell completely on his own steam, alone.'[5]

The officer's theory gave Miller a new perspective on Watson's predicament. With a sudden clarity, the writer saw in the soldier's anguish the core of what he had been seeking so unsuccessfully in the past two months. Watson was not a rarity. Although more intense, his problem was painfully similar to the dilemma many veterans would be facing when they returned from combat to resume civilian lives. They would have to try to cope with the difficulty of transferring military loyalties back to prior civilian relationships, or be forever 'in that restless, aimless state of emotional thirst which . . . has made veterans the anxious and willing collaborators of any demagogue.' And this is what a man like Watson was finding so hard to do:

He must return to his former group . . . reassume its little prejudices, its hates, its tiny aims. He must lop off . . . that one-time feeling of exhilaration he got from the knowledge that whatever the insignificance of his job, it was helping an enormous mass of men toward a great and worthy goal. Now he must forget that. Now he must live unto himself, for his own selfish welfare. Half of him, in a sense, must die, and with it must pass away half the thrill he knew in being alive. He must, in short, become a civilian again.[6]

He had to return to a private life after profoundly living a public one. He had to return to self-interest after knowing the deepest

[5] *Ibid.*, p.154.
[6] *Ibid.*, p.157.

kind of responsibilty. He had to attach himself to the small, personal units of civilian life—family, business, clubs—but with the disquieting knowledge that they might 'never make up in largeness or vitality for the goal he left behind.'

What could be done for this man, Miller asked himself. 'What could civilian America possibly give to Watson that it did not give?' There was only one answer as far as he could see, and he summarized it in his definition of Belief:

> Say it this way. If when he returned . . . he walked in the cities and towns and all about him he sensed and heard evidence that the people were unified in one concept—that he, Watson, had gone forth to rescue something very precious, and that had he not gone forth, and had that thing been lost, the people would have been in mourning for the rest of their lives.[7]

Watson had been linked to his buddies by

> an emotional unity born of common danger and the common military goal—they *knew* each other through that and they were one with each other, because of it. What links Watson with the civilians at home, though? A parade? Sympathy? . . . The only means by which Watson can rejoin himself with America is by sharing with civilian America a well understood Belief in the rightness, justice, the necessity of his fight.[8]

The naïveté of this observation is obvious. First, the conclusion that veterans were inevitably disappointed in their homecomings is not the most felicitous example of clear inductive reasoning. Secondly, the premise that every American fighting man was 'exhilarated' at being part of 'a great and worthy goal' is at best tenuous and at worst the same kind of maudlin sentiment that Miller had deplored in all those celluloid epics he was attempting to contradict. In his understandably fervent commitment to the moral rectitude of the war, he refused to acknowledge anything less than the most selfless motivations for his country's military, and the possibility that a man could fight and kill solely to save his own skin, or even for the sheer sadistic pleasure of the action, seemed not to cross the young writer's mind. Finally, the concept

[7] *Ibid.*, pp.158–159.
[8] *Ibid.*, pp.158–159.

of Belief, with its portentous capital lettering, is, for all its obvious sincerity, a rather glib and remote panacea for a highly complex problem.

Nevertheless, despite the weaknesses of Miller's conclusions, they retain a certain validity. If he oversimplified the dilemmas of returning veterans, he still touched upon problems faced by many of them; and even though his analyses of the soldiers were often superficial and his resolutions ingenuous, his delineation of a basic lack of communication between the combat veteran and the world to which he was returning was frequently accurate. The rootlessness and dissatisfaction of many ex-servicemen in postwar America proved to be a sadly eloquent testimony to this impression.

For Miller, Watson was partially the victim of a society that had not provided him with a sense of connection extending beyond the praiseworthy but limited loyalties to self and family. Like Chris Keller of *All My Sons*, whose prototype he clearly is, Watson could not readjust to a world which, for all its slogans, had not really absorbed the profound experiences and truths he had. Unlike his fictitious successor, Watson was unable to probe the implications of his experiences. Viewing his outfit as the definitive social group of his life, the veteran was ultimately betrayed by the narrowness of his otherwise laudatory commitment. Consequently cut off from his inner world by circumstance, he found himself adrift in an outer world he could not understand. The man Arthur Miller met in the OCS barracks was alone and afraid, caught between a meaningful allegiance he could no longer maintain, and another which had quite lost its meaning.

If Watson's plight pointed to major themes in *All My Sons*, it also embodied a motif that the playwright would not dramatize in depth until two decades after his fateful meeting with the young veteran: the relationship of separateness and betrayal.

Sincerely loving the men of his platoon, Watson nonetheless was betraying that love by failing officers candidate school. Although he could honestly talk about dying for any one of his friends, he could not wholly stifle the ambivalent relief at being removed from their peril, and the dichotomy between his earnest words and his reluctant actions was agonizingly clear. As Miller walked out of his life, Watson remained a man torn by fear and guilt, frustrated and yet never wholly comprehending the meaning of his frustration. In *Situation Normal*, Miller did not explore the ramifications of this conflict between self-preservation and commitment. The time and place were not conducive, and the writer was still subordinating psychological insight to didacticism; but twenty years later, in *After the Fall, Incident at Vichy,* and *The Price,* the exploration would be made, with some conclusions that would have shocked the idealistic and impressionable young author of *Situation Normal.*

The book continues with Miller meeting Ernie Pyle to compare observations, and the differences between the two men are quickly confirmed. Miller was puzzled and disappointed by the famous war correspondent, who seemed polite but totally unreceptive to his moral earnestness. In almost all of Pyle's battlefield reports, Miller had found graphic descriptions of combat, stripped bare of any theorizing, and now he discovered the same sparseness in the man himself. At first the playwright was disconcerted by Pyle's apparent lack of deliberation about the war, but the longer he spoke with him and pondered his approach, he gradually began to realize that the correspondent was not just photographically recording events:

> Ernie Pyle's thought *was* in his columns. His thought is people. His thought is details about people. War is about people, not ideas. You cannot see ideas bleeding. . . . Ernie knew most soldiers were not being visibly changed by ideas. He understood completely that they could be, but it was not his business to write about what could be. He had enough to do writing about what is. Now.[9]

Miller wanted to do both.

> Because the truth is a larger thing than what man feels or knows at any particular time in his life. This war is not merely about a lot of guys who are doing something which will have significance when their uniforms are moth-eaten and don't fit any more. Ernie knows this better than I, but it is not his business to deal with it.[10]

Miller made it his.

Situation Normal concludes with the writer on a plane, observing

[9] *Ibid.,* p.166.
[10] *Ibid.,* p.167.

a young Naval officer on his way home from combat duty in the Pacific. He imagines the homecoming of the serviceman, his reunion with his family and sweetheart, and his awkward attempts to establish some kind of meaningful communication with them. Finally, he visualizes a scene between the young officer and his mother, at the breakfast table, as she asks him to describe his experiences overseas.

'Well in the beginning it was pretty bad,' the lieutenant mutters in Miller's imaginary conversation. 'But after a while . . . it was all right.'

And then, trying to be gentle with his mother, he attempts to abort the painful conversation.

'Oh, hell, let it go at that. It doesn't matter anyway.'

But the young man is struck by a sudden afterthought.

'Does it?' he asks himself.

For Arthur Miller, the question was—and is—rhetorical.

7

'An adjustment of distance to make

a clear image'

When he went job hunting after his high school graduation in the early 1930s, Arthur Miller first experienced the acrid taste of anti-Semitism. As he worked in the Brooklyn Navy Yard during the war, he again sampled its sour, bilious flavor.

He had been sharing a job with a Czech welder, with whom he had struck up a casual friendship. One day, while they were idly talking during a lunch break, the other man suddenly revealed a viciously anti-Semitic bias. Although it was not directed at Miller, whom he did not even suspect of being Jewish, the writer was so stunned by the vehemence and ugliness of the outburst that he 'just couldn't believe it.' The incipient friendship was rapidly dissolved, but the bitter memory of the incident remained with Miller for a long time.

No clearly defined line connects this event with Miller's novel, *Focus*, but its influence upon the book is pervasive. The senseless, unreasoning hatred that arbitrarily breaks through the apparently placid and genial exterior of an individual provides the oppressive climate in which the action of the novel takes place.

Originally *Focus* was conceived as a play, but as the idea took form, Miller felt that the situation and mood could best be realized within the structure of the novel, which would enable him to tell the story in the third person while simultaneously sifting the events through the mind of the central character, Lawrence Newman. Although he was not yet ready to attempt it on the stage, Miller was employing in *Focus* the technique he would perfect in *Death of a Salesman*.

The action unravels dualistically, through a series of external incidents leading in an accelerating arc to an explosive climax, but even more importantly, through the protagonist's hypersensitive impressions of and reactions to these events. A humiliating job interview, a subway ride (approximating a descent into a Plutonian underworld), the icy glare of a hostile neighbor, an overturned garbage can—all become chilling manifestations of a nightmare world that despite its proximity to external reality takes on a frightening meaning of its own. And because Newman's fevered perspective is set against an objective frame of reference, the reader can note his dislocation without being totally drawn into its vortex. Not until the climactic struggle in the book, a bizarre and brutal battle on a dark, snow-swept street, does the objective world finally coalesce with Newman's impressions of it, fusing the nightmare into reality.

Focus tells the story of the macabre disorientation of a New York personnel executive. A nondescript little man, he is wholly unsympathetic in his patronizing attitude toward those whom he considers inferior and in his fawning subservience before the personages who occupy the rungs above him in the politely anti-Semitic corporation for which he works. Compulsive, fastidious, and apprehensive, he is like a mouse on a conveyor belt, scurrying feverishly to maintain his shaky equilibrium.

Possibly he might have maintained it, and his existence would probably have yawned into a grey infinity, were it not for a rather ordinary occurrence which abruptly detours his life. Because of failing sight, Newman is forced to get a pair of spectacles, which, to his chagrin, make him appear decidedly Semitic. This embarrassing new look rapidly leads to a series of situations in which he is increasingly persecuted and victimized by a world wherein he had considered himself secure.

At first he is demoted from his job in personnel because his new countenance is detrimental to the organization's image. Enraged at this humiliation, he hastily resigns, only to find that his troubles are just beginning. In a series of job interviews he is treated with the same placid condescension he had previously shown to applicants before him, and even though he finally obtains a new position he accepts it out of desperation rather than preference. The neighbors on his block begin to doubt him, and when he marries a woman who also looks Jewish, they openly shun him. Because they are trying to maintain a restricted neighborhood, their cold indifference finally flares into overt hostility, and Newman is forced to undergo a number of petty harassments. Increasingly he finds himself being pushed into an unwilling alliance with the only real Jew on the block, a storekeeper named Finkelstein, who has incurred his neighbors' wrath by refusing to move.

At his wife's urging Newman makes a final effort to reinstate himself in the good graces of his former companions by attending an America-First rally as proof of his loyalty and ethnic purity, but his Semitic appearance elicits suspicion, and the evening degenerates into a fiasco when he is thrown out of the hall after he finds himself surprisingly unable to applaud the featured speaker.

The book reaches its climax when the Newmans are waylaid by a few hired thugs who hope that a beating will persuade them to move. As his wife flees, Newman is saved from serious injury when Finkelstein rushes to his aid, and even though the two men are beaten up, they manage to fight off their assailants. Newman then helps the injured Jew to clean up and puts him to bed. When he gets home his wife pleads with him to see the neighbor who instigated the attack. She explains that from a conversation she has just had with the man, she is sure that he is now convinced that the Newmans are not Jews and is ready to accept them. But Newman turns from her in disgust, walks out of the house, and goes to the local police station to report the assault. When the officer on duty assumes that he is Jewish, Newman affirms the assumption, and in so doing feels 'as though he were setting down a weight which for some reason he had been carrying and carrying.'[1]

Focus is a flawed book. The plight of an individual forced into becoming the victim of prejudices with which he had aligned himself most of his life rings with an honest dramatic irony. But the devices Miller employs to sustain this irony are sometimes as authentic as Uriah Heep's humility.

The triangular structure of the block, with a Jew on one end, the most outspoken bigot on the other, and Newman conveniently in between, is established more with an eye to symmetry than to credibility. So too is Newman's literal and figurative movement toward Finkelstein, which is balanced neatly by his movement away from his former friends. Concomitantly, the series of interviews which find the protagonist on the opposite side of the desk from which he begins the story, to patly reinforce the obvious pattern of reversals upon which the book is structured. Finally, Newman's

[1] Arthur Miller, *Focus* (New York: Reynal & Hitchcock, 1945), p.217.

relationship with his wife, Gertrude, is cluttered with contrivance. Rejected by him in a job interview because he thought she was Jewish, she then appears as *his* interviewer, and before you can say peripeteia she not only gets him a position but rather hastily manages to reel him in as well. Her Semitic appearance serves her husband rather badly but the demands of the plot quite well, by verifying the suspicions of the neighbors. However, this bit of coincidence pales alongside her final function in the story. She is able to convince Newman's harassers of his loyalty because—and this almost ruptures the concept of a small world—she has formerly been involved with the same superpatriotic organization they represent.

If his wife teeters perilously on the rim of the credible, Newman's mother never quite rises from the depths of the unrealized. She is an invalid who lives with Newman and who appears to be a determining factor in his neurotic existence, but she never emerges from her shadowy limbo. The dramatic possibility inherent in the confrontation between her and her son's new wife remains totally unexplored. She has no existence of her own, and blends finally into the darkness of the room which encloses her.

Several reviewers of the book felt that another of its drawbacks was the contrived use of the eyeglasses to initiate and sustain the action. To an extent this criticism is valid. In employing the spectacles as the immediate reason for Newman's reversals, Miller is on firm dramatic footing, particularly in his portrayal of the reaction of Newman's employers to his altered appearance. They do not suspect him of being Jewish; they are simply chagrined that one of their top personnel interviewers looks Semitic. But when the author asks his reader to believe that friends who have known a man for years begin to suspect him of being a Jew because he puts on spectacles, he is wading into murky waters. The writer might reply that the absurdity of the reaction is precisely his point, since the irrationality of prejudice is one of the book's main premises. Nevertheless, dramatizing senselessness is almost as difficult as dramatizing luck: it puts an enormous strain on credulity. For example, the possibility of trying different spectacles in the hope of finding a more flattering pair never seems to occur to the bedeviled Mr Newman. It should at least occur to Mr Miller.

Still, although they are obviously a device, the glasses are integral to the purposes of the novel and, ultimately, are well worth the calculated risk which Miller took with the laws of probability. Like many of the playwright's subsequent heroes, Lawrence Newman suffers from myopia; he cannot see things distinctly. Obviously his physical ailment is symbolic of a more pervasive and crucial moral affliction.

Focus is defined by *Webster's New World Dictionary* as '*an adjustment of distance to make a clear image*,' and this is precisely the definition Miller has in mind. At first the figurative adjustment of Newman's moral outlook parallels his literal reaction to the glasses: vision is narrowed and intensified, but also distorted. As he gains focus, his view becomes sharper but circumscribed, concentrating inward. Then it begins to expand beyond the self, encompassing others. It is this double focus, inward and outward, leading to greater clarity and comprehension, which provides the movement of the book.

Despite its structural flaws and occasionally inchoate characterization, *Focus* is a taut and exciting novel. Newman's demotion, his initial attemps to cope with the glasses, the melee at the America-First rally, and the night attack in the snow are only a few of vividly etched scenes that underscore the birth pangs of Newman's second nativity; and although some sequences are luridly highlighted, others blend smoothly into the fabric of the book. Newman's dream of the carnival, his entrapment in the glass office, the movie that he sees just prior to his assault, and the allegory of Itzik the Jew all beautifully enhance the action and substantiate the meaning of the story. And even though Newman's wife and mother are unsuccessful characterizations, Newman himself is skillfully realized.

Not only is Lawrence Newman a most reluctant hero, but throughout most of the novel he is a genuinely offensive bundle of eccentricities and prejudices. In his forties, he has had no relationship with a woman, due partially to his fear of involvement as well as to his sickly attachment to his invalid mother. His sexual frustration manifests itself in two particular ways: in a recurring dream about a faceless, fleshy female whose thighs dominate his fevered imagination, and in his obsessive preoccupation with his car. He is in fact pleased that gasoline rationing has forced him to store the automobile in the garage because he is now able to lavish care and attention on it.

Without admitting it . . . he enjoyed the car much more . . . when it was on the blocks. . . . On these war Sundays he took the immaculate storage battery, which he kept in the basement, and installed it in the car and ran the engine for a few moments. And then he disconnected the battery and hauled it back into the cellar, and walked around the car looking for rust spots, and turned the wheels a little . . . to keep the bearing grease mobile, and generally did each Sunday what the manufacturer had advised doing twice a year.[2]

It is hardly coincidental that Newman's delight in handling and nursing the passive automobile is markedly contrasted to the 'terrorizing experience' he undergoes the other days of the week when he sits exposed 'in full view of the stenographers' on the sixteenth floor of the skyscraper in which he works.

Newman's feelings of sexual inadequacy are also sublimated in an obsessive fixation with order. Like Mr Prufrock's existence, Newman's is measured out with coffee spoons, the same number of grains falling daily, like sand, into the hourglass urn of his life. Each day is marked by a precise routine that involves his immaculate attire, subway trips into the city, the perfectly timed return home, the ritual of the evening meal and paper, and the exact dispensation of clothing to proper closets, hangers, and hatboxes. (Indeed, an initial sign of Newman's dislocation is his forgetting to put his hat away for the night.) He even takes a particular comfort in noting the similarity of the houses on his block. 'The memory of their sameness soothed his yearning for order.'

This yearning also manifests itself in the office he has designed for himself:

Several years ago, in his zeal to serve his employers as they had never been served, he had conceived of an office with glass walls to be set on one side of the floor. The arrangement was adopted, and from then on he could work at his desk and simply look up to tell at a glance whether the whole floor was in order.[3]

But this glass-enclosed room soon proved glaringly detrimental to its creator. Not only does it place him in full, naked view of

[2] *Ibid.*, p.14.
[3] *Ibid.*, p.14.

all seventy stenographers on the floor, but with his eyesight failing, he is put at an overwhelming disadvantage, since everyone can see into the office while he cannot see out. The plate glass cage literally isolates Newman without endowing him with any of the comforts of privacy. Metaphorically it describes his entire life.

In every area of his existence he remains figuratively imprisoned in a glass office, staring blurrily at people but unable to communicate with them. In his business and in the social life of his neighborhood, Newman is a man apart, quarantined by his annihilating insecurity and fear of self-assertion. Torn between a covert contempt for individuals he envies and resents and an ambivalent desire for some sort of communal existence, his whole life can be defined by Prufrock's question: 'How should I presume?' His toadying eagerness to please his superiors, his continual anxiety about his position with the firm, and his compulsive need to soak up his neighbors' comradery all emanate out of that single query.

Newman's weaknesses strongly emphasize the difficulty of the reluctant trek he must make from murkiness to illumination, and render his ultimate victory all the more significant in the light of the obstacles barring his way. Even more importantly, by making Newman unappealing, Miller can suspend the reader's sympathy and allow him to view the protagonist analytically as well as sentimentally.

The fact that Newman is a Gentile rather than a Jew also fulfills Miller's intentions. Aside from enabling the writer to dramatize the irony of his protagonist's plight, Newman's background also allows Miller to avoid triteness and sentimentalism. One of the salient points made in the book is that its central character is a victimizer as well as a victim, who, like many of the Salemites in *The Crucible*, is swept into a whirlpool of evil for which he is partially accountable.

Newman's responsibility for his predicament is exhibited in numerous ways. In the book's opening incident, a woman is attacked in the street below his window. But although he can hear her cries for help and see her struggling with her assailant, he does nothing, closes his window, and returns to bed. He refuses to help the woman because he is understandably afraid of getting into trouble; but he rationalizes his behavior by noting her Puerto Rican accent. Considering her nationality, and the lateness of the hour, he is able to satisfy his conscience with the assumption that 'she was abroad at night for no good purpose,' and that she could probably 'take care of herself because she was used to this sort of treatment. Puerto Ricans were, he knew.'

His observation of her ethnic background is more than just a convenient justification for turning his back on her; it is a manifestation of the prejudices that bubble beneath his immaculately groomed exterior.

It is precisely the blandness of Newman's prejudice that makes it so terrifying, and in this complacency his moral myopia manifests itself most repugnantly. He does not observe individuals; he sees types whose cardinal sin is being different. Even when circumstances draw him into a begrudging alliance with Finkelstein, Newman can barely comprehend the man as anything more than a stereotyped representative of an alien group.

'You don't understand,' he says to the storekeeper in dumb sincerity, 'it's not what *you've* done, it's what others of your people have done.'

Finkelstein's reply slashes to the core of Newman's affliction. 'In other words,' he answers sardonically, 'when you look at me you don't see me.'

Although the apparent impersonality of Newman's bigotry is so exasperating for Finkelstein, this intolerance is much more a part of Newman's germplasm than his neighbor realizes. Evolving out of the insecure little man's isolation, his bigotry has become a compensatory mechanism against it. In his particular alienation Newman has been forced into the figurative role of the Jew long before the eyeglasses turned him into a literal pariah. In fact he is infinitely more alone than Finkelstein because he lacks the storekeeper's family ties, sense of tradition, and inherent dignity.

Consequently, Newman's resentment of the Jew is partially the outgrowth of his semiconscious identification with him. Secretly detesting the weaknesses which isolate him from his society, he transfers his self-disgust to this convenient surrogate self. For Lawrence Newman, the Jew becomes what Miller in *Incident at Vichy* is to call 'the Other.' Not only is he the object upon whom Newman can vent his ambivalent aggressions, but he is also the scapegoat who provides, in their mutual detestation of him, the diseased bond between Newman and the community with which he is uneasily allied. Newman is never wholly alienated as long as he is willing to join in the persecution of the historical alien. To avoid

victimization he becomes the victimizer. Still beyond his comprehension is the possibility that a man can refuse the former and still
prevent himself from becoming the latter.

Finkelstein has transformed this possibility into fact. The storekeeper also has his prejudices, but he recognizes them for what
they are, and rather than rationalizing he continually attempts to
fight them.

'The other day,' he confides to Newman, 'a colored man—I
never seen him before—he comes into the store for Camels.'

> I ain't got Camels and I tell him. . . . 'Who was you saving
> them for?' he says, 'the Goldbergs?' If we was outside . . .
> I would have hit him with a box. On times like that I get
> a certain feeling about those people. To me they ain't regular.
> *But I try to stop my thoughts about them.* I say to myself, after
> all, how many colored people do I know? Better I should
> be saying, this colored person and that one I don't like. But
> I got no right I should condemn the whole people, you under-
> stand me? If I never seen California redwood trees what right
> I got to say they ain't so big? You understand me?—I got no
> right.[4]

Finkelstein's determination not to be a victimizer is the corollary
of his resolve not to be a victim. During a visit to his father's
grave, he recalls a story his father used to tell about a Jewish
peddler named Itzik who lived in Poland at the turn of the century.
Cheated and betrayed by a wealthy baron into becoming the victim
of an anti-Semitic pogrom, Itzik passively accepted his fate, and
suffered the destruction of his family and fortune. When questioned
as to the meaning of the story, the elder Finkelstein had replied:

> What it means? It means nothing. What could this Itzik do?
> Only what he had to do. And what he had to do would end
> up the way he knew it would end up, and there was nothing
> else he could do, and there was no other end possible. That's
> what it means.[5]

It is an answer dredged out of the blood of two thousand years
of persecution and victimization which have made the Jew consider

[4] *Ibid.*, p.166. Italics my own.
[5] *Ibid.*, p.148.

injustice as the immutable factor of his existence. But for Finkelstein the reply is insufficient. Brooding over his father's grave, he
notices a few nearby gravestones knocked over and defaced with
swastikas, and as he fights back angry tears he reconfirms his
rejection of his father's interpretation of the story:

> That Itzik, that peddler—there was a meaning to his story.
> And it was not that the Jew was fated to a bloody end. . . .
> The meaning . . . was that this Itzik *should never have allowed
> himself to accept a role that was not his,* a role that the baron
> had created for him . . . he should have allowed his indignation
> to carry him away and gotten on his wagon and driven directly
> home. And then when the pogrom came, as it would have no
> matter what he did, he could have found strength to fight.
> *It was the pogrom that was inevitable, but not its outcome.*[6]

On his return from the cemetery, Finkelstein buys three baseball
bats to keep in the store for protection. He will neither try to in-
gratiate himself with his neighbors, nor will he let them banish
him from his home. Either alternative would find him playing a
'role that is not his.' If a pogrom is mounted in the neighborhood,
he will accept only its factuality, but not the inevitability of its
outcome.

> If there are others who have something to be ashamed of, let
> them hide and wait for this thing that is happening, let them
> play the part they have been given and let them wait as though
> they are actually guilty of wrong. I have nothing to be ashamed
> of and I will not hide. . . . I am no Itzik. God dammit to
> hell . . . they are not going to make an Itzik out of me.[7]

The most profound difference between Finkelstein and Newman
is that for too long Newman played the false role by surrendering
his conscience and self-respect in return for the uncertain blessing
of security. It is this difference which the action of *Focus* relentlessly narrows. At the conclusion, Lawrence Newman also refuses
to play Itzik.

Just as he literally moves toward Finkelstein in a series of reluctant encounters that culminate in his care for the other man

[6] *Ibid.,* pp.149–150.
[7] *Ibid.,* p.150.

after their back-to-back struggle in the wintry street, Newman
figuratively closes the moral distance between himself and his unlikely neighbor. It is Finkelstein the individual whom Newman
comprehends as he progresses from his ambivalent relationship
with the archetypal Jew to his clear recognition of a particular one.

He achieves his first breakthrough on his way home from the
disastrous rally, when he is accosted by the storekeeper. Drawing
Newman into conversation, Finkelstein asks him what he sees
when he looks at him. Newman's evasive and embarrassed answer
is aborted when he suddenly realizes that the seemingly casual
question has been voiced in a deep but controlled anger.

> And standing there, looking into [Finkelstein's] angry face,
> Newman's idea of him altered. Where once he had seen a
> rather comical, ugly, and obsequious face, now he found a
> man . . . throbbing with anger. And somehow his anger made
> him comprehensible to Mr Newman. . . . And for a moment
> he felt intensely ashamed that Finkelstein, this adult and not
> at all comical man, was identifying him with the moronic
> mob at the hall. For he did not know how to answer Finkel-
> stein as a Fronter, as a man consumed by hate. The fact of
> the matter was that he had no complaint against Finkelstein
> in particular and he could not face the man like this—and he
> was a man now—and tell him that he disliked him. . . . looking
> at Finkelstein now, Newman saw that he had not really hated
> *him*, he had simply always been at the point of hating him. . . .[8]

Newman's new concept of Finkelstein is painfully confusing.
Just as the new glasses blurred all the images of a familiar and
ordered world, so too does this altered perspective jumble the old
ideas and prejudices which had fit so neatly into the narrow but
regulated pattern of his life.

> A spasm of distress began to take hold of Mr Newman's
> stomach. It was as though all the tokens of the known world
> had been switched, as though in a dream his own house
> numbers had been changed, the name of his street, the location
> of the 'ell' in relation to his corner, as though all the things
> that had been true were now catastrophically untrue. He felt
> he was going to throw up and cry. . . . The eyes of Mr Finkel-
> stein were on his back, hurting him more. If the man would

just disappear, just go away . . . for God's sake go away and
let everybody be the same! The same, the same, let us all be
the same![9]

Newman's attempt to deny Finkelstein is a measure of his reluctance to accept himself, an unwillingness which has marked all
of his actions since the day he tried on the glasses. From the
moment he is thrust into his bizarre new role he tries harder than
ever before to compromise. He continually alters his routine in the
desperate hope of ironing out the unexpected wrinkle in his life,
but each effort only increases his frustration. At first he is outraged at the gruesome irony that has made him the victim of his
own bigotry. But as his new identity is pressed upon him by his
firm, his neighbors, and the inescapable image in the mirror, his
rage is channeled into timorous acceptance. He changes some of
his gestures because he is afraid of seeming too forward, and in
a restaurant he even overtips the waitress and refuses to count his
change rather than be taken for a mercenary Jew. His groveling
becomes so marked that even his wife, a thoroughgoing bigot, is
enraged at his debasing attempts at accommodation.

However, as one exit of compromise after another slams shut
in his face, Newman still holds out against his truth. Even when his
assailants approach him and strike, he makes a last, desperate
effort at concession. Seconds before Finkelstein rushes to his rescue, Newman tries to divert the attack to the Jew. 'He stood there
and he saw then that his hand was pointing, pointing toward the
store. "Go!" he shouted.' It is not until the final exit is closed to
him, and he is literally back-to-back with Finkelstein that Newman
strikes back at his assailants.

Nonetheless, his counterattack is a blind backlash, the instinctive
reaction of any trapped animal. It is really the prelude to the important choice which occurs later that evening when Newman has
the opportunity to rejoin the persons who instigated the assault.
Faced with reentering this dubious Eden, he has only to nod his
head.

But he does not, and his negative reaction provides the most
positive moment of his life—his moment of commitment. The
way to it was paved by the brutal fight, in which he experienced a
new sense of awareness.

[9] *Ibid.*, p.170.

In all his life he had never known such calm, despite the torrent of blood rushing through him. Within his raging body a stillness had grown very wide and very deep and he stared at his image feeling the texture of this peace. It was almost a tone he seemed to be hearing, level and low and far away. He stood there listening to it.[10]

But it was also paved earlier, in the maelstrom of lesser indignities, when Newman walked through the city, 'and his honor stalked him, demanding its due. And it drained away his inner ease, it burdened him with a secret new personality.'[11] With each increasing humiliation his indignation had also increased, and when he strides toward the police station to report the attack, this identity, conceived in shame, but tempered in anger, is irrevocably certified. He feels that he has lived 'an honest five minutes . . . the first five minutes he had ever spent unafraid.' Situation has forced him to choose, but his ultimate choice is an act of will, a commitment to his integrity.

Ostensibly about anti-Semitism, *Focus* is also dramatizing something more. Anti-Semitism is one ugly manifestation of a distortion and perversion of human relationships which pervades the entire society in which Newman lives, and it is against this dark and treacherous swamp beneath the fragile veneer of civilization that Miller sets his story of a man's agonizing reevaluation of himself and his allegiances.

Throughout the novel, Newman is plagued by a recurring dream. He visualizes a large, spinning carousel that is fixed atop an underground factory in which something vaguely frightening is being manufactured. Finally he comes to realize that the carousel is a metaphor for civilization and the terrible thing churning beneath it is the unreasoning hatred and bigotry that manifests itself in the rationalizations for closing a window on a woman in trouble, and more pointedly in the sickening laughter Newman hears in a darkened theater when Jews are shown being victimized in a war movie. Anti-Semitism is a particular form that this evil takes, but it is the pervasive and cancerous quality of this savagery that Miller is probing in the story of Lawrence Newman.

Newman finally challenges this evil by rejecting his previous

[10] *Ibid.*, p.212.
[11] *Ibid.*, p.185.

alliance with it. He does not discover himself in his community, but in his alienation, and more precisely in his preference for this isolation than for acceptance into the camouflaged and scented barbarism that had previously infected him.

At the conclusion of *Focus*, he and Finkelstein remain communal pariahs; but each man has faced and overcome the monster beneath the tinkling carousel. And in the lacerating process, a minority of one has become a minority of two. Thus, Newman's responsibility to Finkelstein evolves out of his new responsibility to himself. Achieving personal dignity, he can no longer deny another man his. This is the relatedness that Newman achieves, and herein is the sombre premise and hope which underlies so much of Arthur Miller's work: a tough-minded faith—not in group action and far-ranging social panaceas—but in the inherent need of some individuals to find their integrity, and in the process, to recognize and strive for any other man's right to do the same.

8

'To him they were all my sons,

and I guess they were'

Focus helped to heal some of the wounds to ego and bank account that had been opened by the failure of *The Man Who Had All the Luck*. The book received essentially favorable reviews and sold more than ninety thousand copies, but although Miller was being touted as a promising novelist, he was already at work on another play. The theater was still his first love and strongest challenge, and he was determined not to let *The Man Who Had All the Luck* provide his curtain call.

Like the idea for his previous play, the stimulus behind his current project was provided by an actual event. During a casual evening at home, a relative ('a pious lady from the Middle West') told the Millers about a family in her neighborhood that had been destroyed because the daughter had reported her father to the authorities after discovering that he had been shipping faulty materials to the Army during the war. Later in the evening, the lady asked Miller how he came by the ideas for his stories. His reply was a masterpiece of understatement.

'I just pick them up here and there,' he murmured politely.

Although his reply may have seemed rather tame to his visitor, the effect of her story on him was galvanic.

'The girl's action astounded me,' he recalled. 'An absolute response to a moral command.'

> I knew my informant's neighbourhood, I knew its middle-class ordinariness, and I knew how rarely the great issues penetrate such environments. But the fact that a girl had not only wanted to, but had actually moved against an erring father transformed into fact . . . what in my previous play I had only begun to hint at. I had no awareness of the slightest connection between

the two plays. All I knew was that somehow a hard thing had entered into me, a crux toward which it seemed possible to move in strong and straight lines. Something was crystal clear to me for the first time since I had begun to write plays, and it was the crisis of the second act, the revelation of the full loathesomeness of an anti-social action.[1]

Even before his relative's tale was completed, he had transformed the daughter into a son, and visualized the second act's climactic confrontation between the young man and his father.

But if the conception of the play was immediate and lucid, its development was not. Miller had been deceived before by ideas he could not integrate into a meaningful dramatic structure, and he was not about to make the same mistakes again. In *The Man Who Had All the Luck*, he had attempted to grasp a sense of mystery, the 'wonder of how things and people got to be what they are,' but this effort had betrayed him. With his new play, he was determined to

seek cause and effect, hard actions, facts, the geometry of relationships, and . . . hold back any tendency to express an idea in itself unless it was literally forced out of a character's mouth; in other words to let the wonder rise up like a mist . . . from the gradual remorseless crush of factual and psychological conflict.[2]

Or, to state his intentions somewhat more prosaically, he would brush up on his Ibsen and write a well-made play.

However, the effort was more easily prophesied than accomplished. Throughout 1945 and 1946, Miller wrestled with causes and effects, and the 'geometry of relationships.' The drama, which he called *The Sign of the Archer*, limped into its fifth and sixth drafts without coalescing, and Miller finally became so depressed that he considered abandoning the theater.

What finally pulled the play out of the quicksand was his recognition that it lacked a crucial balance because he had been trying to give too many characters equal importance. The mother, particularly, was overshadowing her husband and son, and dwarfing

[1] Arthur Miller, 'Introduction,' *Collected Plays*, p.17.
[2] *Ibid.*, p.15.

their conflict with her neuroticism. As Miller again revised the drama, he subordinated her problems to the relationship of father and son, and for the first time felt reasonably sure of himself. This alteration also necessitated a change in the play's title, and a few days before its trial run in New Haven, Miller discarded *The Sign of the Archer*, which was oriented toward the mother's astrological beliefs, for *All My Sons*, a line pertinent to the father's dilemma. When he subsequently put the finishing touches on the 110-page working script, Miller could look back on seven hundred pages of trial heats and exploratory drafts. Now the young writer knew exactly why the venerable Mr Ibsen sometimes needed as much as two years to hammer out a play.

Ibsen's influence on *All My Sons* is direct and pervasive, and Miller has never hesitated to acknowledge it. Like most of the Norwegian's dramas, Miller's play is carefully structured and tightly plotted. It begins with a late point of attack, very close chronologically to its climax, and—like Ibsen's *Ghosts*—proceeds, through a series of revelatory conversations, to expose a guilt-laden past. Thus, the interrelationship between previous actions and present consequences, which marks so many of Ibsen's works, is crucial to the pattern and meaning of *All My Sons*.

Another similarity between Miller's drama and the realistic plays of Ibsen is exhibited in their motifs. The themes of the sins of the parents visited on the children, and of the house built on a lie, which are threaded through Ibsen's dramas, are also woven into the fabric of *All My Sons*.

But although Miller owes much to Ibsen, his relationship to the nineteenth-century Viking is not merely predicated on an amalgam of situations and themes ripe for the American dramatist's picking. Miller did not discover themes in Ibsen. He found, first of all, an expository form that struck him as eminently suitable for the purposes of *All My Sons*, but which he would not hesitate to abandon in any subsequent play where it would not be integral to its meaning. Secondly, and of much greater significance, Miller was deeply impressed by the way Ibsen's dramas revealed 'the evolutionary quality of life,' the phenomena of 'process, change, (and) development.'[3]

Basically, then, it is Ibsen's involvement with a character's entire history and his insistence upon 'valid causation' as the essential

[3] *Ibid.*, p.21.

dramatic method that Miller found so appealing. Ibsen's realism was not an attempt to reduce the mystery and complexity of life to logical and reasonable formula, but an effort to define and explain the human condition insofar as it could be explained without losing its essential wonder.

> His basic intention [was] . . . to assert nothing he had not proved, and to cling always to the marvellous spectacle of life forcing one event out of the jaws of the preceding one and to reveal its elemental consistencies with surprise. In other words, I contrast his realism not with the lyrical, which I prize, but with sentimentality, which is always a leak in the dramatic dike. He sought to make a play as weighty and living a fact as the discovery of the steam engine or algebra. This can be scoffed away only at a price, and the price is living drama.[4]

The thematic image of *All My Sons* is a circle within a circle, the inner depicting the family unit, and the outer representing society, and the movement of the drama is concentric, with the two circles revolving in parallel orbits until they ultimately coalesce.

All My Sons relates the story of Joe Keller, a small factory owner who, in order to save his wartime government contract, allows a number of cracked cylinder heads for airplane motors to be shipped to the Air Force. His hopes of escaping detection are shattered when twenty-one fliers crash to their deaths in the faulty planes and the damage is traced back to his plant. Although he escapes a long prison sentence by maneuvering his partner into taking the blame, everyone knows that he was equally guilty. But undaunted by the surreptitious whispering of his community, Joe returns to his business, rebuilds it, and by the time the war is over, is operating it smoothly and successfully.

When his son Chris returns from the Army, he suppresses his doubts about his father, and reenters the business. Eventually he becomes engaged to Ann Deever, the daughter of Joe's ex-partner and the fiancée of Chris's brother Larry, who was killed in the war. But their future is soon threatened by ghosts from the past. Mrs Keller is against their marriage because she refuses to believe that Larry is really dead. Relying increasingly on omens and astrological signs, she will not be swayed by the arguments of her hus-

[4] *Ibid.*, p.22.

band and son. Still another cloud that hangs over Chris and Ann's future is the living specter of her imprisoned father.

For the first half of the play, the attempts of Chris and Ann to overcome the obstacles to their relationship form the central action. For a while they appear to be successful. With Joe's help they override Mrs. Keller's objections; and even after Ann's brother George arrives, and tries to break up the engagement, the elder Keller placates him by convincing him that his father was solely responsible for shipping out the defective parts.

But the uneasy calm is soon shattered when an inadvertent comment by Joe about his health proves that the cold that supposedly kept him at home when the cylinder heads were sent out was a ruse. George storms out of the house, demanding that Ann follow him. Although she eventually rejoins Chris, their relationship suddenly becomes secondary as the dramatic emphasis shifts from Chris, Ann, and Mrs Keller to Chris and Joe; and the confrontation between the guilty father and the prosecuting son quickly explodes into the central conflict of the play.

With driving intensity the drama focuses on these two, as Joe desperately tries to justify his actions while Chris relentlessly and agonizingly allows him no quarter. But despite his son's attempts to make him comprehend the enormity of his act, not until Ann reveals a letter from Larry which discloses his intention of committing suicide on a combat mission as an atonement for his father's crime, does Joe Keller perceive the ultimate meaning of his deed. Finally taking full responsibility upon himself, he too seeks expiation in death.

The first act of *All My Sons* is a graphic example of Miller's attempt to particularize his theme by letting it emerge out of a specific communal context. Through leisurely pacing, casual conversations, and an accumulation of realistic detail, the act slowly and meticulously establishes a credible portrait of a typical midwestern town. Unlike their predecessors in *The Man Who Had All the Luck*, the secondary characters in *All My Sons* are integral to their play as they reinforce the domestic and communal insularity of the Keller's environment. For it is precisely this insularity that provides the buffer between Joe Keller and his awareness of a relationship to a world beyond his front porch and backyard.

Perhaps the salient feature of the elder Keller is his affability. He is a pleasant man who enjoys the heartiness of a poker game with the boys, the relaxation of a Sunday afternoon in an easy chair, and the antics of the neighborhood children, a rather genial and somewhat bullish self-made man who is justifiably proud of his business and his imposing position in the community. Keenly aware of his lack of education and sophistication, he continually makes self-deprecating comments, but under the guise of this apparent humility, he cheerfully broadcasts his influence and connections.

Although he is intensely possessive toward his business, he is hardly a ruthless and scheming tycoon dominated by a lust for power. In fact he does not view the factory as an end in itself, but as the means by which he can give his family the security they presently enjoy, and enable his son to make the best possible life for himself.

Joe's ambitions for Chris are not entirely selfless. He wants the young man to have everything he can give him, but on Joe's terms. As a projection of his father, Chris must not only be as good as Joe, but greater. Nonetheless, to define this expectation as ruthless egotism masquerading under the guise of paternal love is to distort the entire relationship between these two men. Joe's hopes for his son contain the egocentricity of any father's unconscious desire to combat his mortality through the promise and potential of his children. The elder Keller would be appalled at any suggestion that his motivations toward his wife and son were in any way selfish or ambivalent.

This conscious and avowed dedication to his family manifests the flaw in Joe Keller's character which will eventually prove catastrophic. He is myopic. So preoccupied is he with the world of the inner circle that the outer world is a blur, and he is unable to recognize the external ramifications of what he considered a private act. This is why he can honestly refer to the deaths of twenty-one men as a 'mistake,' and why he is able to advise Ann that when her father is released from prison he should follow Joe's example and return to the town that has ostracized him.

'Till people play cards with him again,' Keller doggedly assures her, 'and talk with him, and smile with him—you play cards with a man, you know he can't be a murderer. And the next time you write him I like you to tell him just what I said.'[5]

A man simply cannot be a murderer if he is a good husband,

[5] Miller, 'All My Sons,' *Collected Plays*, p.81.

loyal father, and all-around nice guy. In the inner circle he did not commit a crime; he was involved in an accident, and consequently the guilt he feels does not involve the twenty-one fliers nearly as much as it does the man whom he allowed to take all the blame for the 'mistake.'

Because Joe views his act as private, he is able to rationalize it in two ways. He can accept the lie that he never gave his partner the order to ship out the parts as necessary for the preservation of his family—an end which justifies any means for Joe. He can also visualize a wonderfully simple atonement. He will give Deever a job with the firm as soon as he is released; through his connections he will establish the man's son in a career; and finally he will take the daughter into his own family, thus making his partner's grandchildren heirs to the Keller legacy. A most reasonable and generous restoration. The consideration that atonement for twenty-one deaths is not quite as simple does not cross Joe's mind because they belong to the outer circle, which is still bewilderingly out of focus.

There is nothing extraordinary about Joe Keller's morality. Like his immediate neighbors and the community at large, he is a man with quite common, narrow loyalties, who might have lived a long, bland and complacent existence had he not become involved in an unusual situation. Ultimately it is not the monstrousness but the conventionality of Joe's outlook, actions, and rationalizations which provides the underlying horror of the play.

In two major confrontations with Chris, Joe expounds everything he believes in and stands for. At the end of the second act, when he is forced to admit his responsibility for sending out the defective cylinder heads, he begs his son to understand his reasons:

> What could I do! I'm in business, a man is in business; a hundred and twenty cracked, you're out of business; you got a process, the process don't work you're out of business; you don't know how to operate, your stuff is no good; they close you up, they tear up your contracts, what the hell's it to them? You lay forty years into a business and they knock you out in five minutes, what could I do, let them take forty years, let them take my life away? I never thought they'd install them. I swear to God. I thought they'd stop 'em before anybody took off. . . . Chris, I did it for you. I'm sixty-one years old, when would I have another chance to make something for

you? Sixty-one years old you don't get another chance, do ya?[6]

In Joe Keller's eyes there is nothing dishonest in a plea to the two values upon which he has based his life: the worth of individual effort and the sanctity of family loyalty born of love. His second appeal extends beyond the individual and the family, but still is defined by the inner circle.

'You want me to go to jail?' he cries to his son. 'If you want me to go, say so.'

> What's the matter, why can't you tell me. . . . I'll tell you why you can't say it. Because you know I don't belong there. . . . Who worked for nothin' in that war? When they work for nothin', I'll work for nothin'. Did they ship a gun or a truck outa Detroit before they got their price? Is that clean? It's dollars and cents, nickels and dimes; war and peace, it's nickels and dimes, what's clean? Half the goddam country is gotta go if I go! That's why you can't tell me.[7]

It is an appeal to a world beyond family but still lacking responsible human relationships, a world in which practicality has created its own particular brand of morality. Joe's problem is not an inability to differentiate between right and wrong. Although his family represents an absolute right for him, his preceding comments to Chris strongly emphasize his recognition that his actions in behalf of his wife and son were wrong. But he takes refuge in numbers, stressing that the only difference between his situation and thousands of similar ones lies in the gravity and the publicity of the consequences. Joe Keller does not claim moral rectitude for his actions: he claims family loyalty as an unshakable end, and social expediency for the less defensible means.

He is both victim and victimizer. His society has inculcated false values in him, and to the extent that these enable him to justify his behavior, society is partially responsible for his actions. But Joe has sinned against society also. Because of his intense and narrow allegiance to his family, he has committed a crime against the outer world. To protect those closest to him he has sacrificed others. The fascination of *All My Sons* lies precisely in its dramatization, not

[6] *Ibid.*, p.115.
[7] *Ibid.*, pp.124-125.

of good versus evil, but of a conflict between two forces, family and society, each of which is inherently good. The tragedy of Joe Keller's life is that a basically decent motivation has precipitated the catastrophe. The tragic irony of the play is that his crime against the outside world eventually becomes a crime against his own family as well, and in destroying those to whom he considers himself unrelated, he finally destroys those to whom he is most intensely bound.

Although Joe Keller's crime is the sale of defective parts to the government, this crime is the consequence of the pervasive illness of unrelatedness. It is this bland but lethal disease that is so frightening for Miller because it plunges into jungle anarchy all civilization's attempts at order and meaning. And it is against this barrier of unrelatedness that Chris Keller hurls himself.

Chris is his father's antagonist, the individual who offers idealism as the possible antidote to Joe's expediency. It is an idealism contained in his explanation to Ann of what the war has meant to him.

'They weren't just men,' he says, referring to the soldiers in his platoon.

> One time it'd been raining several days and this kid came to me, and gave me his last pair of dry socks. Put them in my pocket. That's only a little thing . . . but . . . that's the kind of guys I had. They didn't die; they killed themselves for each other. . . . And I got an idea—watching them go down. Everything was being destroyed, see, but it seemed to me that one new thing was made. A kind of responsibility. Man for man . . . to show that, to bring that on earth again like some kind of monument and everyone would feel it standing there, behind him, and it would make a difference to him. And then I came home and it was incredible. I . . . there was no meaning in it here; the whole thing to them was a kind of a—bus accident. I went to work with Dad, and that rat-race again. I felt . . . ashamed somehow. Because nobody was changed at all. It seemed to make suckers out of a lot of guys.[8]

With very few embellishments this is the speech in which the soldier Watson tried to tell Miller what the war meant to him, and it is this idea—and his intense disillusionment at its failure to

[8] *Ibid.*, p.85.

take root in his own home—which Chris flings in the teeth of his father's plea that he acted in the young veteran's behalf:

> For me! Where do you live, where have you come from? For me!—I was dying every day and you were killing my boys and you did it for me? What the hell do you think I was thinking of, the Goddam business? Is that as far as your mind can see, the business? What is that, the world—the business? What the hell do you mean you did it for me? Don't you have a country? Don't you live in the world?[9]

Finally, in reply to his mother's question as to what more they can be, Chris extends his idealism to the perimeter of the outer circle.

'You can be better!' he exclaims. 'Once and for all you can know there's a universe of people outside and you're responsible to it, and unless you know that you threw away your son because that's why he died.'[10]

These ringing declarations have been cited by a number of critics to illustrate one apparently glaring weakness of *All My Sons*: a moral didacticism that bogs down the play in a sticky morass of righteousness. They have complained that Chris Keller is just too right, too good, and too insistent on his rectitude and goodness to be any reasonable facsimile of a human being. He has been labelled his author's moral pitchman, verbally clubbing an audience into dazed submission; and the playwright who had insisted on suppressing an idea unless 'it was literally forced out of a character's mouth,' has been sharply criticized for creating a character with a mouth that apparently needs very little forcing.

Although this criticism is valid, it must be sharply qualified, for the younger Keller is much more than a thematic megaphone through which the dramatist is trumpeting the play's message. He is an individual caught in a human conflict, and even though he often speaks for the author and his didacticism is not always controlled by the playwright, Chris certainly does not receive Miller's unconditional approval, nor does he warrant it. A great gulf looms between Chris's ideals and his actions, and anyone who fails to make this observation misses the crux of the son's relationship to his father.

[9] *Ibid.*, pp.115–116.
[10] *Ibid.*, pp.126–127.

Beneath the conflict of the two different systems of value Joe and Chris represent is the agonizing struggle between a father and a son, and although the ethical relationship between the two is clearly delineated, it is rooted in a complex personal involvement that defies any glib resolution. From an abstract moral perspective, Chris is Joe's prosecutor, the man who must show him his wrongness; but more pointedly, he is a son torn apart by the conflict between his devotion to his father and his concept of justice and humanity which that selfsame parent has outraged. Consequently, while they herald his idealism, Chris's exhortations ultimately exhibit his ineffectuality as prosecutor. The louder he declaims, the more he signals his inability to become the disinterested moral voice he is often accused of being.

Chris cannot be the impartial prosecutor for three basic reasons. Anticipating Biff Loman, he is a son overwhelmed by the revelation of paternal guilt. All his life his view of his father has been so magnified that Joe's sins are not proof of human frailty, but evidence of the collapse of a deity.

'I never saw you as a man,' Chris exclaims in horror when the elder Keller begs for understanding. 'I saw you as my father.'

In this context, 'father' means the personification of goodness and infallibility, and when this image collapses Chris can only feel the terrible betrayal of a childhood faith. Each man bears the burden of responsibility—Joe for casting himself in a role he cannot fulfill, and Chris for adamantly maintaining his adolescent adoration of an impossible idol—and each pays for the dichotomy between reality and the illusion he has fostered.

Secondly, Chris cannot shake the realization that whatever his father did, he did for him. Thus, despite all his protestations, he knows that circumstance has made him a dominant factor in his father's degradation, and this knowledge continually complicates his desperate attempts to separate Joe's actions from their motivations.

Thirdly, and most significantly, Chris's shame and rage are not directed solely against his father; they are also aimed at himself. For all his lip service to humanitarian ideals, Chris is torn by guilt at what he considers to be his sellout to the same society and values he detests. And his shame is intensified because in working for his father he must suppress any suspicion he has held since the older man's arraignment. Thus, although sincerely felt, Chris's

idealism is tinged with a hollowness that an unsympathetic neighbor labels hypocrisy. The wife of a physician whom Chris has been
urging to abandon a lucrative practice for a research career, she
pours out her resentment to Ann:

> My husband has a family, dear. Every time he has a session
> with Chris he feels as though he's compromising by not giving
> up everything for research. As though Chris or anybody else
> isn't compromising . . . . Chris is working with his father, isn't
> he? He's taking money out of that business. . . . Who is he
> to ruin a man's life? Everybody knows Joe pulled a fast one
> to get out of jail. . . . I've got nothing against Joe. But if
> Chris wants people to put on the hair shirt, let him take off
> his broadcloth. He's driving my husband crazy with that
> phony idealism of his.[11]

Chris's idealism is not phony; it just eludes its spokesman. Not
only is the conflict between idealism and expediency manifested in
the struggle between son and father but also in Chris alone; and
not until he is presented with the irrevocable proof of the consequences of Joe's expediency can he begin to resolve the struggle in
himself. Even then his initial steps are painfully tentative. He
shouts, thrashes about, and threatens his father, but he cannot do
anything. Each stormy denunciation and exhortation dissolves into
a puddle of indecision.

'What must I do, Jesus God, what must I do?' he cries at the
end of the second act; and at the conclusion of the play the tune
has not substantially changed.

'I can't look at you this way,' he complains to Joe, and then
shamefully adds: 'I can't look at myself.'

His final words, following his father's suicide, further delineate
his paralysis:

'Mother, I didn't mean to . . .' he exclaims, his voice trailing off.

The idealistic veteran meant to, but the son, torn between duty
and love, was never able to enact the ultimate and dreadful condemnation of his father. Only the older man's death can break the
stalemate, and even then Chris's mother must literally push him
out of the stricken house to save him.

But Chris Keller's inability to fully dedicate himself to his beliefs

[11] *Ibid.*, pp.93–94.

does not invalidate them. The moral responsibility he advocates may indeed be Quixotic, but the question might be posed as to whether the fault lies with Chris or with his world. If Miller makes Joe Keller the defendant and Chris the prosecutor, he ultimately compels the audience into becoming the jury. To decide the extent of the father's crime and the son's outrage, we must judge our own standards of value. Interestingly, the strongest positive reaction to the initial production of *All My Sons* came from young veterans.

'They're grateful I'm not a wise guy,' Miller reported in a newspaper interview shortly after the drama's premiere. 'They write that the play is about "the things we feel but don't say for fear of being laughed at." '[12]

Ironically the man who most fully commits himself to Chris's idealism is not the younger Keller but the man who violated every concept of it. It is Joe Keller who arrives at a genuine recognition of the meaning of his crime, and then firmly translates his awareness into action. Significantly, his illumination is not the result of Chris's harangues but of the discovery of his responsibility for his other son's death. Chris has brought Joe to the point of comprehension, but the older man's moral perspective is still blurred. As his son hammers at his unrelatedness, Joe only knows that his family is beginning to disintegrate in spite of his desperate efforts to hold it together, and even when his wife tries to explain that for Chris there 'is something bigger than the family,' Joe still cannot understand.

'Nothin's bigger than that,' he insists defiantly. 'I'm his father and he's my son, and if there's something bigger than that I'll put a bullet in my head!'[13]

Joe's comments in the final moments of his life illustrate his growing uncertainty and despair. Despite his attempts to regain assurance he plunges deeper into bewilderment, and almost everything he says twists into a question.

'What must I be forgiven? . . . He wouldn't do that—would he? . . . What am I gonna do, Kate? . . . Then why am *I* bad? . . . Well talk to me!—what do you want me to do?'

He desperately longs for the certainty he is positive Larry would have provided.

[12] Arthur Miller, quoted in *New York Times*, Theater Section, February 23, 1947 p.1.

[13] 'All My Sons,' *Collected Plays*, p.120.

'Goddam, if Larry was alive he wouldn't act like this,' he complains, contrasting Chris to his late brother. 'He understood the way the world is made. He listened to me. To him the world had a forty-foot front, it ended at the building line.'[14]

Not until this last bastion of his defense is demolished does Joe's vision freeze into clear and terrible focus. With his realization that like Chris's world, Larry's also extended far beyond 'the building line,' Joe finally understands how circumscribed his own has been, and how his narrow commitment to it has caused him to defile the one outside. When his wife pleads with him not to surrender to the authorities, by attempting to convince him that Larry would never have advocated such a move, Joe gazes solemnly at the letter from his son.

'Then what is this if it isn't telling me?' he replies. 'Sure he was my son. But I think to him they were all my sons. And I guess they were, I guess they were.'[15]

No wonder Miller selected this line when he revised the play's title. Emerging as it does from the morass of Joe's defensive declarations and groping questions, and set against the impassioned and strained rhetoric of Chris's exhortations, its simple and dignified finality poignantly testifies to its speaker's profound self-awareness and relatedness to a world he only dimly knew existed.*

To debate the necessity of Joe Keller's suicide is fruitless. Given his character and the situation acting upon it, he has no other alternative. That he acts out of a sense of guilt is unquestionable; but his death is not just the result of a lacerated conscience. By this final deed, Keller takes upon himself the responsibility from which he fled in his life, and thus establishes a significance through death that had been previously lost to him. He dies to regain his conscience, to establish an integrity defined by its moral commitment. The final irony lies in the fact that while Joe eventually comprehends the meaning of his relationship to the outer circle, it is precisely this perception that renders him more alone than he has ever been before. In the last moments of his life he is totally

[14] *Ibid.*, p.121

[15] *Ibid.*, p.126.

* The dialogue of *All My Sons* is often intentionally banal, not only to suit the characters, but to illustrate the intense difficulty of meaningful communication. Uncommunicated truth is a major motif in the play, and the language, in its bland, clichéd conventionality, graphically exhibits this problem.

isolated from the family and the community, the familiar world
that ends at the building line. The man who asked everyone for
answers comes to realize that only he can supply the ultimate ones.
Like Lawrence Newman, he must rely finally on his particular
conception of himself and his personal definition of the word
dignity.

A powerful but far from perfect drama, *All My Sons*, is perhaps
the weakest structurally of Miller's major plays.* When the dramatist praised Ibsen for seeking to 'make a play as weighty and living
a fact as the discovery of the steam engine or algebra,' he failed
to mention that a drama can suffer as much from overweight as
underweight. In many respects, *All My Sons* is a rather corpulent
case in point.

Most of the extra poundage accrues to the first act. Comprising
almost half the play, the act slowly and painstakingly creates what
Miller termed an 'atmosphere of undisturbed normalcy.' Acknow-
ledging the glacierlike pace of the act, the playwright subsequently
remarked that 'it was designed to be slow. It was made so that
even boredom might threaten, so that when the first intimation of
the crime is dropped, a genuine horror might begin to move into
the heart of the audience, a horror born of the contrast between
the placidity of the civilization on view and the threat to it that
a rage of conscience could create.'[16]

Obviously then, the pacing of the act was a strategic and calculated risk. Unfortunately the intention is not validated by the
results. Not only does boredom threaten, it sets in; and before a
genuine horror moves into the hearts of the audience, an equally
authentic lethargy has softened mind and bone.

Another weakness of the first act is that so much of it is devoted
to creating a tangential line of development. The characters who
dominate the act are Chris, Ann, and Mrs Keller, but although
their situation initially appears to be the play's major concern, it
subsequently proves to be an oblique prelude to the central conflict between Chris and his father, a kind of façade that alternately
conceals and reveals the deeper drama beneath it. Moreover, instead of being dramatically realized individuals, Kate Keller and
Ann Deever are too patently related to the development of the

---

*Excluded from the category of major plays are those dramas, pro-
duced or unproduced, preceding *All My Sons*.

[16] Miller, 'Introduction,' *Collected Plays*, p.18.

plot. Thus, when their conflict over Chris is subverted, they simply fade away and remain only peripherally involved in the situation that they helped to elicit. Similarly, the whole problem of Kate's obsessive delusions about her dead son, which is apparently crucial to the first half of the play, is resolved so rapidly and neatly that one cannot help but suspect the depth of her original dilemma.

Finally, the length of the opening act badly weakens the pacing of the play. So extended and casual is the action, that by contrast the next two acts—and particularly the third—seem quite frenetic. Too much is crowded into too small an area, and the careful causation Miller strove for explodes in a melodramatic burst of fireworks that more closely approximates Alfred Hitchcock than Henrik Ibsen.

But the length of the first act is not the sole cause of the play's harried quality. A number of controlled contrivances turn the second and third acts into a blatantly rigged minefield. Every dramatist uses devices to sustain his action. The trouble with Miller's employment of them is twofold: first, they are rather flagrant; second, they undercut one of his basic intentions in the play, namely the desire to dramatize the integral relationship between actions and consequences. Although the playwright spends an inordinate amount of time and effort constructing a bridge between present and past, when the time comes to draw them together in a causal relationship, he relies more on strategically placed coincidences than on any dramatic interaction of character and circumstance.

These devices are less meretricious than clumsy, but to the extent that *All My Sons* relies in most of its crucial moments on a telephone call by George Deever, a slip of the tongue by Kate Keller and Larry's surprise letter, it manifests a mechanical theatricality that is sharply at odds with the illusion of reality and cause-and-effect inevitability that its author has so earnestly propounded for it. Throughout the play, 'the marvellous spectacle of life forcing one event out of the jaws of the preceding one' needs shots of adrenalin to facilitate the process.

More than any of Miller's subsequent plays, *All My Sons* is a drama in the service of a message. Fortunately the message is dramatic and substantial, and the play is rooted in enough human conflict and complexity so that it never deteriorates into an illustrated editorial. But because its moral earnestness is rather garishly

highlighted by its structural weaknesses, the play reels dangerously
between didacticism and gimmickry. It is to Arthur Miller's credit
as a dramatist that even in this awkward position, *All My Sons*
remains as provocative and powerful as it does.

9

'The play grew from simple images'

All My Sons began the first of 328 performances at the Coronet Theater in New York on the evening of January 29, 1947. Produced by Harold Clurman, Walter Fried, and Elia Kazan, and directed by the latter, it starred Ed Begley and Arthur Kennedy as Joe and Chris Keller. The initial reviews were mixed, and while the majority of the newspaper and magazine critics scored the play's overtly mechanical structure and excessive reliance on devices, they praised what Louis Kronenberger called its 'dramatic sense, human sense, and moral sense.' Most agreed that although the drama was flawed, it was nevertheless an immeasureable improvement over *The Man Who Had All the Luck*, and a marked and noteworthy step forward in the development of a new and important talent.

An additional verification came three months later when the New York Drama Critics voted *All My Sons* their annual Circle Award, bypassing Eugene O'Neill's *The Iceman Cometh* to do so. In retrospect it is fairly obvious that the preference was not the most perceptive choice ever made by that astute body, but it was undeniably a heady tonic for the young playwright.

By May of 1947, a Paris production of *All My Sons* was underway, and three Stockholm producers were bidding for it. Along with *Focus*, it was purchased for the movies, and Miller was asked to write the screenplays for both projects. He declined, explaining that he had worked enough on each. The film version of *Focus* never materialized, although the story was presented subsequently on television with James Whitmore in the leading role; but *All My Sons* was made into an earnest but lackluster motion picture in 1948, with Edward G. Robinson perfectly cast as Joe Keller, and Burt Lancaster somewhat less comfortably jammed into the role of Chris.

With *All My Sons* enjoying a substantial Broadway run, Miller began working on a new play, a 'love story of working people in an industrial city,' which he titled *Plenty Good Times*. At the same time he bought some land in Roxbury, Connecticut, and moved his wife and two children, Robert and Jane Ellen, into the country. As soon as they were settled, he began to build a small shack behind the main house. Working alone, he dug the cellar, poured the concrete foundation, put up the roof, and installed the plumbing. The result was a fourteen-by-fourteen foot, split-shingle, one-room cabin which was to become his workroom, and through the spring and summer of 1948 he put it to use as he labored diligently on *Plenty Good Times*. But by the middle of August he found himself stalemated, and after unsuccessfully trying to break the mental blockade, he finally consigned the play to a desk drawer where it has dustily lingered to the present day.

The frustrations he encountered with *Plenty Good Times* were not new to Miller, who had experienced them with both *The Man Who Had All the Luck* and *All My Sons*, nor would they miraculously cease with his subsequent dramas. His plays are put together as rigorously and carefully as the cabin he erected on his Connecticut acreage, and the procedure is exhausting. His creative process generally unrolls at a slow and deliberate pace, marked by clearly defined stages, evolving painstakingly and often agonizingly either to the completion of a drama or to its termination.

Despite his reputation as a didactic writer, he rarely begins with an encompassing theme, but rather with an event, an individual, or even a few words of dialogue which may suddenly grab and hold his interest. An incident related to him during a casual conversation, a person who says or does something to catch his fancy, or a sudden image that explodes in his mind out of nowhere, or perhaps out of the buried past, is often enough to provide the crucial point of departure for a new play.

Starting then with something specific and concrete, Miller begins to develop and test it in a dramatic context. Often he finds that what enthralled him so greatly at eleven o'clock the previous night has dwindled to Lilliputian proportions in the clear light of a new day, and a potential play is aborted in embryo. But if the new image or idea retains its hold on his imagination and shows promise of evolving into something meaningful, he begins to put it into writing.

The process involves notebooks into which he pours anything he can think of about the event, character, or image that originally stimulated his curiosity. There is scarcely any order or structure to this initial phase of his work. Almost nothing in the ordinary, high-school notebooks even remotely suggests an integrated, comprehensible paragraph. Instead, there are penciled jottings, bits of dialogue, jagged descriptions of a fragmentary scene, sketches for a set design, bedeviling conversations with himself, line after line of plot outline, and a cornucopia of character analysis, much of it about individuals who may still be hovering on the outer perimeter of his mind.

As the notebooks begin to fill up in this random fashion, Miller starts to peck out scenes on his typewriter, hoping that the bits and pieces in the books will begin to gel in their typewritten setting. Often they do not, and scene after scene is quickly relegated to the wastebasket in a growing mountain of crumpled paper. But what may appear to be a singular waste of effort and time, especially since Miller sometimes continues in this manner for weeks at a time, is actually an important creative process for the playwright. Although he eventually discards most of the notebook jottings and early typewritten scenes, he feels the method is invaluable because it enables him to think his way through from the original germ of an idea to a tentative framework. And by continually experimenting and conversing with himself in print, he is able to combat the distraction and inertia that comprise the greatest threats to his progress.

If nothing happens after this point to make him feel that the project has any promise or potential, he may set aside or completely abandon the play. But if the shape and direction finally begin to clarify themselves, Miller gradually relinquishes the jottings and concentrates on particular characters and events. For days at a time he may lean back in his chair, his long legs stretched across his desk, staring blankly out the window while his gaze is really fixed on a character's appearance or on the vital confrontation that is to provide the climax of a particular act. During these ruminations, although he may never pick up a pencil or strike a typewriter key, he is working as hard as at any other time during the creation of his drama.

Gradually the notebooks begin to take on a new appearance. Instead of exhibiting snatches of conversation, drawings, fragmented pieces of character analysis, and sporadic stretches of plot, they display long and detailed passages of dialogue, action, and situation. Miller molds and reshapes these pages until, in his words, 'thinking is left behind [and] everything is in the present tense and a play emerges which has resemblances but little else to the mass of notes left behind.'[1] This leap from the notebooks to the initial draft is perhaps the most difficult part of the undertaking, since it is so uncertain and depends almost as much on circumstance and that vague but crucial element of luck as it does on the writer's creative talent. Miller wryly recalls an overwhelming ratio of notebook plays to typewritten first drafts.

With the typed manuscript, the dramatist launches the play proper. Now he shapes and revises the script meticulously as he attempts to blend character, theme, and action into a structural unity. Sometimes he is able to achieve his goal fairly rapidly, in two or three drafts. Other times it takes a dozen. And there are occasions when not even that many are sufficient to make the play coalesce, and the result may be a drama like *The Man Who Had All the Luck*, which—for all Miller's efforts—remained a disorganized endeavor. Or his labors may result in a play like *A View from the Bridge*, which he revised radically even after its Broadway premiere. He may even produce a script like *Plenty Good Times* that never gets into the hands of a director and cast, dying instead painfully but unceremoniously in stillbirth.

More than once, Miller has amassed a thousand pages of typescript—approximately nine times the amount of a finished manuscript—only to find that they still had not blended into a play. Although bursting with characterization and action, they lacked the cohesion so vital to a successful drama. Tired and disgusted, and realizing that he had taken the venture as far as he could, the writer would then gather up all the material, and in the loneliness of defeat, burn it. Nevertheless, the preceding weeks and months had not added up to a complete zero. In that time he had created characters and situations that might live again in other plays, or might provide the germinal spark for a new project.

Death of a Salesman originated in this manner, with its roots stretching back to an unfinished play Miller had begun at the University of Michigan. Not until he was rummaging through his files

[1] Arthur Miller, quoted in Allan Seager, 'The Creative Agony of Arthur Miller,' *Esquire*, 52 (October, 1959), p.126.

long after *Death of a Salesman* was playing on Broadway did he come across the old manuscript and realize that its protagonist, a salesman, had been evolving in his mind, gathering a kind of momentum that would eventually propel him into the dramatist's consciousness and facilitate the creation of Miller's most famous play.

Death of a Salesman was written in less time than any of his major dramas except *Incident at Vichy*, and although in its inception it adhered to the creative process described above, its development proved to be a notable exception to this procedure.

Hard at work one evening on the ill-fated *Plenty Good Times*, Miller found himself no longer concentrating on an effort that had already become uninteresting, but instead thinking about a salesman he had once known when he worked for his father. As he visualized this man, a flood of images crowded into his imagination. The first, large enough to fill an entire stage, was the salesman's face, which slowly opened to reveal the inside of his head. And from that intensely subjective vantage point, a whole series of smaller images, comprising the man's life and spiraling out of Miller's memories of his own youth and the joys and sorrows woven into these recollections, began to emerge and crystallize with remarkable suddenness. The method that normally would take weeks and months of clarification in the notebooks was accelerated and compressed into no more than a couple of hours.

Sitting alone in the silent room, the playwright saw a small frame house that had once rung with the shouts of growing children but was now deserted and still. And with the man's face and the house that rose out of it providing the central images, a procession of pictures flickered across Miller's mind like a silent film unrolling against a spectral screen.

There were images of futility—'the cavernous Sunday afternoons polishing the car. Where is that car now?' he wondered. 'And the chamois cloths carefully washed and put up to dry, where are the chamois cloths?' And memories of 'endless, convoluted discussions, wonderments, arguments, belittlements, encouragements, fiery resolutions, abdications, returns, partings, voyages out and voyages back, tremendous opportunities and small, squeaking denouements—and all in the kitchen now occupied by strangers who cannot hear what the walls are saying.'[2]

[2] Miller, 'Introduction,' *Collected Plays*, p.29.

Images of old age, of friends and acquaintances gone, 'and strangers in the seats of the mighty who do not know you or your incredible value.' The painful image of a son no longer viewing his father as a god, separated from him by the inevitable process of growing up, his 'hard, public eye upon you, no longer swept by your myth, no longer rousable from his separateness, no longer knowing you have lived for him and have wept for him.'[3] The image of 'ferocity when love has turned to something else and yet is there, is somewhere in the room if one could only find it,' and the image of people who cared deeply for each other gradually turning away from each other in bewilderment and sorrow. The vision, also, of a man's overpowering need to assure his immortality by leaving a 'thumbprint somewhere on the world.'[4]

All these images filled the great open face that loomed out of the darkness of the writer's consciousness. It was the face of a man 'superbly alone with his sense of not having touched and finally knowing in his last extremity that the love which had always been in the room unlocated was now found.' And with this apparition and knowledge, a series of concluding images: a suicide 'so mixed in motive as to be unfathomable and yet demanding statement. Revenge was in it and a power of love, a victory in it that would bequeath a fortune to the living and a flight from emptiness.' And following it, a sense of calm, 'the peace leaving the issues above ground and viable yet.' Finally and comprehensively, the dominant image of a 'private man in a world full of strangers, a world that is not home nor even an open battleground, but only galaxies of high promise over a fear of falling.'[5]

For all the impressions, Miller had only one certain action in his mind: the suicide of the salesman. And with that established he began to weave the rest of the images into a story. He did not care how much the play might wander, since he was primarily interested in enabling his protagonist to relive enough of the past to fully motivate his act of self-destruction, and anything substantiating this deed was ripe for inclusion. Forgotten and momentarily abandoned was *Plenty Good Times* as the dramatist started shaping his new project, which he tentatively called *The Inside of His Head*

[3] *Ibid.*, p.29.
[4] *Ibid.*, p.29.
[5] *Ibid.*, p.30.

in reference to the point of view from which most of the story would be told. The play was to sweep outward from the mind of the salesman.

'There were two undulating lines in [my] mind,' Miller explained, 'one above the other, the past webbed to the present, moving on together in him and sometimes openly joined, and once, finally, colliding in the showdown which defined him in his eyes at least—and so to sleep.'[6]

But sleep was the consideration farthest from the playwright's mind that particular evening. He worked through the night, and by dawn he had completed two-thirds of the first draft in the most rapid and concentrated burst of creative writing in his entire life. The final third proved more of an obstacle, and after almost three months of unsuccessful effort, he put the script aside and made a final attempt to complete *Plenty Good Times*. But the new drama now obsessed him and he soon abandoned the other play for good and returned to it. Refreshed by his respite, he put on a spurt of sustained effort, completed the working draft by the autumn of 1948, and changed the play's title from *The Inside of His Head* to *Death of a Salesman*.

Although he wrote much of the drama at breakneck speed in a state of almost feverish intensity, Miller often found himself laughing aloud as it burst into life under his touch, when he realized that he had said exactly what he wanted to say and had made a scene do precisely what he wanted it to do. Never before had he felt quite so free, so sure, even so cocky about the rightness of his task.

Only once did his confidence waver, when he first read the play aloud to his wife and two friends. He could feel the silence enveloping him throughout the reading; and when he finished and looked up from the manuscript to see only glazed expressions, he could feel a ball of ice slipping from his heart to the pit of his stomach. For a few agonizing moments he heard only the deafening tick of a clock; then, one of his friends haltingly began to murmur how shaken he was, and when Miller looked at his wife, he noticed tears running down her face.

Death of a Salesman was accepted for production by Kermit Bloomgarden and Walter Fried at first glance. Miller's close friend, Elia Kazan, who had staged *All My Sons* and more recently had

[6] *Ibid.*, p.30.

won unanimous critical and popular acclaim for his brilliant handling of Tennessee Williams' *A Streetcar Named Desire*, eagerly
took the directorial reins, and Jo Mielziner and Alex North were
designated to design the challenging sets and compose the incidental music.

But if the play quickly enraptured the individuals who under-
took its production, it did not exactly elicit bouquets—or dollars—
from a few other sharp theater veterans whom its backers approached. Cheryl Crawford refused to join in its financing, producer Leland Hayward cut his investment in half once he pondered
over the script, and Joshua Logan, fresh from the melodious
simplicity of *South Pacific*, dismissed the drama as incomprehensible. And there were others who shared their doubt and
trepidation.

However, the persons committed to the play were so confident
of its commercial success and so intrigued by its novel form and
structure that they refused many of its backers the traditional right
to read the script and make suggestions for its possible improvement. In fact their main reservation was confined to a brief flurry
over the play's title. Bloomgarden felt that *Death of a Salesman*
was simultaneously morose and pedestrian, and feared that it
would frighten potential audiences away. His opinion was rein-
forced by a number of his friends and quite a few theater owners
and ticket brokers for whom *The Dashing Dane* would have been
a marked improvement over *Hamlet*.

Robert Dowling, owner of the Morosco Theater, where *Death
of a Salesman* was scheduled to open in February of 1949, was so
apprehensive about its title that he even thought of keeping it off
the marquee, and went so far as to offer to finance a research poll
to prove to Miller that the name was detrimental. Although the
playwright adamantly refused the offer, a conference was finally
held to determine what to do about this traumatic tempest in a
teapot. As he heard the fate of his play compared to that of the
Titanic, should the title be retained, Miller began to waver. He
was on the verge of capitulating, when one of the backers jumped
the gun and passed around a list of alternate titles. Miller immediately canceled his surrender.

'Pure conceit,' he admitted gloatingly after *Death of a Salesman*'s opening. 'It annoyed me that anybody might think of a
better title for my own play than I could. Also, I was furious that

anybody else could come up with a whole list of titles, like a bunch of bananas.'[7]

Casting the play was a painstaking process. Arthur Kennedy, who had been extremely impressive as Chris Keller in *All My Sons*, was selected to play the pivotal role of Biff Loman, and Cameron Mitchell, a promising young actor, took the part of his brother, Happy. In Lee J. Cobb, a superb actor who had distinguished himself in a number of Group Theater productions before some commonplace Hollywood films, Miller and Kazan knew they had quality, but were uncertain about quantity. Cobb seemed to have too much. A large man, he projected a massive strength that clashed with Miller's conception of his beleaguered protagonist. But the choice turned out to be admirable for everyone involved with the project as Willy Loman became the triumphant and memorable role of Cobb's career.*

Perhaps the most hectic bit of casting involved the part of Willy's wife, Linda. Miller and Kazan were looking for a woman who, in the playwright's words, 'looked as though she had lived in a house dress all her life, even somewhat coarse and certainly less than brilliant.' It was a description that did not apply in the least to Mildred Dunnock. Frail, delicate, and dignified, she impressed the writer and his director as 'a cultivated citizen who probably would not be out of place in a cabinet post.' As diplomatically as possible they told her so at a tryout, and after her initial disappointment she expressed her understanding and left.

The following day, as the line of actresses queued up in the wings, Miss Dunnock was again present. This time she had padded herself from neck to hemline to make herself appear larger and dowdier, and for a moment Miller did not even recognize her. Although she did a reading for him which suggested that she fit the part better than he had previously supposed, he still felt that she was not wholly right for it, and again he turned her down. The following day she was back. The day after that she returned once more. And again the next day. When the time came for the final selection, Miller and Kazan chose Mildred Dunnock. Winning the role on talent and sheer persistence, the actress more than con-

[7] Miller, quoted in Robert Sylvester, 'Brooklyn Boy Makes Good,' *The Saturday Evening Post*, 222 (July 16, 1949), p.98.

* The role was repeated by Cobb, no less triumphantly, for a Columbia Broadcasting System television production of *Death of a Salesman* on May 8, 1966.

firmed the choice by shaping Linda Loman into one of the greatest portayals of a long and illustrious career.*

Any serious doubts about the play's title and cast were quickly dispelled during a highly successful trial run in Philadelphia which saw *Death of a Salesman* garner unanimous critical and popular acclaim. However, as the actors prepared for the Broadway premiere, they knew that all the preceding praise could be dissolved in one chilling deluge from the New York drama critics. Consequently,˙ despite the out-of-town valentines, nerves were pretty frayed when the curtain rose in the Morosco Theater on the evening of February 10, 1949.

Only the playwright seemed blissfully unperturbed. The same sureness which had marked his earliest efforts on the play was in evidence again as he greeted his family and friends with an almost carefree aplomb and strolled backstage before the curtain to bless the cast in mock Brooklynese. He was so confident by the middle of the first act that he left the rear of the orchestra where the deathwatch is usually endured and ambled into the lobby. Confronting the distraught Kermit Bloomgarden, who was chewing dazedly on the splintered remnant of what before its mutilation had been a perfectly good cigar, Miller cautioned his friend against 'smoking so loudly,' and embarked on a leisurely walk down Forty-fifth Street.

If this behaviour approached the classic definition of hubris, the dramatist certainly was not struck down for it that evening, nor for many nights to come. Even as the audience slowly left the theater, still deeply jolted by the emotional experience they had just undergone, the critics of the eight major New York newspapers were formulating their unanimous and unreservedly enthusiastic responses. The performance of *Death of a Salesman* on the tenth of February was the first of 742 that would run deep into November of 1950. With his third produced play, Arthur Miller became a force to be reckoned with in the American theater.

* Miss Dunnock also repeated her interpretation of Linda in the CBS television drama. An additional testament to her ability to impress an author and director was her selection by Kazan and Tennessee Williams for the part of Big Mama in *Cat on a Hot Tin Roof*, a choice which necessitated the author's transformation of the character from a large, gross woman to a female with Miss Dunnock's slight physical appearance.

10

'I am not a dime a dozen!'

Death of a Salesman is the story of a man's life as it is depicted in its final, tortured days. The protagonist is Willy Loman, a traveling salesman who lives in Brooklyn and covers some of the New England territory by automobile. In his sixties, he is physically and mentally exhausted and can no longer meet the rigorous demands of his vocation. Despite the zealously loyal encouragement of his wife, Linda, he knows that his life has not been successful, and the knowledge has brought him, despite intermittent flashes of bravado, to the brink of self-destruction. Depressed by the emptiness of his old age, he is particularly anguished over the inability of his two sons to fulfill his aspirations for them. Happy, a shallow and vain playboy, is mired in a stultifying position with a department store; and Biff, the boy in whom Willy placed his greatest faith, is little more than a hobo and petty thief. It is Biff's return to his father's house after years of drifting that precipitates the action of the drama.

Through an intricate series of flashbacks, originating in Willy's fevered mind, the roots of his family's deterioration are gradually revealed. A man with a semimystical belief in his own concept of success, Willy has spent his life attempting to instill his values into his sons. He has preached his gospel of salesmanship—a brash personality, a ready smile, a fast joke, and a glittering appearance—as the key to fame and fortune; and fostering this gaudy philosophy in his boys, he has overlooked their weaknesses in the golden mist of his grandiose dreams, thus unintentionally but unquestionably paving the way for their ruin.

Following his father's counsel, Happy becomes a frustrated gigolo, and he never really understands why his life has deteriorated into such a hopeless treadmill. Biff's aimless existence, on the other hand, is the result not only of illusions but more pertinently of their sudden and traumatic destruction. As a teenager, Biff surprised his father in a clandestine affair, and stunned by the shattering revelation of a fallen idol, he hysterically branded Willy a fake and a liar and fled into a life of escape and self-pity.

With his sons now home together for the first time in years, Willy makes a final attempt to unite the crumbling family, and succeeds in again sweeping Biff into his vision. But simultaneous visits by Biff and himself to prospective and current employers end disastrously for both men. Seeking a desk job and a raise, Willy is fired instead because of his age and growing incompetence; and Biff spends a fruitless day waiting vainly to see the man he had hoped to sell an incredible promotional scheme. While fleeing from the latter's office with a fountain pen he had stolen in anger and frustration, Biff finally realizes how exaggerated and ridiculous Willy's ideas and dreams have been, and he resolves to free himself from them once and for all by living within the knowledge of his limitations.

In the play's climactic scene, Biff tries to communicate his insight to his father; but his love for the man overwhelms him and he breaks down weeping on Willy's shoulders. Exalted at the revelation of his son's feeling, Willy again prepares to give him the opportunity for greatness that he stubbornly believes can still be Biff's. He roars his car into the night to kill himself and so provide Biff with twenty thousand dollars of insurance money as the means for regeneration. Willy views the final act of his life as both an atonement for past failures and an affirmation of his ideals and love.

The drama closes with a requiem around Willy's grave. In marked contrast to the death of a salesman Willy had always dreamed about, his mourners number only his immediate family, his friend Charley, and Charley's son, Bernard. In a series of fragmentary eulogies, each person attempts to account for Willy Loman's life and death. The scene closes on silence and darkness as the sons help their quietly sobbing mother from the graveside.

Despite basic structural differences, *Death of a Salesman* has many elements in common with *All My Sons*. Both plays involve the interaction of the inner circle of the family with the outer circle of society. However, in *Death of a Salesman* the action is rooted more concretely in the familial arena; man's social responsibility is an important motif, but it is subordinated to the more dominant theme of a father's conflict with his sons.

In both plays, parents of tenuous authority are challenged by their children. Each father has a feminine, tenacious wife who is so absorbed in his welfare and is so unquestionably compliant with his values that her potential for saving him is minimal. In the relationships in both plays, the profound problem is a lack of meaningful communication, particularly between father and son, and despite the close bonds between them. Although to a degree each father has been egocentrically seeking a kind of personal immortality through his sons, overtly his love for his family has been the driving force and justification of his life.

Both dramas are structured around a guilty past which increasingly intrudes itself into the present. In the case of Joe Keller, a definite crime returns to destroy him; in Willy Loman's situation, a lifetime of lies and lapses determine a fate as catastrophic, if not as clearly delineated, as Keller's.

In time each protagonist is brought into the direct path of the consequences he has wrought, and both plays are patterned as personal courts of inquiry in which victimized sons eventually become the unwilling prosecutors of their fathers. The climactic moment in each drama involves a son's agonized and essentially futile attempt to make his father face truth, and each play concludes with the death of the older man as a kind of atonement. In each situation, the father's degradation serves as the ironic but crucial prerequisite for his son's possible salvation.

Nevertheless, for all its similarity to *All My Sons, Death of a Salesman* exhibits the striking artistic development of its author. Structurally it is an achievement of remarkable originality. Like its immediate predecessor, it adheres faithfully to Miller's belief that to know an individual as a dramatic entity one must comprehend his past as well as his present. However in *Death of a Salesman* there is no need to solidify the connections between what the playwright termed 'events and moral consequences, between the manifest and the hidden,' since everything in the play was 'assumed as proven to begin with.'[1] Thus, the process of revelation now consists of bringing things to mind rather than making intricate verbal connections. There is no need for half-veiled intimations of what is

[1] Arthur Miller, 'Introduction,' *Collected Plays*, p.24.

to come, hints of the protagonist's desperation, or allusions to latent relationships and conflicts. Early in the opening scene Willy admits with a frankness born of desperation that he is at the end of his rope, and his first confrontation with Biff jarringly dramatizes the bitterness of their relationship. *Death of a Salesman* does not need the scrupulous expository form of *All My Sons* because its protagonist's character and situation allow him to relive his life before our eyes. Consequently exposition is replaced by illustration.

The structure is a blend of naturalism and expressionism, resulting in an extremely powerful and highly personal form. Although rooted in realistic convention, the play extends the borders of realism without straining credibility because it is mirroring the processes of a disoriented mind. Thus, the form of *Death of a Salesman* is perfectly suited to the nature of its protagonist's psychological imbalance, in which the memory of the past challenges the reality of the present in a surrealistic battle for supremacy.

One important manifestation of this structure is the breakdown of chronological time in order to dredge the important elements from the past into the troubled present. This is not a simple flashback technique by which Willy's life is presented in a neat linear development but rather a complex interrelationship of past and present, illusion and reality, through which character and event emerge concentrically, almost kaleidoscopically, out of the vast whirlpool of Willy's semiconscious existence.

This form is integral to the theme and characterization of the play in at least two ways. First, it indicates the agonizing intensity of the salesman's search for the meaning of his life. He recreates incidents and individuals as if they were all witnesses at an inquest, and reaches out to them in an almost delirious attempt to find answers for his fall.

The second important consequence of *Death of a Salesman's* structure is that by insolubly linking the final days of Willy's life with the years that have shaped them, it gives his life and death a dramatic cohesiveness. Classically, Miller introduces his protagonist shortly before his destruction, but by *showing* the audience Willy's life instead of piecing it together through exposition, the playwright escapes the snare of wordiness and the long, ponderous development which was necessary to the meaning but detrimental to the effectiveness of *All My Sons*. The suspense that would ordinarily precede Willy's death is eradicated, but as the play's title indicates,

Miller did not intend the ending to come as a surprise. More pertinently, the salesman's suicide is graphically joined to the past events which have paved its way.

Miller does not ask the audience to make an unqualified emotional identification with his beleaguered hero. Although the play's power lies in its stunning ability to elicit this sympathy, the intensely idiosyncratic portrait of Willy Loman is a constant reminder that the meaning of his drama depends upon our clear awareness of the limitations of Willy's life and vision. The flashbacks are not scattered through the play at random. Even though Miller does not present them in any tidy chronological order, he selects and arranges them in a definite pattern that gives increasing depth and dimension to the protagonist while simultaneously illuminating the contradictions in his character which continually evade Willy's subjective scrutiny. Emerging out of 1928, the watershed year of Willy's life, each flashback sequence moves us deeper into Willy's consciousness and leads finally to the scene involving Biff's discovery of his adultery, the episode that would understandably issue last out of Willy's recollections since it is the one memory he has tried hardest to repress.

Essentially the flashbacks fall into two categories, each defining a crucial facet of Willy's life. One grouping comprises the events involving Willy and his brother Ben, who appears to Willy's crumbling mind as a cold, righteous, self-assured deity, an objectification by contrast of Willy's uncertainty and insecurity. In every confrontation with Ben, Willy is portrayed as the adoring, fearful, and supplicating child seeking guidance and assurance from the archetypal authoritarian father. Guidance is also the keynote of the second set of flashbacks, but in these Willy is dispensing advice rather than seeking it. This series of episodes, which centers on Willy and his sons, shows Willy the father trying to substantiate his ecstatic belief in the success ideal by superimposing it upon his children.

Both sets of flashbacks culminate in the one involving Willy's infidelity—the fact and symbol of his final degradation, the revelation of his insecurity and failure, and the verification of his bleak loneliness and alienation. Ultimately each event dredged out of his past makes the same point about Willy Loman: his life is caught in an unresolvable dichotomy between fact and fancy. He is unable to separate his individuality from his conception of himself as a supersalesman because he cannot truly differentiate between the two.

Willy's life is a patchwork of errors in judgment, mental and moral lapses, and misdirected hopes, but perhaps his greatest mistake is living far too long with the wrong dream. He verbalizes this dream in the advice he gives to his sons in the initial flashback when he compares them to the bookish and not very personable Bernard.

'Bernard is not well liked is he?' Willy asks rhetorically.

'He's liked,' Biff replies, pompously echoing his father's tone, 'but he's not well liked.'

'That's just what I mean,' Willy exclaims, driving home the proof of his argument:

> Bernard can get the best marks in school, y'understand, but when he gets out in the business world, y'understand, you are going to be five times ahead of him. That's why I thank Almighty God you're both built like Adonises. Because the man who makes an appearance in the business world, the man who creates personal interest is the man who gets ahead. Be liked and you will never want. You take me for instance. I never have to wait in line to see a buyer. 'Willy Loman is here!' That's all they have to know, and I go right through.[2]

This is the success dream to which Willy Loman has dedicated his life and the lives of his sons. Not inherently false, it is nonetheless wrong for him, but he clings to it with a fanatic allegiance that he can ultimately maintain only at the price of his identity. Unknowingly surrendering what one critic has called his 'conscience—that which is most fundamentally himself—for a place in society that was never his,'[3] Willy eventually sacrifices himself and his sons to his deceptive and demanding deity.

Willy Loman's success myth has at least three basic aspects, each one personified by an individual in his life. His brother Ben represents the adventurous spirit of rugged individualism and rapid wealth. Ben is the man who took out on his own to make his fortune in Alaska, but because of his 'very faulty view of geography,'

[2] Miller, 'Death of a Salesman,' *Collected Plays*, p.146.

[3] William B. Dillingham, 'Arthur Miller and the Loss of Conscience,' *The Emory University Quarterly*, 16 (Spring, 1960), p.44.

wound up in Africa, and through a combination of daring and the sheerest dumb luck struck it rich.

'Why boys, when I was seventeen I walked into the jungle,' he pontificates to the awestruck Biff and Happy, 'and when I was twenty-one I walked out. And by God I was rich.'

To which Willy ecstatically adds: 'You see what I been talking about? The greatest things can happen!'

Ironically but characteristically, it is not what Willy has been talking about at all, but his reaction to his brother's oracular autobiography is further proof of the temptation Ben's philosophy holds for him. If Willy is mesmerized by Ben Loman's success story, he is also seduced by some of its ramifications.

'Never fight fair with a stranger, boy. You'll never get out of the jungle that way,' the uncle intones to his nephew, Biff, and it is precisely this stress on the justification of means by ends that enables Willy to overlook or condone the petty thievery in which his sons indulge. He views their misdeeds either as something they will outgrow, like acne, or even more frighteningly, as proof of their All-American razzle-dazzle initiative.

The member of the Loman family who fears and distrusts Ben is Willy's wife, Linda, and her trepidation is quite natural because she manifests an aspect of the success myth—security and stability —to which a figure like Ben is a constant threat. It is Linda who helped influence her husband to settle for the simple security of home, family, and steady job instead of following in the seven-league bootsteps of his legendary brother.

Too often Linda has been oversimplified by audiences and critics who have leaped at an apparent discrepancy between her relationship to Willy throughout the play and her final words over his grave. Pointing to the obvious bewilderment in her heartbreaking 'I don't understand' at the funeral, they have viewed the line as proof positive that Miller mechanically and blatantly altered her character to drain the final emotional ounce out of his already limp audience. How can she fail to comprehend at her husband's graveside, they have sarcastically asked, what she had realized all too well throughout his life? Haven't her conversations with her sons, particularly her 'attention must be paid' exhortation, amply proven that she has always keenly understood Willy and his faults?

The paradox exists, but rather than furnishing evidence of unfair character manipulation, it sharply illustrates the playwright's comprehension of this important and complex individual. The dichotomy between Linda's apparent understanding of her husband throughout their marriage and her bewilderment at his funeral is the result not of any disparity in Miller's mind but in Linda's. She does understand Willy, but only those aspects of his character which are perceptible to her. Other facets of her husband are beyond her comprehension, and it is precisely this uneasy combination of perception and incomprehensibility that is integral to her relationship with the men in her family.

For all her goodness, Linda Loman is a root figure in the catastrophe of her husband and sons. She has a painfully realistic insight into the character and situation of the man she married. She is not fooled by his pretense that the fifty dollars a week he borrows from his friend Charley is his paycheck, but she allows him his lie because she will not rob him of his remaining dignity by informing him she is aware of his petty deception. She realizes, too, that he has been obsessed with the idea of suicide, but although she has quietly subverted his attempts, she again cannot shame him by confessing her knowledge of his plans. And when she angrily replies to Biff's denunciation of Willy as a man with 'no character' by reminding him of his father's devotion to his family, she is fiercely demanding that her son give her husband the respect that is due him.

'There's more good in him than in many other people,' she affirms simply and truthfully. Fully cognizant of his weaknesses, Linda—unlike the son whose love for him is so ambivalent—can also comprehend Willy's decency, loneliness, and heartbreak.

But with all her insights, she has blind spots, and for all her knowledge of Willy as a struggling and weary provider, she can never totally abrogate her faith in him as the Great Salesman. Thus, even while noting his lifelong exertions to barely keep his family going, she can still incredibly label him the trailblazer who opened 'unheard-of territories' for his firm. She knows the truth about her husband but will not wholly face it with him or with herself. Instead she continually helps to inflate Willy's overblown image despite her suspicions of its falsity. In her overwhelming devotion to him, she has helped build a doll's house around him and, consequently, has done to Willy what he has been doing to Biff and Happy. And she has been spurred by the same motivation: love. In being a good wife, Linda Loman has extended her devotion to an extreme that has become destructive not only to her husband but to her sons, who have also become victims of her gingerbread house.

In her well-meaning prudery and naïveté, and in her unswerving loyalty to Willy, she has unconsciously fostered adolescent sexual attitudes in all three of her men by creating an image of herself as the maternal counterpart of the infallible father. The more she is a paragon of virtue to them the less are they able to relate to her as adult males to a wife and mother. Their view of her is pantingly adolescent and distorts all their relationships with women.

'They broke the mold when they made her,' gawks Happy adoringly, never suspecting that his image of Mom as goddess is partially responsible for his shoddy encounters with girls who are never fit to bring home to her, as well as for his father's cheap and pathetic adultery and Biff's traumatic reaction to it.

To a great extent, Linda's mistakes with her husband and sons are the consequence of her longing for security. Theoretically this desire is hardly reprehensible, but for Linda it has become as encompassing and intense as Willy's mystical dreams of conquering the world. Where he equates success with universal adoration, Linda equates it with material well-being, and just as he attempts to condone a lifetime of lapses by embracing his dream with increased fervor, she does likewise with hers. Consequently she can condone her husband's weaknesses because in spite of all his errors he has provided her with the necessary security. Her comments over his grave show how much she has emphasized this materialism and how little, for all her insight, she really knew the man to whom she was married.

'I can't understand it,' she muses, 'at this time especially. First time in thirty-five years we were just about free and clear. He only needed a little salary. He was even finished with the dentist.'

Linda truly cannot comprehend how a man who has paid a mortgage and completed his dental work could want to destroy himself. Charley's reply, almost a rebuke, is lost on her.

'No man,' he says as gently as possible, 'only needs a little salary.'

No man indeed, and Willy Loman least of all. Linda understands the hard-working, self-sacrificing father and husband; she understands the loyal provider. But she never quite comprehends the visionary whose right to dream she has so stalwartly defended. Although she has even occasionally been swept by his dream, she has never been able to recognize its meaning for Willy. This is her failing and her tragedy.

The preceding comments are scarcely intended to portray Linda as the villain of the piece. One of the strengths of *Death of a Salesman* is its refusal to pin blame exclusively on a person, an institution, or even on an entire society. Although Willy Loman's destruction is partly the fault of his family and the failure of certain values propounded by his society, it is no less his own doing. And viewing the play solely as a polemic against modern American capitalistic society is ultimately about as valid as labeling Linda Loman its Lady Macbeth.

Nevertheless, the charge of polemicism has been hurled against *Death of a Salesman* by an inordinate amount of critics who have tenaciously embraced the assumption that the play is a dramatization of a socio-political philosophy, albeit a disturbingly inconsistent one. Thus Eric Bentley complained about what he perceived to be the drama's conflicting points of view. As tragedy, he declared, it is weakened by its extreme social consciousness, and as social drama it is overinflated by its aspirations to tragedy. Consequently it is a peculiar, and unsuccessful, hybrid.

> The 'tragedy' destroys the social drama; the social drama keeps the 'tragedy' from having a genuinely tragic stature. By this last remark I mean that the theme of this social drama, as of most others, is *the little man as victim*. The theme arouses pity but no terror. Man is here too little and too passive to play the tragic hero.
>
> More important even than this, the tragedy and the social drama actually conflict. The tragic catharsis reconciles us to, or persuades us to disregard, precisely those material conditions which the social drama calls our attention to. . . . Or is Mr Miller a 'tragic' artist who without knowing it has been confused by Marxism?[4]

Bentley's review, which appeared soon after the play's opening, was the first of many stinging attacks by critics who initially insisted on a doctrinaire interpretation of *Death of a Salesman* and then compounded their rigidity by scoring it for not fitting neatly into the selected mold.

[4] Eric Bentley, *In Search of Theater* (New York: Knopf, 1953), p.85.

In a much more devastating critique in the June 1949 issue of the *Partisan Review*, Eleanor Clark blithely began with the premise that 'it is, of course, the capitalist system that has done Willy in,' and then, wrapped in the cotton candy comfort of this assertion, clawed at the playwright for trying to conceal this obvious truth 'behind an air of pseudo-universality.' The result for Miss Clark was 'an intellectual muddle and a lack of candor that regardless of Mr Miller's conscious intent are the main earmarks of contemporary fellow-traveling.'[5]

Predictably, critics who adored the play precisely *because* they viewed Miller as a fellow traveler were not wholly satisfied with it either. Writing for *Masses & Mainstream* in 1949, Samuel Siller praised the drama's social content and purpose but found the presence of Willy's capitalistic friend Charley as eulogist a marked weakness. Nor could he accept Miller's tacit approval of Bernard's success in a capitalistic system. Noting the dramatist's sympathy for both these characters, Siller concluded an otherwise laudatory review by admonishing Miller for his apparent fear of carrying his Marxist fervor through to its logical conclusions.

The obvious weakness in these critiques, and a host of similar ones from both the ideological Left and Right, is that they begin with premises that are something less than foolproof, and then go on to castigate the play for not fulfilling them. Miller has insisted that *Death of a Salesman* is neither the left-wing diatribe against American capitalism nor the implicit approval of the system that opposing reviewers have branded it. He has carefully stressed that his play in particular, and drama in general, cannot be simply equated with political philosophies.

I do not believe that any work of art can help but be diminished by its adherence at any cost to a political program, including its author's, and not for any other reason than that there is no political program—any more than there is a theory of tragedy—which can encompass the complexities of real life. Doubtless an author's politics must be one element, and even an important one, in the germination of his art, but if it is art he has created it must by definition bend itself to his observation rather than to his opinions or even his hopes.

[5] Eleanor Clark, 'Old Glamour, New Gloom,' *Partisan Review*, 15, No.6 (June, 1949), p.633. The first appearance of Miss Clark's review was in *Partisan Review*.

If I have shown a preference for plays which seek causation
not only in psychology but in society, I may also believe in
the autonomy of art, and I believe this because my experience
with *All My Sons* and *Death of a Salesman* forces the belief
on me.[6]

The preceding statement is not cited to compel the reader to take
the playwright's word as gospel. It is still a pretty good idea to
heed D. H. Lawrence's advice to trust the tale rather than the
teller. But the tale being told in *Death of a Salesman* substantiates
the teller's observations.

Early Miller dramas like *Honors at Dawn* and *They Too Arise*
are typical products of Marxist orientation and idealism, but although *All My Sons* and *Death of a Salesman* owe a great deal to
these germinal plays, they bend more to their author's observation
than to any political philosophy. They are Marxist only if their
critic assumes that every indictment of a social system must necessarily evolve from *Das Kapital*. Miller berates society for its stulti-
fication of the individual, but he also scores the man who is a
threat to his society. It is this two-pronged attack, providing the
dramatic balance in his work, which confuses and irritates single-
minded observers who refuse to believe that this dualism could
be intentional.* Thus Mr Bentley chided the dramatist for *unintentionally* confusing tragedy with social drama (which the critic
blandly equated with *socialist* drama), assuming that had Miller
concentrated either on one genre or the other, a clearer play would
have emerged. Possibly, but the clarity would have been markedly
superficial. What Bentley and other critics sought in *Death of a
Salesman* was the play Miller refused to write, the one that would
have bent itself to preordained opinion rather than to objective
observation.

This is why Samuel Siller was so miffed by Miller's sympathetic
treatment of Charley and Bernard. Unreservedly accepting the
premise that the writer was indicting everything Charley and his
son represent, the critic could only view Miller's sympathy for

[6] Miller, 'Introduction,' *Collected Plays*, p.36.

* Perhaps the most single-minded and incisive critical commentary on
the play came from the anonymous patron of the arts who stomped out
of the theater on opening night, past the amused playwright, and into
posterity, leaving behind him the immortal line: 'I always knew that
New England territory was no damn good!'

these men as a form of moral cowardice. This is also why Eleanor Clark, although ideologically opposed to Miller, took for granted that the scene in which Willy is 'brutally fired after some forty years with the firm' is directly traceable to 'the party-line literature of the "thirties".'[7] The only trouble with this observation is its complete distortion of character and situation.

The scene is so painful that it makes one wince, but its tone is a blend of pathos and irony rather than indignation and indictment. Here is the aging salesman, determined at last to ask his youthful employer for better working hours and more salary, and receiving instead his dismissal notice. Here is Willy Loman, having just advised his son of the importance of putting on a bold front to impress a prospective employer, now literally groveling before his own boss. Here finally is age giving way fearfully but remorselessly before youth. Indeed, the inevitability of Willy's dismissal, rather than its brutality, is the keynote of the entire episode.

Howard Wagner is no capitalistic ogre; he is a fairly ordinary man in a terribly awkward situation, and it is precisely his *lack* of ruthlessness which makes the incident so painful. The irony of the scene stems from its double perspective. What for Howard is little more than an embarrassing predicament is for Willy nothing less than a life-and-death issue. To expect Howard to comprehend his employee's anguish is to ask for a minor miracle. Nevertheless, it is noteworthy that Howard does not terminate Willy's employment immediately, but only after the salesman has given him an opening by complaining of his inability to meet the demands of his job. Howard could have legitimately fired Willy years ago, but he could not bring himself to do so. That he finally does is much less a manifestation of villainy than of insensitivity and self-absorption.

The tape recorder provides the scene's key image. Howard's preoccupation with it throughout the interview can be viewed as Miller's bitter commentary on a society in which man's involvement with the machine has replaced his responsibility to his fellowman. But as critic Dennis Welland has noted, the implications in this image extend beyond the societal.[8] If the recorder literally contains portions of Howard's past, it symbolically represents Willy's,

[7] Clark, *Partisan Review*, p.633.
[8] Dennis Welland, *Arthur Miller* (New York: Grove, 1961), p.54.

and his hysterical inability to switch it off suggests his helplessness before a life that has careened out of control.

The machine also emphasizes an important similarity between Howard and Willy. Howard has recorded the voices of his wife and children, and it is this preoccupation with his family, rather than with his business, which is partially responsible for his callousness toward Willy. And if his familial pride manifests itself at a devastatingly inopportune moment for the weary salesman, one can only surmise how Willy would have acted if their positions were reversed. The scene may be construed as an indictment of a system, but it must also be understood as an arraignment of Willy Loman. Howard's pride in his son echoes Willy's, differing from it only in intensity, and his callousness to Willy, due partially to this paternal esteem, mirrors Willy's lifelong insensitivity to Bernard. The beleaguered salesman has not collided with a capitalistic despot but, ironically, with a younger embodiment of his own traits.

Ultimately it is not Howard, but Charley who is the truly successful man in the play and who provides the counterpoint to Willy. A profoundly decent person and, as Willy belatedly realizes, 'the only friend I got,' Charley is never blinded by sentiment. His reply to Willy's wonder at how Bernard became a success without his apparent guidance is wholly in character.

'My salvation is that I never took any interest in anything.'

This explanation is hardly an indication of Charley's unrelatedness, because the moment he expounds it he quietly gives his friend fifty dollars to help pay his bills. What Charley means by lack of interest is the ability to live without ecstatic devotion and fanatical commitments. Willy and Charley live in the same neighborhood, have essentially similar backgrounds, are quite comfortable with each other, and yet their views are sharply divergent. But this difference is not ideological. It is the result of a reasoned perspective which Charley maintains, and which Willy has never had.

Miller's approval of Charley manifests not only his acceptance of the man but of the capitalistic system in which he thrives, assuming that for all that can go wrong with it, 'the norm of capitalistic behavior is ethical, or at least can be.'[9] The same assumption underlies *All My Sons* and clearly suggests that the influence of Karl Marx is no more pervasive in these plays than the influence of Groucho, Chico, or Harpo. Miller indicts Willy's society

[9] Miller, 'Introduction,' *Collected Plays*, pp.36–37.

for its success gods and its stress on material accretion as a sign of grace, but he also scores Willy because he has pledged himself to this code so zealously (again the contrast to Charley whose lack of fanaticism makes him a better businessman) that he has betrayed himself and his family.

The result is the situation in which Willy finds himself in the final days of his life. He is a man alone, and his isolation is graphically highlighted by the structure of the play which presents him, even in the midst of his family, as a solitary figure increasingly lost in memories and dreams. His alienation from Biff is the most anguished because their relationship had been the deepest, but Willy is also cut off from Linda, who has been too afraid of hurting him to allow any meaningful communication, and from Happy, who has always figured secondarily in his father's affections and hopes. And just as Willy is alone, so too is each of the others.

Perhaps Happy's isolation is the most pathetic because it most starkly bears the imprint of Willy's influence. Happy is the son who inherits his father's blindness and becomes the dog-eared carbon copy of the older man, the fast-talking hustler caught on a treadmill of loneliness and frustration, filling an empty existence with delusions that only intensify its hollowness. At the conclusion, Happy is Willy's lone disciple, and his final words over his father's grave ring with a grimly humorous irony.

'All right boy,' he challenges Biff, 'I'm gonna show you and everybody else that Willy Loman did not die in vain. He had a good dream. It's the only dream you can have—to come out number-one man. He fought it out here, and this is where I'm gonna win it for him.'[10]

The Loman line. The final tarnished echo of Willy's exuberant credo. Biff cannot even reply, and 'with a hopeless glance at Happy, he bends towards his mother.'

The mordant irony of Willy Loman's existence lies in the fact that his isolation is largely the result of his inability to perceive that he never was the personality man he prided himself on being. He selected a role he could not fulfill, and in his commitment to his choice lost his identity. Happiest at manual labor, planting a small garden, building a swing, or putting a new addition on the house, he is nonetheless unable to comprehend the meaning of the joy and satisfaction he feels at these accomplishments. Not until

[10] Miller, 'Death of a Salesman,' *Collected Plays*, p.222.

his funeral is the contrast between these tasks and the career Willy chose finally verbalized.

'There's more of him in that front stoop than in all the sales he ever made,' Biff murmurs to Charley, who quietly affirms the observation.

'Yeah,' he replies, 'he was a happy man with a batch of cement.'

But Willy became a salesman because this particular profession best symbolized for him the promise and infallibility of his illusion. In an uncharacteristic—and poorly motivated—burst of rhetoric, Charley defines Willy's choice, in the Requiem:

> For a salesman, there is no rock bottom to the life. He don't put a bolt to a nut, he don't tell you the law or give you medicine. He's a man way out there in the blue, riding on a smile and shoeshine. And when they start not smiling back —that's an earthquake. And then you get yourself a couple of spots on your hat, and you're finished. Nobody dast blame this man. A salesman is got to dream, boy. It comes with the territory.[11]

A million or so salesmen might argue that their profession comprises a bit more than this, and Miller, with an intimate knowledge of it, would undoubtedly agree.* Charley's definition is symbolic; the salesman he eulogizes is the epitome of the cult of personality. He does not sow, he does not reap, he does not create anything tangible. He sells. What? Miller never identifies the products in Willy's sample cases because his wares are clearly subordinate to his primary commodity—himself. And when this commodity is no longer marketable, as Charley suggests, the sky grows pale and the sun glints coldly.

---

[11] *Ibid.*, p.222.

* Nevertheless, as recently at March, 1966, the Sales Executives Club of New York felt duty-bound to rectify the distorted image of the salesman that the play was foisting upon an unsuspecting American public, by proposing that certain modifications be made in the script of the CBS television production of the drama, and that a brief epilogue entitled 'Life of a Salesman,' describing the joys and rewards of salesmanship, be added. 'For years the play has been plaguing our "selling as a career" efforts,' the Club complained. The Xerox Corporation, sponsor of the production, and the Columbia Broadcasting System politely, firmly, and with no overt trace of a titter, denied the request. At present, even after a repeat performance of the televised drama, there is every indication that the selling profession and the public have again survived.

But if Charley's eulogy metaphorically catches the anxieties of Willy's profession, it falls far short of summing up Willy. Charley may be correct when he states that a salesman 'is got to dream,' but he is clearly in error when he tries to absolve his friend of all blame. The need to dream is one thing; the sacrifice of self and family to an illusion is quite another. To the extent that Charley views Willy solely as the victim of his vocation, he—like Linda—does not fully understand him.

Paying the price for his choices, Willy is trapped by his adherence to two contradictory ways of life. On the one hand, he burns with a consuming desire to recapture the past, which he views through rose-tinted glasses. It is a quest for a kind of simplicity and innocence that is illustrated in all his spontaneous responses to nature and yesteryear, encompassing even the names he has chosen for his sons, names bursting with naïve exuberance and vigor. On the other hand, he is fervently determined to succeed in his contemporary competitive society, and his obsession is concretized not only in the profession he has chosen but in his adoration of all the household gods of commercialism. In fact his speech is so liberally sprinkled with brand names, business concerns, and products that he unconsciously parodies these selfsame deities. Unable to reconcile the dualistic nature of his quest, he has become a man divided, the agonized victim of an existence which offers him two impossible alternatives: a regression to memories of the past, or the narcotic elation of hoping for future miracles. The past and the future thus consume him because the present has become a vacuum.

In one respect Willy is caught between two cultures: the vanished agrarian frontier that he rhapsodically associates with his father, an itinerant peddler ('a very great and wild-hearted man') who used to wagon his entire family across the country selling handmade flutes; and modern urban society, the tape-recorder civilization of Howard Wagner.

Throughout the play a polyphonic use of images manifests the dichotomy between these two antithetical existences. The drama is dotted with references to the natural world, which includes everything suggested by the flute melody that weaves through the play as a lyrical motif 'telling of grass and trees and the horizon.' But the drama also abounds with references to products and corporations, monetary figures and itineraries, appliances and mortgages, and finally to the omnipotent insurance policy for which Willy offers up his life. Perhaps the controlling image, which bridges both ways of life and illustrates the deterioration of Willy's present condition, is the house itself. Once it was part of a neighborhood of lawns, elms, and open spaces; now the area has shrunken into a mortar and brick vise, enclosing and stifling the house and its inhabitants.

'We are aware,' Miller instructed his set designer, 'of towering, angular shapes behind [the house] surrounding it on all sides. . . . As more light appears, we see a solid vault of apartment houses around the small, fragile-seeming home.'[12]

The implications of this scenery are further elaborated by Willy.

'The way they boxed us in here,' he complains. 'Bricks and windows, windows and bricks.'*

Perhaps the scene that most clearly illuminates Willy's agony is the bizarre sequence in which he makes a final and futile attempt to plant the garden he has previously never had time to cultivate. Humiliated by Howard Wagner and degraded by his own sons, who have abandoned him in a restaurant where they were to have treated him to dinner, he staggers home and in the dead of night makes a ludicrous and grotesque effort to create something out of the soil that is still left to him. It is the crumbling salesman's last vain attempt to accomplish something, the dying ember of the agrarian frontier dream. As he fumbles in the dark with the seed packets, Willy converses feverishly with his brother Ben, the embodiment of that dream, and contrasts the chaotic present with the happiness and promise of the past:

Oh, Ben, how do we get back to all the great times? Used to be so full of light, and comradeship, the sleigh-riding in winter, and the ruddiness on [Biff's] cheeks. And always some kind of good news coming up, always something nice coming up ahead. And never even let me carry the valises in the

---

[12] *Ibid.*, p.130.

* The prevalent atmosphere of the enclosed and constricted house is claustrophobic, a mood that is figurative as well as literal. The apartment houses are the outward manifestations of the inner walls that provide Willy's imprisonment. Just as his home is engulfed by physical barriers, his mind is hemmed in by psychological obstructions, and although it can range through time and space, its motion is always circular, and severely and increasingly circumscribed.

house, and simonizing, simonizing that little red car![13]

Although there is unmistakably a poignant measure of truth in Willy's elegiac reminiscence, it is also saturated in the sentimentality that marks all his recollections. Miller best explained this dichotomy a few years later in a statement he made with respect to his film script, *The Misfits*, which is also concerned with the clash between past and present.

This film is really about the choice between illusion and reality: what has happened to this country is that people cling to the illusion of a frontier—but the only real territory left is relationship to other people. There really never was any other territory, but we are just finding it out. . . . Maturity means living in relation to reality—it means leaving behind all the childhood figures, even if it means leaving behind some of the poetry of those figures too.[14]

In *Death of a Salesman* the final impression of the last frontier is that of a dream, beautiful but woefully insubstantial. And when Willy recalls the joyous past of his youth, his longing for the frontier ethos and values should not be construed simply as a condemnation of present society. His recollections are painful examples of his inability to relinquish 'the childhood figures' and their 'poetry' which is so noticeably lacking in his bleak and promiseless present. They exhibit the vain romantic hope of escaping from the pressures and responsibilities that have propelled him to the brink of destruction.

To an extent, Biff falls under the same spell. However, his future life should certainly not be accepted as the panacea to the cash nexus of the play. Biff has begun to find himself, but his sense of direction, although westerly, is still vague, and his vocation as a cowboy is not the surefire alternative to his problems. If he is going to be happy as a ranch hand, his fulfillment will not be due to the mystique of the last frontier, but to his relocation as a human being.

So far I have stressed the negative aspects of Willy Loman's dream—its emphasis on personality, appearance, and a mystical adoration of success that transforms failure into the penultimate sin. But there is a positive aspect, too, and to ignore it is to overlook

[13] *Ibid.*, p.213.

[14] Miller, quoted in Alice T. McIntyre, 'Making *The Misfits* or Waiting For Monroe or Notes from Olympus,' *Esquire*, 55 (March, 1961), p.78.

a facet of Willy's character that defines him as pertinently as do all his misguided allegiances. His dream is not comprised solely of tinsel and rhinestone; it also contains something profoundly genuine.

The play describes two deaths of a salesman, and they starkly contrast with each other. Willy's closes the drama. Unadorned and unattended by anyone outside the immediate family and friends, it is the direct antithesis of the funeral of Dave Singleman, an elderly salesman whose life and death Willy always dreamt would be his. If Ben and Linda Loman represent two aspects of Willy's success myth, Singleman manifests a third, and perhaps the most important.

When Howard Wagner tries to make Willy face the fact that he is being fired because 'it's a business . . . and everybody's gotta pull his own weight,' Willy counters by attempting to tell the younger man of the effect Dave Singleman had made on him. They had first met when Willy was deciding whether or not to accompany his brother to Alaska.

And I was almost decided to go, when I met a salesman in the Parker House. His name was Dave Singleman. And he was eighty-four years old, and he'd drummed merchandise in thirty-one states. And old Dave, he'd go up to his room, y'understand, put on his green velvet slippers—I'll never forget—and pick up his phone and call the buyers, and without ever leaving his room, at the age of eighty-four, he made his living. And when I saw that, I realized that selling was the greatest career a man could want. 'Cause what could be more satisfying than to be able to go, at the age of eighty-four, into twenty or thirty different cities, and pick up a phone, and *be remembered and loved and helped by so many different people*? Do you know? when he died—and by the way he died the death of a salesman, in his green velvet slippers in the smoker of the New York, New Haven and Hartford, going into Boston—when he died, hundreds of salesmen and buyers were at his funeral. Things were sad on a lotta trains for months after that. *In those days there was personality in it, Howard. There was respect, and comradeship, and gratitude in it.* Today, it's all cut and dried, and there's no chance for bringing friendship to bear—or personality. You see what I mean?[15]

[15] Miller, 'Death of a Salesman,' *Collected Plays,* pp. 180–181. Italics my own.

Howard, who has barely been listening, does not. After all, the incident is not really relevant to the present situation. And yet Howard's inability to grasp the story's meaning for Willy is a fair measure of his shallowness.

Although his recollection begins with references to the security in Singleman's career, Willy is not primarily impressed by the aged salesman's comfortable life. Singleman's telephone sales, green velvet slippers, peaceful death, and large funeral are only the outer manifestations of the truly significant quality that Willy has elicited from the old man's life and death: namely the inherent worth of personal relationships.

There is little doubt that Willy's remembrance of Singleman is as mawkishly exaggerated as his other romanticized recollections. His verbalization of the salesman's death in the smoker of the train pulling into Boston is a characteristic example of his sentimentality. But neither accuracy nor sentiment is the keynote to this sequence. Whether or not the old days contained the personality, respect, comradeship, and gratitude to the degree Willy claims is much less important than his recognition of and insistence upon these values. And it is equally significant that the meaning of personality in this context is much more profound than the slick personableness to which he has paid lip service in so many of his declamations on success.

Willy Loman's destruction is not just the inevitable outgrowth of a stubborn adherence to a false dream. He is also betrayed because the genuine values embodied in his interpretation of Dave Singleman's life have little or no place in Howard Wagner's world. And in emphasizing this part of Willy's dilemma, *Death of a Salesman* indicts society, not in any glib leftist diatribe, but through the drama's deep concern with human destiny in an environment that places only tangential value on the personal worth and dignity of a human being.

But even as the Singleman episode deepens the play's questioning of a society, it further illuminates the character of Willy Loman. Although he recalls true values in Singleman's life, Willy's disastrous error with respect to the old salesman is his failure to perceive that Singleman's success was due to his character rather than his vocation. It was the man, not the job, who elicited the respect and love that Willy so desperately desires. To the extent that he confuses the human being with the salesman, Willy is guilty of a misjudgment. To the extent that he has dedicated his life to an attempt to buy love, respect, and dignity as if they were marketable commodities, Willy is blameworthy. To the extent that he allows personal values to manifest themselves in the impersonal gods of the business world, Willy is culpable. And to the extent that he searches in the public world for the devotion he always had in the private, he must and does bear his share of responsibility.

But responsibility notwithstanding, the question of whether Willy bridges the enormous gulf between pathos and tragedy is difficult to answer. This problem, which has intrigued critics and audiences since the drama's premiere, is not just academic. It is inextricably linked to the meaning of the play, and even further, to the unresolved but vital debate about the possibility of tragedy in modern drama.

Predictably, the initial supporter of Willy Loman's tragic stature was Miller himself, who put the case before his audience in a highly charged emotional tirade by Linda toward the end of the play's first act. Defending her husband against Biff's charge that 'he's got no character,' she replies angrily:

> I don't say he's a great man. Willy Loman never made a lot of money. His name was never in the paper. He's not the finest character that ever lived. But he's a human being and a terrible thing is happening to him. So attention must be paid. He's not to be allowed to fall into his grave like an old dog. Attention, attention must be finally paid to such a person.[16]

Not necessarily.

Aside from the fact that Miller is aiming this outburst at the audience with the delicacy and grace of a Baptist preacher at a revival meeting, the argument makes a weak and confused plea for Willy's tragic potential because it delineates the one attribute that negates it: his littleness. If 'attention must be paid' because Willy is human and suffering, then it is the attention one pays to any televised soap opera with its veritable menagerie of anguished wretches writhing in the throes of ceaseless agonies. No one will deny Willy's suffering, but the question is whether it ultimately manifests anything more than pain, whether it precedes and en-

[16] *Ibid.*, p.162.

genders any insight or knowledge that would render his destruction something more than pitiful waste.

It is not an easily answerable question. In the climactic scene of the play, Biff makes a final desperate effort to force Willy to face reality. Having confronted the bitter facts of his own existence, the son tries to crash through his father's incredible and tenacious fantasies.

'I am not a leader of men, Willy, and neither are you,' he exclaims.

> You were never anything but a hard-working drummer who landed in the ash can like all the rest of them! I'm one dollar an hour, Willy! I tried seven states and couldn't raise it. A buck an hour! Do you gather my meaning? I'm not bringing home any prizes any more, and you're going to stop waiting for me to bring them home![17]

Willy's immediate reaction is the assumption that Biff is trying to spite him in revenge for his disillusionment, but the young man grabs him and cries, 'Pop, I'm nothing! I'm nothing, Pop. Can't you understand that? There's no spite in it anymore. I'm just what I am, that's all.' He literally tries to pound this message into his father, but his anger bursts and dissolves. In the play's most shattering moment he breaks down on the older man's shoulders, sobbing uncontrollably. 'Will you let me go, for Christ's sake?' he begs. 'Will you take that phony dream and burn it before something happens?'[18]

As Biff regains his composure and moves away, Willy pauses 'astonished' and 'elevated.' 'Isn't that remarkable?' he exclaims, 'Biff—he likes me!' And reassured of this simple but treasured truth by Linda and Happy, he cries out his promise—'That boy— that boy is going to be magnificent!'—and rushes ecstatically into the night and into death to give his son the one thing Biff never really wanted from him: money.*

Unable to break the shackles of commercialism that have both defined and limited his life, Willy apparently seeks death as the most feasible resolution to an increasingly desperate dilemma. He will repay Biff's love with cash by putting himself up as collateral.

[17] *Ibid.*, p.217.
[18] See note 17 above.
* So unimportant is the money for which Willy kills himself that it is not even mentioned by anyone in the Requiem over Willy's grave.

Arthur Miller

His suicide will be both an atonement for past errors and a stimulus to his son's future success.

Unquestionably Willy's death is marked by blindness. Performed in the language and context of a bankbook, his final action rings with a familiar and mocking irony. But Willy's blindness is partial rather than pervasive, and to construe his limited comprehension as total obtuseness is to simplify him to the point of distortion. Within the depth and scope of Willy's consciousness there is a great deal of room for perception, and if his final movements are enacted in both figurative and literal darkness, they are still motivated by a clear personal vision that cuts like a beacon through the omnipresent gloom.

Bewildered and lonely over the years since Biff left him, Willy experiences a realization on the last day of his life that dwarfs all his disappointments: the knowledge of his son's love. This love, upon which he had staked his existence, now suffuses his life with new meaning and justifies him as a father.

The bond between father and son is the most important relationship in *Death of a Salesman.** Four generations of Lomans, beginning with Willy's father and continuing through Willy's fervently anticipated grandchildren are either dramatized or discussed in the play. Three generations in Charley's family, culminating in Bernard's two sons, are relevant; and all three generations of the Wagner family—Howard, his father Frank (whose memory Willy

---

* A salient feature of Miller's dramas is his depiction of the father-son relationship. A union simultaneously integral and abrasive, embodying love and resentment, it is undoubtedly what the playwright himself has termed 'the secret drama' in many of his plays, and several studies have concentrated on this covert drama in *Death of a Salesman.*

Some psychological interpretations of the play have noted the Oedipal situation in the Loman family, and have stressed the unconscious motivations and drives of Willy and his sons.

Be this as it may. Miller is too sophisticated a writer not to comprehend the psychological implications in his work, and a psychoanalytical interpretation of his dramas is certainly valid. What is perhaps questionable, though, is the ultimate relevance of such interpretations as 'keys' to the meaning of the playwright's work.

Although Miller has admitted that he finds psychoanalytical studies of his plays fascinating, he has always insisted that he is not overtly writing psychoanalysis. Thus, while *Death of a Salesman* has its subliminal drama, its main concern is with the social and ethical manifestations of the psychological relationships and conflicts. And if the play utilizes the psychological element, it apparently does so to motivate and particularize them, but not to supersede them.

reveres with the same adoration he holds for Dave Singleman),
and Howard's son and daughter—provide important glosses to
the Loman family.

In all, ten generations of father-son relationships are woven into
the tapestry of *Death of a Salesman,* and in each case a father is
involved in passing something on to his son. But no father is more
intensely and zealously committed to his child than Willy, and
out of this network of relationships the love between Willy and
Biff is the deepest and most anguished. It has received the highest
inflation, the most shattering blow, and finally the most poignant
reconciliation; and it is this restoration for which Willy Loman dies.

Unquestionably the situation is imbued with terrible irony, for
at the moment when Biff threatens to break through Willy's dream
world, the realization of his son's love reinflates the illusion and
propels the father on the last lap of the hopeless quest that has
dominated his whole existence. But if the relocation of Biff's love
helps to propagate Willy's delusions, it simultaneously bestows upon him the identity he vainly sought as a worshipper of the success
deities. That he immediately sacrifices this identity to those selfsame gods is ludicrous; but he does not die just to give Biff money.

'Why can't I give him something and not have him hate me?'
he asks earlier in the play.

At the conclusion it is this 'something,' this undefinable manifestation of his overpowering love, for which he sacrifices his life.
And precisely because he finally has a reason for living, his choice
of death, for all its senselessness and irony, becomes an act of
heroism.

Matching the complexity and challenge of the question of Willy's
ultimate insight and knowledge is the problem of his tragic stature.
In her previously cited defense of him, Linda Loman emphasized
her husband's ordinariness and littleness in an attempt to suggest
that even small men are fit subjects for tragedy.* The proposition

* In his essay 'Tragedy and the Common Man,' (*New York Times,*
Feb. 27, 1949), written two weeks after the premiere of *Death of a Salesman,* Miller noticeably qualified Linda's small-man-as-tragic-hero theory
by sharply differentiating between smallness of station and smallness of
spirit. Starting with the proposition that the common man is an apt subject
for tragedy the playwright then qualified the proposal by limiting his
concept of commonness to social position, as opposed to inherent dignity,
moral capacity, and sense of commitment. Although this crucial difference
may perhaps be implied in Linda's passionate defense of Willy, it is certainly not clarified.

is at best tenuous, and generally critics who have shared Linda's observations have used them to mitigate Willy's tragic potential. For example, in his book *The Spirit of Tragedy*, Herbert J. Muller has noted that

> as the study of a little man succumbing to his environment rather than a great man destroyed through his greatness, [the play] is characteristically modern. There is no question of grandeur in such a tragedy; the 'hero' may excite pity, but nothing like awe.[19]

From Gerhart Hauptmann's *The Weavers* to Samuel Beckett's *Waiting For Godot*, the spectacle of the little man futilely bucking the glacial crush of his environment has been the dominant characteristic of realism that, for all the philosophical and structural mutations it has undergone, is still the primary dramatic genre of the twentieth century. And with its emphasis on social and psychological determinism, realism is profoundly antithetical to tragedy, which stresses the crucial balance between individual will and fatalistic forces. But the antithesis of realism to tragedy still does not rule out the possibility of tragedy in modern drama. The question is how far a playwright is willing and able to depart from the inherent limitations of realism so that he can work meaningfully within its necessary frame of reference without wholly succumbing to its philosophical implications.

In *Death of a Salesman*, Miller makes this departure. Just as the play supersedes the strictures of realism, structurally, it breaks through the philosophical barrier by refusing to impale its protagonist on the horns of necessity. Rightly noting the effects of his environment on Willy, Mr. Muller walks an unsteadier line when he attempts to define the beleaguered salesman wholly in terms of that environment. The facts of Willy's story simply do not substantiate this thesis.

If Willy Loman is, as Eric Bentley labeled him, 'the little man as victim,' he is more the victim of his choices than of his environment. He does not suffer will-lessly, but for his conception of dignity and respect, misguided as that concept may be. He is a totally committed man, clinging to his personal dream with a frenzied intensity that lifts him far beyond the ordinary. He refuses

[19] Herbert J. Muller, *The Spirit of Tragedy* (New York: Knopf, 1956), p.316.

to surrender either his vision of himself or his expectations for his
son, and it is this fanaticism which endows him with a stature
clearly at odds with the littleness that is too glibly associated with
his name and profession.*

'That boy is going to be magnificent!' he exults as he imagines
Biff exercising the potential the insurance money will unleash in
him. For all his references to the objects of the business world,
Willy is not a materialist but a mystic, for whom money is not an
end in itself but a means to grandeur. 'Greatness' and 'magnificence' are two words that abound in his vocabulary and define him
more accurately than his sales and front stoop put together. Willy
Loman dies for his son, but he also dies for his concept of magnificence and the exalted hope that it will be realized in Biff.

It will not. Biff will live because he finally realizes and *is willing
to accept* his essential littleness.

'Pop!' he exclaims with crushing finality, 'I'm a dime a dozen
and so are you!'

Willy's enraged rebuttal cuts to the core of his being.

'I am not a dime a dozen!' he replies in a last thundering assertion of his vision. 'I am Willy Loman and you are Biff Loman!'
The cry carries with it a terrible sense of awareness, the simultaneous knowledge of and refusal to concede frustration, loneliness, and
failure.

Had Willy been wholly unaware of the dichotomy between his
ideals and his inability to fulfill them, he would not have experienced much of the anguish that has marked a great deal of his life.
As Miller has suggested, he would have died rather serenely, perhaps while 'polishing his car, probably on a Sunday afternoon with
the ball game coming over the radio.'[20] The form of the play points
to the inescapable fact that Willy is tortured by his awareness of
the falsity of his existence, so anguished that he constantly searches
for indications of where and how it went wrong.

At times Willy's inability to comprehend the contradictions of
his life provides moments of grim and pathetic humor. He reacts
to Biff's latest thievery with outraged surprise even though he has

---

* The play's co-producer, Walter Fried, recalled that when Elia Kazan
drew Miller's attention to the rather blatantly symbolic connotations in the
name Loman, the playwright registered total surprise, claiming he had
never considered it figuratively.

[20] Miller, 'Introduction,' *Collected Plays*, p.34.

recalled instances in the past where he has encouraged it. He spends one moment praising his car as 'the greatest ever built' and then condemns even its manufacturer when he learns he has to pay a repair bill. His advice to Biff on how to approach a man from whom he wishes to borrow a large sum of money is rife with ludicrous contradictions.

'Be quiet, fine, and serious,' he cautions. 'Everybody likes a kidder, but nobody lends him money,' and then concludes with the advice to 'walk in with a big laugh. Don't look worried. Start off with a couple of your good stories to lighten things up. It's not what you say, it's how you say it—because personality always wins the day.'[21]

This to a man who is going to borrow money from an ex-employer who once fired him for stealing basketballs, from a man who is about to be fired because his personality has never won a day of his life.

Willy can relive the most crucial events of his life and still wonder how he has erred in raising his sons. His memory is active and his search for answers intense, but his ability to perceive the meaning of these answers is limited. He can still sincerely ask Bernard near the end of the play what the secret of success is.

But although these instances manifest the previously cited blindness of Willy, they are matched by moments when he is keenly aware of the inconsistencies in his life. In the initial flashback in which he advises his sons how to succeed in business without really trying, he admits to Linda only moments later that he is not succeeding even though he is trying desperately. But she bolsters his flagging spirits, and the dream, like a grotesque balloon, is reinflated. Throughout the play, in the past and present, Linda, Ben, and Charley hear Willy describe the doubt and pain of his life with pinpoint accuracy. His anguished appeal to Biff to understand the motives behind his adultery is further evidence of his self-awareness, and the suicide attempts that stain his present existence are the most awesome manifestations of his insight into the wreckage of his hopes and dreams.

Throughout his life Willy's illusions are threatened by harsh realities. Sometimes he cannot comprehend them, but more often he stubbornly refuses to face their implications. That he cannot define reality and separate it from the illusions that have haunted

[21] Miller, 'Death of a Salesman,' *Collected Plays*, pp.168–169.

his existence is a measure of his obtuseness; that he *will not* is an indication of his obdurate refusal to face utter humiliation. And in that refusal he exercises his choice and adamantly asserts his will in the face of necessity. For Willy, greatness or death are the only alternatives. He will not be little. To live in the light of Biff's knowledge would be to accept smallness; to die when he does, as he does, is to reach out one last time for magnificence. This may not be sensible; it may even be patently ridiculous. But very few tragic heroes were not also damn fools. Charley is sensible, but no one has written a tragedy about Charley.

Death of a Salesman does not conclude with its protagonist's death; it continues through his funeral, a solitary affair in marked and bitter contrast to the one Willy envisioned, and the dichotomy between appearance and reality is nowhere more graphically dramatized than in the disparate funerals of the play's two salesmen. But the Requiem serves still another purpose. It concludes the sound and fury of Willy's life on a note of silence, as the accusations, justifications, and arguments dissolve in a haunting and elegiac solitude.

A lyrical tone poem, the Requiem is an appropriate coda to the symphony that preceded it. For the first and only time the rest of the major characters in the drama are assembled and in their brief parting eulogies expound their various judgments of Willy Loman. The story is finally freed from his tortured mind, and the audience is given an opportunity to view him outside of his perspective.

Ironically, each viewpoint casts more light on its holder than on the mystery of Willy. Linda cannot understand his death; Happy defies anyone to sully his father's dream, totally oblivious to how it has and will sully him; Charley eulogizes Willy's profession but fails to comprehend that the vocation and the man always maintained the most uneasy of alliances. Perhaps Biff comes closest to enunciating the truth about his father.

'The man didn't know who he was,' he repeats twice, and thereby strikes the basic philosophical chord in the play, a chord to which no one else responds.

But for all its apparent validity, even Biff's recognition does not entirely clarify the final picture of Willy. For if the salesman did not know who he was, he knew who he wanted to be. And who he did not want to be. And this is a kind of knowledge, too.

Death of a Salesman is a drama thoroughly centered in the main-

stream of American theater. It presents a critical outlook on contemporary American society; it employs dramatic forms more
expressive than the realistic technique in which it is rooted, succeeding as do the best works of O'Neill and Tennessee Williams
in developing a poetic drama based upon the mores, language, and
experience of American life; and it manifests the primary struggle
of American dramatists to present the common man (broadly
speaking) as the focus of dramatic imagination.

Willy Loman is intrinsically American, but in his particularity
he also attains universality. Shot through with weaknesses and
faults, he is almost a personification of self-delusion and waste, the
apotheosis of the modern man in an age too vast, demanding and
complex for him. But without abrogating his intense individuality,
he is also the archetypal father, not far removed in his hopes, mistakes, catastrophe, and reconciliation from that most ludicrous and
sublime of all archetypal parents, King Lear. Finally, he personifies
the human being's desire, for all his flaws, to force apart the steel
pincers of necessity and partake of magnificence, and in this need
he becomes a profoundly relevant man for all ages.

Willy Loman is a daemonic figure in a shabby business suit, a
man unable to compromise his dream, who—like the tragi-comic
Spanish Don who hurled himself foolishly and wonderfully against
the world's windmills—must pursue his conception of himself
wherever it will lead him with an intensity that most definitely
passes understanding. He is finally destroyed because he seeks a
kind of ecstasy in life which by its very nature is impossible to
maintain. Nevertheless, his inherent humanity and his capacity for
love and self-sacrifice sympathetically and poignantly qualify this
destruction.

If there is a measure of waste in the death of this salesman, it
is more than compensated for by a measure of worth. And in the
balance, delicately but firmly, is poised a play.

11

'To demonstrate that Ibsen
is really pertinent today'

Shortly over a month after *Death of a Salesman* concluded its Broadway run, a new offering by Arthur Miller opened at the Broadhurst Theater. Staged by Robert Lewis and starring Frederic March, Florence Eldridge, and Morris Carnovsky, Miller's adaptation of Henrik Ibsen's *An Enemy of the People* premiered on the evening of December 28, 1950. Although, according to the playwright, it was written 'to demonstrate that Ibsen is really pertinent today,'[1] the demonstration fell considerably short of its backers' expectations, and despite the prestige of authors and cast, the play folded after a meager thirty-six performances. The fault was not exactly Ibsen's.

The drama which Miller chose in his Americanization of Ibsen is one of the Norwegian writer's more intriguing and humorously bitter problem plays. A cross between a jeremiad and a Jonsonian comedy, it concerns the trials and tribulations of one Dr Thomas Stockmann, a well-meaning but superbly naïve small-town physician who has helped to develop the mineral baths that are hopefully going to make his community a bustling tourist attraction. With the baths completed, he is rewarded with a lucrative position as their inspector. However, in the exercise of his new responsibility, he discovers that the waters are being contaminated with typhoid germs from waste products of nearby tanneries. In a burst of idealistic integrity, he proposes to publish his findings and have the baths torn down and rebuilt in a safer location. Elated that he has discovered this potentially catastrophic situation in time, he is confident that the village will hail him as its saviour, and his illusion

[1] Arthur Miller, 'Preface.' *An Enemy of the People* (New York: Viking, 1951), p.8.

is further inflated when he apparently wins over several communal leaders.

Hovstad, the local newspaper editor, and his assistant, Billing, vow their support, seeing in the doctor's declaration a means by which they can embarrass the governing establishment. While not endorsing the editor's radicalism, Aslaksen, the printer, pledges the loyalty and support of 'the compact majority,' the small businessmen who comprise the town's middle class and who ostensibly would lose their starched shirts if their customers were to fall prey to a typhoid epidemic. In fact the only important political figure who does not rally round Stockmann's banner is his brother, the mayor. Instead he reminds the good doctor and his supporters that refurbishing the baths will cost an enormous amount of money, at least two years of hard labor, and a nonexistent livelihood in the interim. Proposing an alternate plan, he suggests that the baths be kept in operation while repairs are made gradually and covertly, thereby accomplishing the desired ends through more moderate means.

Although Dr. Stockmann tries to convince his brother that as long as the baths remain in use a typhoid epidemic is imminent, Mayor Stockmann's appeal to monetary self-interest is much more persuasive than Thomas' appeal to integrity and self-sacrifice, and in rapid order each of the doctor's allies deserts him. Puzzled and angered by their rejection of truth and honor for a false material security, he takes his case before the entire village; but his previous supporters, now firmly aligned behind the mayor, incite the crowd into a howling, hostile mob. Frustrated and enraged by this reception, Stockmann finally condemns the community to perdition and is branded by popular vote an enemy of the people. As the play concludes, although he has lost his job and he and his family have been violently ostracized by the town, he refuses to be silenced and vows to continue his battle for truth and enlightenment.

In his adaptation, Miller closely followed this skeletal plot line. The most obvious alterations involved language and structure, and in both cases the dramatist streamlined the play to suit the tastes of a twentieth century audience. Working from what he termed 'a pidgin-English, word-for-word rendering of the Norwegian,' Miller modernized the dialogue by pruning it of the archaisms of its Victorian translators. Consequently, the literal translation 'well, what do you say, Doctor? Don't you think it is high time that we stir a little life into the slackness and sloppiness of half-heartedness and cowardliness?' became a snappier but quite effective 'well, what do you say to a little hypodermic for these fence-sitting dead-heads?'

Structurally, Miller's alterations further honed the play for maximum theatrical effectiveness. The adaptation is approximately two-thirds the length of the original, with Ibsen's five-act structure reduced to three acts and five scenes. Where Ibsen constructed his drama along the lines of the French well-made play, with each new arrangement of characters signifying a separate scene, Miller ran his scenes into each other, eliminating the awkward passages of transitional dialogue and rendering the action more continuous and cohesive.

A few of the wordy confrontations were deftly scissored, along with some of Ibsen's lengthy and repetitive expository and argumentative statements. The pace of the latter half of the play was accelerated, and the resolution was linked dramatically to the climactic meetinghouse sequence instead of being separated from it by a series of repetitious conversations.

To this day, *An Enemy of the People* is Miller's only attempt at adapting another man's work. It was written because the playwright was positive that the iconoclastic old Viking who had once shocked a Victorian society out of its moral stays was far from ready to be relegated to the dubious honors of dramatist emeritus. Miller contended that Ibsen was alive for modern audiences, particularly in his belief that the stage was a forum for ideas, and in 'his insistence, his utter conviction, that he is going to say what he has to say, and that the audience, by God, is going to listen.'[2] Miller thus saw Ibsen as sharing his own conviction 'that the dramatic writer has, and must again demonstrate, the right to entertain with his brains as well as his heart. It is necessary that the public understand that the stage is *the* place for ideas, for philosophies, for the most intense discussion of man's fate.'[3]

For Miller the dominant idea in Ibsen's play was the central theme of his own society:

Simply, it is the question of whether the democratic guarantees

[2] *Ibid.*, p.7.
[3] *Ibid.*, p.8.

protecting political minorities ought to be set aside in time of crisis. More personally, it is the question of whether one's vision of the truth ought to be a source of guilt at a time when the mass of men condemn it as a dangerous and devilish lie. It is an enduring theme . . . because there never was, *nor will there ever be an organized society able to countenance calmly the individual who insists that he is right while the vast majority is absolutely wrong.*[4]

Miller personalizes this theme in the conflict between the Stockmann brothers. Mayor Peter Stockmann is the voice of corporate authority who presents the argument that Dr. Stockmann will challenge and demolish in the course of the play.

'You're like a man with an automatic brain,' the mayor admonishes his brother, '—as soon as an idea breaks into your head, no matter how idiotic it may be, you get up like a sleepwalker and start writing a pamphlet about it. . . . You're always barking about authority. If a man gives you an order, he's persecuting you. Nothing is important enough to respect once you decide to revolt against your superiors.'[5]

He continues his attack in the meetinghouse scene when he publicly holds the doctor up as a dangerous foe to communal stability:

Has any of us the right, the 'democratic right,' as they like to call it, to pick at minor flaws in the springs, to exaggerate the most picayune faults? And to attempt to publish these defamations for the whole world to see? We live or die on what the outside world thinks of us. I believe there is a line that must be drawn, and if a man decides to cross that line, we the people must finally take him by the collar and declare, 'You cannot say that!'[6]

In reply to this demagogic appeal to both private interest and public duty, Dr. Stockmann challenges the concept of obedience to majority will:

[4] *Ibid.*, pp.8–9. Italics my own.
[5] Miller, *An Enemy of the People*, p.55.
[6] *Ibid.*, p.90.

I proclaim it now! I am a revolutionist! I am in revolt against the age-old lie that the majority is always right! . . . And more! I tell you now that the majority is always wrong, and in this way! Was the majority right when they stood by while Jesus was crucified? Was the majority right when they refused to believe that the earth moved around the sun and let Galileo be driven to his knees like a dog? It takes fifty years for the majority to be right. The majority is never right until it does right.[7]

The references to Jesus and Galileo are Miller's additions. So too is the doctor's ensuing analogy:

A platoon of soldiers is walking down a road toward the enemy. Every one of them is convinced he is on the right road, the safe road. But two miles ahead stands one lonely man, the outpost. He sees that this road is dangerous, that his comrades are walking into a trap. He runs back, he finds the platoon. Isn't it clear that this man must have the right to warn the majority, to argue with the majority, to fight with the majority if he believes he has the truth? Before many can know something, *one* must know it! It's always the same. Rights are sacred until it hurts for somebody to use them.[8]

It is quite obvious that Miller rather blatantly set up Mayor Stockmann's position for the crisp counterattacks of his idealistic brother, and it is equally apparent that in the process he laced into some of the weaknesses inherent in any democratic system of government. The mayor, Hovstad, and Aslaksen continually attempt to conceal their pettiness and moral cowardice behind high sounding words like 'democracy,' 'community,' 'public duty,' and 'majority rights,' which they shuffle around with the deftness—and integrity—of a sideshow barker practicing the shell game.

One of the profound lessons Thomas Stockmann learns from this pack of scoundrels and their dupes is that the democratic processes can become woefully inadequate in a crisis. In the first half of the play he appeals to these courses of action and is sadly disillusioned to discover that they work better theoretically than

[7] *Ibid.*, pp.94–95.
[8] *Ibid.*, p.95.

practically. In the second half he finds that these processes can easily be exploited by any clever demagogue. The meetinghouse fiasco is a graphic example of the democratic procedure degenerating into mob hysteria through clever manipulation by vested interests.

Thus, not only does Miller's adaptation of *An Enemy of the People* again manifests his concern with the human being in his social context, but it also illuminates, more clearly than in some of his previous works, the paradoxical tension in his drama between his theoretical adherence to the concept of harmony between the individual and society and his deepening conviction that this concept cannot work. Unlike *All My Sons* and *Death of a Salesman*, which objectively balance the clash between the private man and the world in which he lives, *An Enemy of the People* radically upsets the equilibrium by demonstrating that society by its very nature is antithetical to personal choice and fulfillment.

'There never was, nor will there ever be an organized society able to countenance calmly the individual who insists that he is right while the vast majority is absolutely wrong.'

And this rectitude is precisely what Thomas Stockmann insists upon. He is hardly a manifestation of Marxist ideology or modern liberalism. More clearly he resembles a Nietzschean *Ubermensch*, the iron-willed man of truth who ultimately owes his primary allegiance to his personal sense of integrity. And in this respect he is similar to a host of Ibsen heroes who carry on their lonely and courageous revolts against the social, ethical, and theological systems that threaten to envelop them in quagmires of conformity. Stockmann is the Dionysian figure whom Ibsen pitted time and again against the Galilean ethic,* the impulsive man seeking freedom in his defiance of a social system that stresses obedience and duty, individual subordination to the corporate will.

Nevertheless, very few Ibsen heroes ever received his unqualified approval. For all his admiration of his Dionysian protagonists, the Norseman had the almost diabolical knack of perceiving and dramatizing their flaws and weaknesses—and the embattled Dr. Stockmann proved to be no exception. While he liked him, Ibsen regarded his crusader with a cocked eye and a wry, almost cynical, grin.

* Most notably in Ibsen's long and rambling philosophical drama, *Emperor and Galilean*.

Miller did not. Eyes fixed and mouth grimly set, he thoroughly admired and supported Stockmann. And this earnest commitment was the main reason for his radical alteration of the doctor's speeches in the meetinghouse sequence.

Two particular statements are missing in the adaptation. The first is Stockmann's comment about biological superiority and inferiority:

The masses are only the raw material from which a People can be made. It's the same thing in all other forms of life. Fine animals are created by breeding and selection. Take an ordinary common hen, for instance—she's not much better than a crow's eggs—or a raven's; she can't be compared with a really fine strain of poultry. But now take a Japanese or Spanish hen—a pheasant or a turkey—and you'll soon see the difference! . . . We're all animals . . . What are we else? But there aren't many well-bred animals among us. There's a tremendous difference between poodle men and mongrel men.[9]

The second is the doctor's heated denunciation of his brother and the other pillars of the community.

'They stand in the way of free men and hamper them at every turn,' he fumes. 'For my part I'd like to see them exterminated together with all other predatory creatures.'

And a few moments later this condemnation is expanded to include the entire town.

'A community based on lies and corruption deserves to be destroyed,' thunders the erstwhile savior of his village. 'Men who live on lies should be wiped out like a lot of vermin.'[10]

In the preface to his published play, Miller explained his deletions by noting the curiously extremist character of the statements. Positive that Ibsen was not in the least fascistic—'the man who wrote *A Doll's House*, the clarion call for the equality of women, cannot be equated with a fascist. . . . the whole cast of his thinking was such that he could not have lived a day under an authoritarian regime of any kind. He was an individualist sometimes to the point of

[9] Henrik Ibsen, 'An Enemy Of The People,' *Six Plays by Henrik Ibsen*, translated and edited by Eva LeGallienne (New York: Random House, 1951), p.229.

[10] *Ibid.*, p.232.

anarchism and in such a man there is too explosive a need for self-expression to permit him to conform to any rigid ideology'[11]—Miller still could not accept Stockmann's previously cited comments as anything less than fascistic.

The way out of the dilemma? He skirted the moral morass by happily concluding that if Ibsen had written his play after the sickening experiences of World War II and its concomitant horrors, he would not have allowed his protagonist to go overboard in his otherwise laudable condemnation of the smug, self-seeking majority.

Miller's misreading of Ibsen is devastating, for he has done nothing less than interpret a polemic comedy as a glowering tragedy. Rendering Dr Stockmann his personal spokesman throughout his adaptation, he blandly assumed Ibsen was doing the same in the original. Nothing could be farther from the truth. Had he approached the drama with less zealous determination and with more objectivity, Miller might have perceived that the speeches that so embarrassed him were included by Ibsen precisely because they *were* extremist, but that his employment of them in no way implied his endorsement.

One of the considerations in the Norwegian's play is the ambiguous and ambivalent nature of truth. Where Ibsen strongly advocated the need for honesty as the antidote to the lies and delusions that were distorting the lives of the characters in *A Doll's House* and *Ghosts*, his perspective shifted in *An Enemy of the People*. Stockmann's cause is undeniably right, but his increasing inability to separate it from his inflated and bruised ego is vivid proof of how tenuous his kinship to Nora Helmer is, and how closely he is bound to Gregers Werle, the supremely cockeyed and destructive idealist of *The Wild Duck*. Miller correctly recognized that Ibsen had 'too explosive a need for self-expression to permit him to conform to any rigid ideology,' but he missed the crucial fact that Ibsen's crusading physician does become an ideologist, with the cult of Self as his basic credo. There is no mistaking the fanaticism of his screeching attack on majority rule when he pompously proclaims that

> the majority is never right—never. . . . I think we must all of us agree that from one end of the world to the other the proportion is overwhelmingly in favor of the fools. And are

[11] Miller, 'Preface,' *An Enemy of the People*, pp.10–11.

wise men to be ruled by fools? What could be more senseless!
. . . The majority has the power, unfortunately—but right is
on the side of *people like me*—of the few—of the individual.
It's the minority that's always right![12]

Unquestionably Ibsen was lashing out against a society that
attempted to stifle the minority voice of dissent, but the blade of
his anger cut two ways: simultaneously slashing the hotheaded
reformer who, in his disappointment at being personally rejected
by his society, would force it to either submit to his truth or be
destroyed entirely. Thus the ultimate and provocative irony: the
man who begins the drama by fighting to save the community from
ruin curses it with hellfire and damnation at the conclusion because
he has been personally humiliated.

Ibsen viewed his protagonist as both heroic rebel and fool. Missing this tantalizingly ambivalent attitude, Miller saw him essentially as the former, the individualist claiming his inviolable dignity
in the face of adversity with an insistence that already characterized the protagonists of *All My Sons* and *Death of a Salesman*, and
would increasingly define the heroes of *The Crucible* and *A View
from the Bridge*.

This endorsement backed the playwright into a moral quandary:
unable to recognize Ibsen's sardonic criticism of his all-or-nothing
idealist, Miller was equally unable to extend his approval of Stockmann as far as he thought Ibsen had extended his. Admiring the
strong man, he nevertheless balked at following his philosophy to
its extreme, so he cut across the play and headed off his Nietzschean hero at the ideological pass. Scrubbing him clean of any
apparent traces of Hitlerian thought, he dipped him generously in
a cool bath of Emersonian individualism and stamped him gently
but firmly with the unspoken motto, 'whoso would be a man must
first be a noncomformist.'

At the conclusion of Miller's play, the beleaguered doctor stands
at his window as an angry mob hurls curses and rocks at him and
exclaims to his family with a 'trembling mixture of trepidation
and courageous insistence':

But remember now, everybody. You are fighting for the

[12] Ibsen, 'An Enemy of the People,' *Six Plays by Henrik Ibsen*, p.226.
Italics my own.

> truth, and that's why you're alone. And that makes you strong. We're the strongest people in the world . . . and the strong must learn to be lonely![13]

Compare this valedictory to Ibsen's final lines. Stockmann, exultant rather than fearful, defies the rabble to drive him away. They cannot, he cries, because he is the 'strongest man in town,' indeed 'one of the strongest men in the whole world!' And then, gathering his sons about him, he informs them of his 'great discovery'—that 'the strongest man in the world is the man who stands alone.' The fact that his devoted wife smiles wanly, shakes her head, and murmurs, 'Oh, Thomas, dear!' does not deter him a moment from his exalted personal vision.

Ibsen's protagonist is a two-fisted, slightly paunchy Don Quixote, suited for action and enjoying every minute of his situation, exhilarated in his alienation, bloody, barely beaten, definitely unbowed, and ready and willing to combat the forces of ignorance and decadence single-handedly. He is an anarchic conglomeration of courage, egotism, naïveté, and inanity. Miller's hero noticeably lacks the latter characteristic. Drawing himself up at the end in a kind of solitary grandeur, he is prepared to face a bleak future with a mixture of doubt and granite dignity that would have been quite alien to the ebullient idealist after whom he is patterned.

The difference between the two characterizations of Dr. Stockmann emphasizes more than just two separate points of view. It also illuminates the glaring weakness of Miller's adaptation. Unwilling and unable to view Stockmann with anything approaching Ibsen's awareness, or even his own acute perception of Joe Keller and Willy Loman, Miller allowed his unwaveringly solemn admiration to tip the play over into a loud and heavy-handed defense of everything for which his hero stands. There is a lot of noise in the original, but it helps to delineate the protagonist's muddle-headedness, as well as his opponent's nastiness. In Miller's drama the noise, like the moral perspective, is too neatly identifiable: pitched against the sour sounds of the demagogues and their dupes are the good, clean, pure tones of the Defender of Individual Rights.

Miller constantly has had difficulty balancing off his human situations and conflicts with his predisposition for making the big thematic statement. *All My Sons* is saved from becoming a strident

[13] Miller, *An Enemy of the People*, pp.124–125.

thesis play because of its highly qualified endorsement of Chris Keller and the intelligent and complex characterization of Joe. Despite its 'attention must be paid' admonition to the audience, *Death of a Salesman* never allows its didacticism to replace the intensely human dilemma as the center of dramatic focus. Both plays, in fact, gain a vital strength precisely from the interrelationship of general theme and specific characterization and situation. But in *An Enemy of the People* the human dilemma is woefully subordinated to the pedantic, and the result is a series of solemn declamations and measured stances that one-dimensionalize the entire drama.

Instead of individuals and passions, we are presented with attitudes and proclamations. Consequently—for all its streamlining and modernizing of the older version—in its thematic leadenness Miller's adaptation seems far more academic and ponderous than the original.* It does not so much dramatize Ibsen's pertinence for modern audiences as it awkwardly attempts to demonstrate Miller's, proving in the process that a demonstration and a drama need not be synonymous.

Actually *An Enemy of the People* is a preview of *The Crucible* in Ibsen's clothing. In his next effort Miller will create another Stockmann figure in the person of John Proctor of Salem and pit him against an inimical social order. But fortunately for the new play, the didacticism will be strictly subordinated to the human drama, and the characters will be endowed with just the complexity and depth that Stockmann and company lack.

*An additional irony lies in the fact that in a few anthologies of modern drama, the Miller adaptation of *An Enemy of the People* is included as the literal translation of the Ibsen original. Obviously, Miller is not the only one who has misread Ibsen's play.

12

'Because it is my name!'

The idea for *The Crucible* was resurrected rather than created out of the corporate national hysteria of the 1950s. Miller had been fascinated by the witch trials of seventeenth century Salem, Massachusetts, but he did not envision them as the stimulus for a drama until the lunacy and terror called McCarthyism struck the country with hurricane force. Although the political aspects of the phenomenon were harrowing enough, the playwright was particularly intrigued by another manifestation of the events—

something which seemed much more weird and mysterious. It was the fact that the political, objective, knowledgeable campaign from the far Right was capable of creating not only a terror, but a new subjective reality, a veritable mystique which was gradually assuming even a holy resonance. The wonder of it all struck me that so practical and picayune a cause, carried forward by such manifestly ridiculous men, should be capable of paralysing thought itself, and worse, causing to billow up such persuasive clouds of 'mysterious' feelings within people. It was as though the whole country had been born anew, without a memory even of certain elemental decencies which a year or two earlier no one would have imagined could be altered, let alone forgotten. Astounded, I watched men pass me by without a nod whom I had known rather well for years; and again, the astonishment was produced by my knowledge, which I could not give up, that the terror in these people was being knowingly planned and consciously engineered, and yet all they knew was terror. That so interior and subjective an emotion could have been so manifestly created from without was a marvel to me.[1]

[1] Miller, 'Introduction,' *Collected Plays*, pp.39–40.

The more Miller thought about the situation, the more horrifying it became for him, and as he tried to explain to himself the cancerous growth of such corporate and individual fear, his mind fastened on a proposition. He theorized that the self-debasing social compliance that characterized so much of the public's reaction to McCarthyism was in some way aligned to a sense of private guilt which a person felt he could alleviate by acceding to the dictates of a public confessional.

> There was a new religiosity in the air. . . . I saw forming a kind of interior mechanism of confession and forgiveness of sins which until now had not been rightly categorized as sins. New sins were being created monthly. It was very odd how quickly these were accepted into the new orthodoxy, quite as though they had been there since the beginning of time. Above all, above all horrors, *I saw accepted the notion that conscience was no longer a private matter but one of state administration. I saw men handing conscience to other men and thanking other men for the opportunity of doing so.*[2]

The central image and motif for a drama was formed in that observation.

'I wished for a way to write a play,' Miller later confided, 'that would be sharp, that would lift out of the morass of subjectivism the squirming, single, defined process which would show that the sin of public terror is that it divests man of conscience, of himself. It was a theme not unrelated to those that had invested the previous plays.'[3]

With these ideas churning in his mind, the playwright thought again of the Salem tragedy, and what had previously been 'an inexplicable darkness' for him now took on a kind of comprehensibility, particularly the phenomenon of surrendering conscience, which had always seemed 'the central and informing fact of the time.'

He drove up to Salem and carefully and laboriously began to examine the records of the trials. As he pored over the elaborately detailed accounts of one of the grimmest episodes in American history, he was struck by two items in particular: the stubborn and

[2] *Ibid.*, p.40. Italics my own.
[3] *Ibid.*, p.40.

adamant refusal of one of the defendants, a farmer named John
Proctor, to submit to an authority he felt to be wrong; and the
mysterious circumstances involving Proctor, his wife Elizabeth,
and the servant girl, Mary Warren, who was their principal
accuser.

As soon as he began to study the large, handwritten folios,
Miller was intrigued by Proctor. Although the New England farmer's testimony is one of the least elaborate in the records, it is
centered in an amazingly liberated outlook. He was one of the few
Salemites who not only refused to acknowledge any league with
the Devil but who carried his defense into a stinging and scornful
attack against his prosecutors, branding the entire proceedings as
trickery and sham.

The second item to catch the dramatist's attention was Mary
Warren's testimony, which—despite the urgent promptings of the
judges—was directed almost wholly against Elizabeth Proctor and
markedly away from her husband. This apparent desire on Mary's
part to see Mrs. Proctor convicted, quickly crystalized Miller's conception of the play. The petty spite of this internal situation as contrasted to the perverse grandeur of the public spectacle gave the
writer the dramatic hub for which he was searching. It was the
first of a succession of mordant proofs that 'the great "issues"
which the hysteria was allegedy about were covers for petty ambitions, hardheaded political drives, and the fantasies of very small
and vengeful minds.'⁴

With the central conflicts and character in mind, Miller then
began to block out his play. Although at times he used verbatim
transcript from the court records, he also made some important
changes in the historical context. He tightened the relationship
between John and Elizabeth Proctor by omitting the historical but
undramatic fact that she was his third wife and stepmother to his
children; he changed her accuser from the bewildered Mary Warren
to Abigail Williams, the foremost instigator of the hysteria; and
since Abigail was only eleven years old at the time of the trials,
Miller increased her age to a more temperamental and provocative
seventeen, thus leaving no doubt about her feelings for Proctor.
Finally the playwright centralized the authority of the prosecution
into a single, dominant figure: Deputy Governor Danforth.

⁴ Miller, quoted in Allan Seager, 'The Creative Agony of Arthur Miller,'
Esquire, p.124.

In marked contrast to *Death of a Salesman*, *The Crucible* was hammered into shape slowly and painstakingly. But if Miller was not as buoyant about it as he had been about his previous drama, he was still quietly confident as he waited through its premiere on a chilly January evening in 1953.

His confidence was somewhat undermined by a mixed critical response. While the play was generally accorded polite approval with adjectives like 'sound' and 'eloquent,' the majority of reviewers deemed it a lesser work than *Death of a Salesman*, and many scored it for its apparent polemicism.

Quite obviously, the parallels between the subject matter of *The Crucible* and the political situation into which it opened strongly influenced its reception. Critics both favorable and adverse insisted on viewing it primarily through politically-tinted glasses, and the play was bathed in shades of red, white, blue, and ubiquitous pink, as proponents of the Left, Right and center leaped to convenient ideological interpretations. The *Death of a Salesman* syndrome was revived and Miller was alternately hailed for writing a leftist onslaught against the Right or damned for not taking his attack far enough. He was praised by some for his courage in challenging McCarthyism full tilt and chastened by others for hiding behind a remote period of American history.

Adhering zealously to the a priori assumption that Miller was a leftist liberal dramatist, Howard Fast praised the play as an allegory about the trial and execution of the convicted atomic spies, Julius and Ethel Rosenberg. From a different corner, but clinging to the same initial assumption about the playwright, Robert Warshow wrote a devastating review of *The Crucible* in the March 1953 issue of *Commentary*, in which he took Miller to task for wholly missing the Puritan experience upon which his play was presumably based. Attacking the dramatist for 'his intelligent narrowness of mind' and for 'his almost contemptuous lack of interest in the particularities—which is to say, the reality—of the Salem trials,' Warshow berated him for completely overlooking the fact that the victims of Salem chose to die, not for a cause, not for civil rights, but 'for their own credit on earth and in heaven . . . they lived in a universe where each man was saved or damned by himself, and what happened to them was personal.'[5]

There is no doubt that Warshow was quite right about the

[5] Robert Warshow, *Commentary*, 15 (March, 1953), p.266.

Puritans. There is also no doubt that he was quite wrong about *The Crucible* and in his wrongness betraying the selfsame narrowness and contemptuous unconcern for the play that he professed to find in its author's attitude toward American history.

In his eagerness to claim Miller's pseudo-intellectual scalp, Warshow overlooked the fact that with the exception of John Proctor, those in the play who choose to die rather than confess falsely are definitely oriented toward a state of grace, and that even Proctor is more historically accurate than a superficial glance would indicate.

As Miller portrays him the New England farmer is an atypical Puritan. His exclamation at the end of the second act that the witchcraft hysteria will provide a dark mirror for the inhabitants of Salem—'we are only what we always were, but naked now!'—rings with modern existentialist overtones. And his decision to die rather than break faith with those who have not confessed is the product of a temporal rather than transcendental commitment. At the conclusion of the play he speaks of what his sons, not God, will think of him, and so doing keeps faith with the continuum of man rather than with a hypothetical afterlife.

But if the preceding attitudes belong to Miller's protagonist, there is no indication that the historical John Proctor would have been puzzled by them. The trial records show that he was profoundly his own man, that he was notably free-thinking and aloof from his church, and that his decision to hang rather than to submit to an authority he deemed tyrannical and corrupt was apparently not greatly motivated by transcendental thought. And as protagonist of *The Crucible*, even if he is not heavenly oriented, he most certainly dies for his 'own credit on earth,' and his salvation or damnation is decisively 'personal.'

Undoubtedly *The Crucible* was inspired by the social and political climate of the United States in the 1950s. Miller was the first to make this admission. Although he never claimed that McCarthyism was a literal resurrection of the Salem witchhunts—Communists after all have a higher degree of corporeality than witches—he openly acknowledged that his reading of the court records was colored by the contemporary experience, and that he found in the transcripts pretty much what he was looking for. Still, it is infinitely too simple to suppose that because a work is influenced by something, it cannot encompass more than the particular stimulus which inspired it. It is hardly accidental that as the McCarthy fervor has waned, critical response to *The Crucible* has grown appreciably favorable. Scarcely the result of the few dialogue changes Miller subsequently made, it is in all probability the consequence of judgments based upon the play's genuine qualities rather than upon its political pertinency. *The Crucible* is topical. However, it is as pertinent to Inquisitorial Spain, the France of Robespierre and Danton, Nazi Germany, and Stalinist Russia as it is to McCarthyite America. Not to mention Salem, Massachusetts of 1692.

But if *The Crucible* is not a contemporary political allegory, neither is it an historical narrative. It is a dramatic exploration of the conditions of corporate hysteria. For all its adherence to history, the play is poetry, self-contained and defined by its aesthetic framework, and as such it ultimately stands or falls. Consequently its validity is no more dependent upon its complete fidelity to the Puritan theocracy than *Julius Caesar* and *Saint Joan* are to their historical antecedents.

Miller was neither re-creating all the particulars of the witch trials nor camouflaging current events when he chose Salem as the location for his drama. He was seeking perspective. He viewed the trials not as an isolated historical phenomenon but as part of a continuing tragedy, not exclusively Salem's child nor the twentieth century's, yet claiming kinship to each.

The playwright was particularly fascinated by the people of Salem. Because of their characters and the historical situation in which they found themselves, they possessed the moral consciousness which he wanted to dramatize. For good or ill, they were individuals who were supremely aware of the nature of their struggle.

> I was dealing with people very conscious of an ideology, of what they stood for. The revolution they had lived through was still in their minds . . . they were special people and could voice the things that were buried deep in them. . . . They knew why they struggled . . . they knew how to struggle . . . they did not die helplessly. The moral size of these people drew me . . . they didn't whimper.[6]

Not only was their awareness razor sharp and diamond hard, but their power of articulation was eloquent. Thus, by choosing the

[6] Miller, quoted in John and Alice Griffin, 'Arthur Miller Discusses *The Crucible*,' *Theatre Arts*, 37 (October, 1953), p.33.

Salemites for his subject, Miller could circumvent the dilemma
which had confronted him in his previous works: the inadequacy
of the modern realistic hero's dialogue to convey his consciousness.
He had explored what he termed the 'subjective world' in *Death
of a Salesman*, and now he wanted to create a more conscious and
intelligible protagonist. The Puritans afforded him the opportunity.

> The society of Salem was 'morally' vocal. People then avowed
> principles, sought to live by them and die by them. Issues of
> faith, conduct, society pervaded their private lives in a con-
> scious way. They needed but to disapprove to act. I was
> drawn to this subject because the historical moment seemed
> to give me the poetic right to create people of higher self-
> awareness than the contemporary scene affords.[7]

Still another reason for Miller's choice of the historical context
for his play was inherent in the structure of the Puritan theocracy.
Its religion stressed the innate bestiality of man and his singular
inability to remedy this woeful state. And since the source of man's
depravity was the flesh, which linked him to the organic world
and provided a constant source of temptation, the individual's—
and society's—primary struggle was against this enticement, which
was credited to the devil and which had to be resisted by constant
and obsessive vigilance.

Miller also took note of the socio-political aspects of the theocracy. Although as the ruling orthodoxy of its time it still demanded an intense commitment from its members, by the final
decade of the seventeenth century, the theocracy was being badly
strained by a number of socially disruptive pressures. From within,
the Puritan codes were no longer as binding to a new generation
as they had been to previous generations who had relied on their
discipline to see them through a rigorous existence in a new and
harsh land. From without, land titles were in dispute in Salem
because of edicts from Boston and London, and the community
was unsure of its future, increasingly fearful and beset by mounting
anxiety.

Given then a morbid religion, in a geographical setting of continual hardship and danger, a social climate of spiraling bewilder-

---

[7] Miller, 'Introduction,' *Collected Plays*, p.44.

ment and fear, and a psychological atmosphere of repression and guilt among people predisposed to blaming Satanic stimuli for unexplained phenomena, there is little wonder that even the most petty motivations and circumstances could engender a terror that would rapidly paralyze all common sense and reason.

The Crucible dramatizes a society's dissolution into a vortex of hysteria. Beginning slowly and then gaining momentum and power, the drama chronicles the storm that breaks over Salem. It starts innocuously as a group of adolescent girls are discovered by the local minister, the Reverend Parris, carousing clandestinely in the forest under the tutelage of a superstitious Barbados servant, Tituba. To forestall their punishment, some of them—including Parris' daughter Betty and niece Abigail Williams—fall into 'mysterious' trances. Two of their neighbors, the farmer John Proctor and the respected matron Rebecca Nurse, recognize the girls' shenanigans for what they are, and Rebecca's reasonable and compassionate comments on the situation momentarily dispel the burgeoning apprehension.

'I have eleven children, and I am twenty-tix times a grandma, and I have seen them all through their silly seasons,' she advises the balky and fearful elders who huddle around the bedside of the apparently stricken Betty Parris. 'And when it come on them they will run the Devil bowlegged keeping up with their mischief. I think she'll wake when she tires of it. A child's spirit is like a child, you can never catch it by running after it; you must stand still, and, for love, it will soon itself come back.'[8]

'Aye, that's the truth of it,' Proctor affirms.

Little does he know that that is not the truth of it in Salem. The climate of the town is dread and it provides the whirlpool out of which the specter of witchcraft begins to spiral.

Threatened with hanging for instigating the strange forest rituals, Tituba confesses to demonism. Abigail, who had previously admitted privately to Proctor that the whole business was a prank, now embraces the convenient excuse provided for her by the helpless servant and the fearful community, and also cries out witchcraft. And as the names of villagers roll murderously off her lips, hysteria breaks loose over Salem. It is quickly and furiously fanned by many of the community's inhabitants, partially out of superstition, partially out of uncomprehended guilts and frustrations,

[8] Miller, 'The Crucible,' *Collected Plays*, pp.243-244.

and partially out of clearly realized desires for material gain and vengeance.

Ann Putnam, whose daughter is one of the afflicted and whose other eight children did not survive infancy, is sure that demonic forces have caused her misery, and her words to Rebecca Nurse are etched in disappointment, pain, and jealousy.

'You think it God's work you should never lose a child, nor grandchild either, and I bury all but one,' she exclaims in agony. 'There are wheels within wheels in this village, and fires within fires!'[9]

Her husband, Thomas, is also quick to embrace demonism in Salem, but his reasons are blatantly more materialistic and vicious than his wife's. Squabbling for years with his neighbors over land and politics, Putnam is eager to revenge some of his legal reverses and gain more substantial chunks of real estate by piously condeming his adversaries as witches.

Unlike the ghost-ridden Mrs Putnam and her cruelly acquisitive husband, the Reverend John Hale of Beverly, who has been summoned as an authority on witchcraft, views the spectacle as a challenge to his calling, a leprous plague on the people of the community that he, like a dedicated physician, is duty-bound to exorcise. His intentions irreproachably above suspicion, he unknowingly begins to pave the way to hell with them.

And with this snowballing amalgam of superstition, malice, and crusading zeal muffling the few voices of reason, the avalanche of terror is launched.

At first Proctor tries to sidestep the lunacy by returning to his farm and family; but his withdrawal is short-lived. Learning that Rebecca Nurse and other friends have been accused and taken by the newly established tribunal, he determines to go back to Salem to help them. However, he quickly finds that the choice is no longer his. Abigail Williams, who had worked for the Proctors and had indulged in a brief, empassioned affair with the farmer, has accused his wife Elizabeth of witchcraft. As she is taken, Proctor realizes the landslide has engulfed him.

The third act of *The Crucible* is the trial scene. The inquisition is presided over by Deputy Governor Danforth, who agrees to hear the testimony of Proctor's current serving girl Mary Warren, whom

---

[9] *Ibid.*, p.245.

the farmer has convinced to give the lie to the girls' accusations. But although she makes a determined effort she falters, and in desperation Proctor confesses to his adultery to prove the real motives behind Abigail's arraignment of his wife.* However, when Elizabeth is summoned to verify his story, she lies to protect his name, and even though Hale believes Proctor's charge and attempts to convince Danforth of the naturalness of a wife's deception in behalf of her husband, the Deputy Governor remains adamant.

Just as Hale turns to condemn Abigail, she circumvents his accusation by shamming hysterics, and the other girls, including the impressionable Mary Warren, are swept along until Mary frenziedly charges Proctor with witchcraft. Appalled at the proceedings, Proctor condemns the tribunal and its judges.

'You are pulling Heaven down and raising up a whore!' he cries to Danforth. And his indictment is echoed when the Reverend Hale denounces the trial and quits the court.

The final act is Proctor's. It is the morning of his scheduled execution. His wife's life has been temporarily spared because she has been found pregnant, but Rebecca Nurse has been sentenced to die with him. Giles Corey, an old friend, has already perished under torture. For a moment hope is expressed that the death sentences will be commuted because of a delayed general reaction against the trials and the hangings.

'There are orphans wandering from house to house,' a desperate Hale reminds Danforth. 'Abandoned cattle bellow on the highroads, the stink of rotting crops hangs everywhere, and no man

---

* Between the play's initial production in 1953 and subsequent ones, Miller included a brief pretrial scene between Proctor and Abigail in which he tells her of his intention to denounce her if she persists in falsely accusing his wife. However, maddened with religious frenzy and frustrated desire, Abigail does not believe that he will carry through his threat and accuses him of secretly hoping that Elizabeth will hang so that he will be free to marry her.

Although the scene is gripping, it is unnecessary. Given Proctor's character, and his discovery of Abigail's viciousness, it is extremely unlikely that he would initiate a clandestine and compromising rendezvous with her in the hopes of changing her mind. Secondly, his disclosure of his intentions prior to the courtroom sequence only serves to weaken the dramatic impact of the moment when he publicly bares his adultery.

The interpolated scene is awkward, and although some productions of *The Crucible* still employ it, Miller has deleted it from subsequent publications of the play.

knows when the harlots' cry will end his life.'[10]

But the hope is aborted when the Deputy Governor refuses to put off the executions and vows to intercede in Proctor's behalf only if the farmer will confess to his collusion with demons. Hale and Parris plead with Proctor to relent, and Elizabeth is summoned to add her persuasion.

At first he looks to her for a decision, but she can only reiterate what he already knows: that the ultimate choice must be his. As time becomes the remorseless enemy, John Proctor fights the most difficult battle of his life. Finally he yields and signs a confession; but when Danforth informs him that it must be shown to all the inhabitants of Salem he recants and tears it to shreds. He cannot betray those who have died before him and are dying the very day he could be given his life. The play closes on Danforth's icy rage, Hale's mortification, and Elizabeth's anguished love. Most importantly, it ends with Proctor's final realization that he can indeed die for what is summed up by the sound of his name. It concludes on the wonder and pride of discovery in the face of death.

The Crucible contains a gallery of sharply etched characters who are skilfully woven into the fabric of the play. With almost two dozen speaking parts, the cast is large; but Miller handles his people deftly and his minor characters flare into life and comprise an essential, highly charged environment for the drama's action.

Three of these individuals—Reverend Parris, Abigail Williams, and Giles Corey—are particularly important to the meaning and development of their story. Each is a gem of in-depth characterization who simultaneously provides a dramatic gloss to the play's main characters and themes.

The Reverend Parris is a root factor in the hysteria that he helps to unleash. His fear of expulsion from his position—'there is a faction that is sworn to drive me from my pulpit'— coupled with his horror at discovering apparent abominations in his own family —'now then, in the midst of such disruption, my own household is discovered to be the very center of some obscene practice'— causes him to cast about for any scapegoat who will rid him of the filth at his door. A graphic personification of the surrender of conscience as a method of survival, Parris might possibly have qualified as a sympathetic figure were it not for the fact that his

[10] *Ibid.*, p.319.

conscience is so paltry to begin with. He is not so much evil as he is petty, but is it precisely this kind of self-seeking meanness upon which the hysteria feeds.

At the close of the play, Parris has changed his tune and begs Danforth to deal mercifully with Proctor and the rest of the condemned; but his turnabout is not a change of character on the part of a repentant man who is horrified at the consequences of his selfishness and hypocrisy. Parris remains odiously consistent. He is not interested in saving the victims' lives. Instead, he would 'postpone these hangin's for a time.' And when he explains why, his baseness is again delineated.

He has been threatened—'tonight when I open my door to leave my house, a dagger clattered to the ground . . . there is danger for me. I dare not step out at night!'—and is afraid of the personal repercussions of subsequent executions. He has helped foster a monstrous evil to protect himself; now he wants to check that evil, not because of any new moral awareness, but out of the same selfishness. Parris has not changed, the situation has. An instigator of the hysteria, the minister finally becomes one of its potential victims and, in the process, illustrates with grim irony the backlashing nature of the storm that swept Salem.

Abigail Williams also personifies the personal spite and hatred at the core of the public spectacle: She is bitterly frustrated after John Proctor has aborted their affair. As the instigator of the midnight pranks, she is fearful that her already tarnished reputation will increase her punishment, so she lunges at witchcraft as the first saving line that is cast her way. Self-preservation is her initial motive, but others supersede it. Soon the thrill of wielding authority acts like a heady wine and she revels in her drunkenness. Initially the girl's lust for Proctor impels her to use her new power against Elizabeth, but with her hopes for a life with the farmer dashed by his public rejection of her, vengeance becomes Abigail's driving force.

Although the urges propelling her are violent and complex, Abigail is far from a Medea or even a fledgling Lady Macbeth. She is no monstrous harridan or ambition-ridden tigress, caught in the nets of her own violence and deception. Rather, she is a shrewd, cruel girl able to use her spite and repression to create a destructive frenzy because the situation is ripe for it. Just as the constricting atmosphere of Salem is partially responsible for her initial violations of the communal codes, so too does it feed the terror she has helped incite. And like so many of the others she is ultimately betrayed by it. When she leaves the play—as she left history—quickly, anticlimactically, and with most of the cash in her uncle's strongbox—she is a pathetic figure, twisted into something subhuman by a situation which allowed all the petty cruelties of a frustrated adolescent to be magnified into a perverse holiness.

One of the most intriguing characters in *The Crucible* is that irascible old man, Giles Corey, whose martyr's death precedes John Proctor's and strongly influences his final decision. Pressed to death by stones, Corey refuses to confess himself a witch, and his final words to his tormenters are fraught with the strength of a terrible challenge: 'More weight.'

Despite the similarity of their fates, however, Giles Corey's relationship to Proctor is more one of contrast than comparison. Like the Reverend Parris, Corey is a most consistent man, but unlike the craven minister, he is an individualist whose commitment to his land supersedes all other loyalties.

'He were not hanged,' Elizabeth tells her husband when he asks about Corey's fate. 'He would not answer aye or nay to his indictment; for if he denied the charge they'd hang him surely, and auction out his property. So he stand mute and died Christian under the law. And so his sons will have his farm. It is the law, for he could not be condemned a wizard without he answer the indictment, aye or nay.'[11]

Corey will not have the land for which he worked and fought taken from him on what he believes to be a technicality. On the last day of a life marked by numerous lawsuits in behalf of his property and possessions, Corey again finds himself embroiled in litigation. And even more galling to him than the loss of his land is the strong possibility that he stands to lose it to Thomas Putnam, the enemy he has already bested in court on a couple of occasions.

Giles thus dies as he has lived: battling for all he considers his, at the center of a circumscribed universe. The rest of the world does not concern him. In some respects this is true of John Proctor at the beginning of the play, but hardly at the conclusion. Proctor arrives at a new knowledge; Giles Corey does not. The painfully

[11] *Ibid.*, p.322.

naïve creature, who unwittingly helped condemn his wife by voicing
his suspicion of her reading habits, dies in an aura of innocence.
He does not realize that his death might involve something more
significant than his few acres; the greater connections escape him.

He is indeed 'the fearsome man' Proctor succinctly eulogizes,
but his fearsomeness is self-contained. Ultimately he is a comic
character caught in a profoundly serious situation, and even as
his death is tragic, Giles is not. His last words are supremely eloquent in their rustic brevity, but if he had been capable of a last
gesture it probably would not have been toward his Maker or his
destroyers; it would in all likeliness have been a final, defiant fist
waved triumphantly under the nose of a sonofabitch named
Thomas Putnam.

While other subsidiary characters, including the calculatingly
vicious Putnam, his pathetic and neurotic wife, Ann, the common-
sensical and courageous Rebecca Nurse, and the confused and
frantic Mary Warren, join the Reverend Parris, Abigail Williams,
and Giles Corey in providing a vital context and atmosphere, the
four dominant figures of *The Crucible*—John and Elizabeth Proctor, the Reverend John Hale, and Deputy Governor Danforth—
propel the play's action and meaning to its dramatic crescendo.

The marriage of Elizabeth and John Proctor is the crucial relationship in the drama, for out of its ambivalence springs Proctor's adultery with Abigail and the choking guilt that accompanies
it. In their initial scene together John's exclamation to Elizabeth
manifests this guilt and defines the inadequacy of their marriage:

You forget nothin' and forgive nothin'. Learn charity, woman.
I have gone tiptoe in this house all seven month since she
is gone. I have not moved from there to there without I think
to please you, and still an everlasting funeral marches round
your heart. I cannot speak but I am doubted, every moment
judged for lies, as though I come into a court when I come
into this house![12]

Like Kate Keller and Linda Loman, Elizabeth Proctor is one of
Miller's 'good' wives, duty-bound to her husband, loyal, trust-
worthy, obedient. And destructive. However, although Elizabeth is
similar to Kate and Linda in her commitment to husband and

[12] *Ibid.*, p.265.

family, she differs markedly from them in her self-appointed role as her spouse's moral guardian. She is not vociferous in her judgment, but Proctor can feel it over him constantly, hanging about his conscience like the symbolic albatross. At one point he begs her to look for some goodness in him instead of judging him and continually finding him wanting. She claims that she is not his judge, and then in the next breath contradicts herself.

'I never thought you but a good man, John,' she remarks, 'only somewhat bewildered.'

His answer is etched in bitter laughter: 'Oh, Elizabeth, your justice would freeze beer!'

Elizabeth Proctor is a product of her time and community. A zealous adherent to the Puritan ideal of duty, she is simultaneously the victim of Puritanical strictures. She has uncomprehendingly witnessed her rigid devotion cast a chilling pall over her house and drive her husband into the arms of another woman. Her sense of duty has enabled her to take him back, but without understanding either him or herself. Thus their life together is a kind of grim charade, in which a dignified façade barely conceals the hollowness beneath it.

But if Elizabeth initially lacks the capacity for compassion that characterizes Linda Loman, she grows in the course of the play's development. Unlike Linda, whose plaintive bewilderment closes her play, Elizabeth achieves an awareness of herself and her husband which allows her to sound a depth of feeling that was almost impossible for the young woman trapped in the coils of a rigid and constricting ideology at the beginning of the drama.

In the final moments of their lives, the Proctors are closer to each other than ever before. And in the last scene of the play John, who earlier had begged his wife not to judge him, now relies on this new intimacy and pleads for her counsel and judgment. Although her final refusal to be his judge bears a superficial resemblance to her previous comments, it is totally different. No longer the cool, condescending reply of a mother to an errant child, her decision embodies the anguished truth of a woman who has finally judged her own character and found it wanting.

I have read my own heart this three month, John. I have sins of my own to count. It needs a cold wife to prompt lechery. . . . You take my sins upon you, John . . . John, I counted

myself so plain, so poorly made, no honest love could come
to me! Suspicion kissed you when I did; I never knew how
I should say my love. It were a cold house I kept![13]

And finding herself less than perfect, she is at last able to perceive the goodness in her husband, a quality she had found easy to
overlook in her quest for perfection.

'Forgive me, forgive me, John,' she asks in total sincerity, 'I
never knew such goodness in the world!'

Elizabeth cannot judge her husband any longer because she
knows that he must provide his own tribunal in this most agonizing moment of his life. He must be his own master.

'There is no higher judge under Heaven than Proctor is!'

In the moments before their parting, the Proctors' marriage
gains the tenderness and substance it had always lacked, and
Elizabeth's final words as her husband is led to his death are a far
cry from her earlier statements.

'He have his goodness now,' she weeps, 'God forbid I take it
from him.'

If the relationship of John and Elizabeth is the personal main-
spring of Proctor's involvement in the events of *The Crucible*, his
conflict with Deputy Governor Danforth provides the broader and
deeper implications of these events. The two men confront each
other twice in the play: in the trial scene and on the day of Proctor's scheduled execution—and in these two confrontations the
dramatic experience of *The Crucible* flares into fierce life as the
age-old rivalry for the human spirit between catholicity and the
protestor is vividly recreated.

Many critics have pointed out the similarities between the trial
scene in *The Crucible* and its counterpart in Bernard Shaw's *Saint
Joan*. Both scenes dramatize the struggle between the individual
and corporate authority, both precede the martyrdom of the protagonist, and in both the hero initially capitulates before recanting
when the ultimate implications of his confession become clear.
However, underlying the rather obvious similarities of the two
trials is a profound difference. Whereas Joan's inquisition, as depicted by Shaw, is scrupulously fair, Proctor's ordeal is marked by
a monumental unfairness.

It is useless to wish that Miller would have tempered the fana-

[13] *Ibid.*, p.323.

ticism of his judges and made them more reasonable, thereby
rendering the conflict between the accused and the accusers less
strident. The premises underlying *The Crucible* and *Saint Joan* are
quite dissimilar and necessarily demand different types of inquisi-
tors. Although in both plays these adversaries are adamantly determined to kill in order to uphold the rectitude of their positions,
Joan's antagonists are able for the most part to separate their
causes from their egos; Proctor's are not. The evil of *The Crucible*'s
prosecutors is a manifestation of a total and blind commitment of
mind and will to a concept that eventually eradicates all lines between reason and lunacy. Shaw is dramatizing the rationality of
Joan's antagonists; Miller is focusing precisely on the irrationality
of Proctor's. Their characterizations cannot possibly be similar.

A couple of years after he wrote the play, Miller even voiced
his regret at not having made Danforth more purely evil than he
originally rendered him.

> I was wrong in mitigating the evil of this man and the judges
> he represents. Instead, I would perfect his evil to its utmost
> and make an open issue, a thematic consideration of it in the
> play. I believe now, as I did not conceive then, that there
> are people dedicated to evil in the world; that without their
> perverse example we should not know the good. Evil is not a
> mistake but a fact in itself. . . . I believe . . . that, from what-
> ever cause, a dedication to evil, not mistaking it for good,
> but knowing it as evil and loving it as evil, is possible in
> human beings who appear agreeable and normal. I think
> now that one of the hidden weaknesses of our whole approach
> to dramatic psychology is our inability to face this fact—to
> conceive, in effect, of Iago.[14]

In America particularly, from Emersonian Transcendentalism,
which viewed evil as the vacuum left by the absence of good, to
more recent environmental and psychological rationalizations, the
modern writer has often manifested a marked propensity for mini-
mizing evil as a self-creating and self-perpetuating phenomenon.
The problem with Miller's newly-minted 1955 conception of evil
does not lie in its degree of validity—and he is certainly far less
idiosyncratic in his 'discovery' than the tone of his statement

---

[14] Miller, 'Introduction,' *Collected Plays*, pp.43–44.

indicates—but in its application to the judges of *The Crucible*.

That the sadism that Miller eventually recognized in these men was actually a part of the Salem experience is not at all unlikely; but to have made 'an open issue, a thematic consideration of it in the play,' would have obscured the significantly more important consideration of evil with which the drama is concerned. To have rendered Danforth any more monstrous than Miller initially made him (and he is hardly an Oliver Wendell Holmes as he stands) would have drastically and irreparably distorted his function in the play.

Although generated and nourished by superstition, repression, and fear, the evil which envelops Salem becomes increasingly greater than the malice or error of any specific member of that society, be he the covetous Thomas Putnam, the vengeful Abigail Williams, or even the cruel and rigid Danforth. It is not sustained by any diabolical wickedness in any of its progenitors, but by an absolutist belief in the rightness of a cause, a commitment so fanatic that common sense, decency, and honesty are swept away before its gale force.

In Salem these people regarded themselves as holders of a light. If this light were extinguished, they believed, the world would end. When you have ideology which feels itself so pure, it implies an extreme view of the world. Because they are white, opposition is completely black.[15]

This fanaticism is graphically exhibited in Danforth's final reasons for continuing the hangings even after he is confronted with substantial evidence that he no longer has the support of the majority of the community. He must go on killing, he claims with bone-chilling logic, lest the guilt of those already executed be doubted and the rightness of his cause be questioned. There is of course sadism involved here, but the moral absolutism of the Deputy Governor's position—the single most terrifying fact of the actual trials—is the overwhelming horror of *The Crucible*, and to make a primary consideration of anything less would be to distort and dissipate this crucial issue.

Danforth's great fault is not his *inability* to come to any new

[15] Miller, quoted in John and Alice Griffin, 'Arthur Miller Discusses *The Crucible*,' *Theatre Arts*, p.34.

knowledge, but his *refusal* to admit even to himself that any new knowledge exists. In the course of the play John Proctor finally becomes what Danforth always was—a totally committed man. But unlike Proctor—and the divergence is crucial—Danforth's commitment is blindly divorced from the lessons of human experience. Like Elizabeth and Hale, Proctor is able to face knowledge that runs counter to his concept of the world and his place in it, but Danforth, in his self-imposed righteousness, is not.

On seeing the falsity of the trials, although previously committed to their purpose, Hale rejects them; but Danforth will not because he is finally unable to set himself apart from his cause. His ego and his mission have fused into a monstrous unity that has completely dehumanized him. At the end of the play he desperately wants Proctor's confession, not so much to save his adversary's life, but as public proof of the validity of the inquisition. It is this awesome antagonist, and not just a sadistic killer, against whom John Proctor is pitted.

Unmistakably the protagonist of *The Crucible*, Proctor is nevertheless a markedly reluctant hero for most of the play. Like Lawrence Newman of *Focus*, he does not choose his heroic destiny but finds it forced upon him slowly and painfully until all his alternatives are pared down to two, between which he must make a final, agonizing choice.

To a degree he is a victim of a choice he has already made: his adultery with Abigail. The consequences of this act eventually recoil on him and help propel his destruction. However, *The Crucible*'s resemblance to the pattern of *All My Sons* ends with this superficial similarity. Miller was quite aware that Proctor's brief fling with his serving girl hardly warranted a trip to the gallows. On the contrary, the fact that the Salem trials became a perverse kind of public retributive justice for private follies, not only allowing but even eliciting the disclosure of personal affairs to public scrutiny, is one of the main points of the play. Proctor's transgression was personal; that it should be dragged into the harsh glare of public administration does not illustrate the soundness of cause-and-effect relationships, but the monstrous absurdity manifested in the gulf between the alleged aims of the trials and the bedrock reality in which they were riveted.

However, Proctor is not simply a victim of corporate authority's manipulation of private conscience. Although his sense of guilt is a determining factor in his reluctance to become involved in Salem's troubles, it is not the sole reason for his detachment. To begin with, he just cannot believe that the mischief of the girls will engender anything more virulent than a few sound spankings. Secondly, disgusted with the hypocrisy and greed of some of Salem's leading citizens, particularly the Reverend Parris and Thomas Putnam, Proctor simply wants nothing to do with them. He is weary, too, with the theology Parris thunders from his pulpit, a religion focused constantly on the depravity of man and the punishment that awaits him (obviously a topic about which Proctor feels he needs no additional information). Finally, and perhaps most significantly, Proctor is too intensely committed to his personal privacy to involve himself in matters that he thinks are scarcely his business.

'I have a crop to sow and lumber to drag home,' he comments matter-of-factly as he walks away from the gathering thunderheads. Like Joe Keller, he initially views his world and his responsibility to it as ending at the building line; and like previous Miller heroes he is to discover that he is more involved in the world beyond that questionable line than he ever intended to be.

His initial entanglement is rapid and involuntary. Through Mary Warren he learns that the 'mischief' has erupted into a full-fledged maelstrom of hysteria, and even as he promises his wife to 'think on' her proposal that he go to Salem and speak out against the ugly proceedings, he discovers that some of his closest and most respected friends have been taken. Before he can recoil from this news, Elizabeth is arrested, and with this development the man who, out of private guilt, public disgust, and personal inertia has attempted to remain aloof from the outside community, suddenly finds himself at its frenzied center. Proctor finally decides to go to Salem, but rather late and with very little choice.

In the third act he tries to rescue Elizabeth by arguing her case before Deputy Governor Danforth and the other judges. In so doing he attempts two things: he is resorting to reason and legality, and he is still trying to remain as personally uninvolved as possible. Both efforts are doomed to failure. Danforth's explanation of the nature of the trials puts a chilling end to any hopes Proctor may have had in reason and in due process of law.

'In an ordinary crime, how does one defend the accused?' the judge asks rhetorically.

One calls up witnesses to prove his innocence. But witchcraft
is *ipso facto*, on its face and by its nature, an invisible crime,
is it not? Therefore, who may possibly be witness to it? The
witch and the victim. None other. Now we cannot hope the
witch will accuse herself; granted? Therefore, we must rely
upon her victims—and they do testify, the children certainly
do testify. As for the witches, none will deny that we are most
eager for all their confessions. Therefore, what is left for a
lawyer to bring out? I think I have made my point. Have I
not?[16]

If Proctor was awaiting a reply to his earlier question, 'Is the
accuser always holy now?' Danforth has supplied it in an icy
affirmative.

With the appeal to common sense shattered, so too is Proctor's
attempt to remain detached, and by accusing Abigail of willfully
plotting his wife's murder, he bares his private life and his personal
guilts to the inquisition. However, his desperate confession is useless when the vengeful girl utilizes the climate of hysteria to trap
him. As Proctor stares in horror at the accusations hurled against
him, the private man has finally become inextricably enmeshed
in the public situation he so steadfastly strove to avoid. And his
cry to Danforth at the close of the act flames with the realization
of what his uninvolvement has helped foster.

'A fire, a fire is burning!' he exclaims in a frenzy of awareness.
'I hear the boot of Lucifer, I see his filthy face! And it is my face,
and yours Danforth! For them that quail to bring men out of
ignorance, as I have quailed, and as you quail now when you know
in all your black hearts that this be fraud—God damns our kind
especially, and we will burn, we will burn together!'[17]

They will not. In whatever hell he has created for himself, Danforth will burn alone. Proctor's development has brought him to
the realization of his complicity in the evil around him, but in *The
Crucible* the awareness of guilt is not the raison d'être of the
action.

'There was an attempt to move beyond the discovery and unveil-
ing of the hero's guilt, a guilt that kills the personality,' Miller subsequently explained.

[16] Miller, 'The Crucible,' *Collected Plays*, p.297.
[17] *Ibid.*, p.311.

I had grown increasingly conscious of this theme in my past work, and aware too that it was no longer enough for me to build a play, as it were, upon the revelation of guilt, and to rely solely upon a fate which exacts payment from the culpable man. Now guilt appeared to me no longer the bedrock beneath which the probe could not penetrate. I saw it now as a betrayer, as possibly the most real of our illusions, but nevertheless a quality of mind capable of being overthrown.[18]

The unraveling of the drama substantiates its author's commentary. Proctor's recognition of his complicity in the situation is not the final certification of guilt, but rather the critical prerequisite for transcending it. He has come to a new and lacerating awareness. Still remaining is the thorny problem of what course of action this knowledge will elicit.

Even after the mockery of a trial and the hardships of months in prison, Proctor's involvement is still not synonymous with his responsibility, and he is not yet ready to commit himself to his fellow prisoners and against their persecutors. Trying to understand and act upon the promptings of his conscience, he seeks additional help from his wife, his God, from anyone temporal and transcendent.

'Then who will judge me?' he cries out. 'God in Heaven, what is John Proctor, what is John Proctor?'

The third person reference, which is continued through to the conclusion of the play, illustrates his desperate attempt to view himself objectively in a final effort at some new recognition and verification. The result is the awareness of his isolation, the realization that no one else can judge him and either condemn or justify his course of action.

Torn between signing the prepared confession or mounting the gallows, he chooses his life and makes ready to put his name to the document, justifying the act by reminding himself of his unworthiness and inability to play the demanding role of hero-martyr.

'I cannot mount the gibbet like a saint,' he equivocates. 'It is a fraud. I am not that man. My honesty is broke . . . I am no good man. Nothing's spoiled by giving them this lie that were not rotten long before.'[19]

[18] Miller, 'Introduction,' *Collected Plays,* pp.40–41.
[19] Miller, 'The Crucible,' *Collected Plays,* p.322.

The statement is less a manifestation of Proctor's self-awareness than of his desire to escape from his responsibility through self-deprecation, the hope of submerging himself in the tepid and masochistic security of acknowledged guilt. But even though he is ready to sign the confession, he balks at incriminating those who have not signed.

'They think to go like saints. I like not to spoil their names.'

Against Danforth's insistence that he implicate the others, Proctor remains adamant; his confession must be private.

'I speak my own sins,' he reminds the Deputy Governor, 'I cannot judge another. I have no tongue for it.'

Danforth's urgency is cooled by Hale's and Parris' arguments that Proctor's confession is sufficient to impress the town, and as Danforth relents, his adversary finally makes his signature. It is Proctor's last attempt to escape from commitment into the ambivalent relief of disengagement.

However, Miller seals the remaining exit through which his protagonist hopes to flee by way of compromise. With Danforth's revelation that the confession must be nailed to the church door for all to see, Proctor's retreat into anonymity is cut off. The noman's-land of compromise between private and public commitment has been wiped out, and he must now either align himself against the condemned—wholly and publicly—or with them, just as totally and just as overtly.

As Danforth avidly reaches for the piece of paper, Proctor exercises his final choice. He snatches it up, 'a wild terror . . . and a boundless anger . . . rising in him,' and holding the confession away from the Deputy Governor, he hurls his fury at his tormentors.

'I have confessed myself!' he cries. 'Is there no good penitence, but it be public? God knows how black my sins are! It is enough!'

The revelation that the confession must be publicized is made by Danforth after it has been signed, but Proctor's reversal is hardly the consequence of the Deputy Governor's final stipulation. Proctor has known all along what Danforth intended to do with his confession. Certainly Parris' earlier explanation that it would 'strike the village that Proctor confess' because his is 'a weighty name' has left little doubt in the farmer's mind as to what purposes his confession would be used. Why then the signature and the immediate and violent recantation?

Simply, Proctor requires the final proof that his compromise will still not allow him to evade his responsibility. Just as Lawrence Newman needs the last humiliation of a beating to bring his moral vision into the sharpest possible focus, so too must Proctor face the ultimate indignity—the written certification of the betrayal of his friends—before he can act on what he already knows: that he cannot buy life at the price of conscience.

'I have three children,' he states with simple but terrible finality. 'How may I teach them to walk like men in the world, and I sold my friends? . . . Beguile me not! I blacken all of them when this is nailed to the church the very day they hang for silence!'[20]

The private man and the public man have coalesced, not like Danforth, blindly unaware of the line of demarcation between ego and principle, but in Proctor's ability to finally comprehend that his inviolable commitment to his personal integrity is wholly bound to his responsibility to a world beyond himself. It is all summed up in his defense of his name.

When Danforth asks him why he will not allow his signature to be made public. Proctor replies 'with a cry of his whole soul':

Because it is my name! Because I cannot have another in my life! Because I lie and sign myself to lies! Because I am not worth the dust on the feet of them that hang! How may I live without my name! I have given you my soul; leave me my name![21]

John Proctor is wrong. In refusing to yield his name he keeps his soul, for the two are synonymous. Miller restated the situation in an interview shortly before *The Crucible*'s opening in 1953, when he remarked that:

nobody wants to be a hero. You go through life giving up parts of yourself—a hope, a dream, an ambition, a belief, a liking, a piece of self-respect. But in every man there is something he cannot give up and still remain himself—a core, an identity, a thing that is summed up for him by the sound of his own name on his own ears. If he gives that up, he becomes a different man, not himself.[22]

[20] *Ibid.*, p.327.

[21] *Ibid.*, p.328.

[22] Arthur Miller, quoted in *New York Herald Tribune*, Jan 25, 1953.

In *A View from the Bridge*, Miller is to dramatize in Eddie Carbone, that 'different man,' the individual who gives up the name. However, in keeping faith with others, Proctor retains his, for the idea of 'name' is never entirely personal. In maintaining his identity, he helps substantiate the identities of Rebecca Nurse and Giles Corey. Like the rest of Miller's heroes, Proctor is not a glib altruist. His primary concern is with his private conscience. But he learns in the pressure of the crucible that ultimately there is no differentiation between private and public integrity. Consequently his final choice is inevitable. At the end, like Newman and Keller, Proctor stands committed, though ironically more isolated than he has ever been, alone in the realization that he makes his final choice without the aid of anybody or of any carefully constructed and guaranteed philosophical plan.

Unlike Keller's, Proctor's choice to die is not ambivalent. He has not yielded his conscience in an act of betrayal. Thus his death is not an atonement, but an unqualified affirmation. He does not die out of guilt, which he has finally transcended, but out of responsibility.

The triumph of Proctor is dramatically highlighted by the defeat of John Hale, the individual in the play who loses everything that the 'name' symbolizes for the New England farmer. A man who profoundly believed in the rightness of his cause, Hale makes the most complete turnabout in the drama, and in so doing acts as a kind of balance between Danforth and Proctor. In contrast to the Deputy Governor, Hale is able to reject his allegiances when he finds they are wrong.

'I denounce these proceedings, I quit the court!' he exclaims after Proctor is condemned.

But the realization comes too late. In his zeal to combat the evil of witchcraft he has compromised his conscience and relinquished his name. Consequently his new knowledge cannot free him; it can only erode. At the conclusion, the degree of erosion is manifested in his agonized attempts to make Elizabeth convince her husband to cling to his life.

'Let you not mistake your duty as I mistook my own,' he warns her.

I came into this village like a bridegroom to his beloved, bearing gifts of high religion: the very crowns of holy law I brought, and what I touched with my bright confidence, it died; and where I turned the eye of my great faith, blood flowed up. Beware, Goody Proctor—cleave to no faith when faith brings blood. It is mistaken law that leads you to sacrifice. Life, woman, is God's most precious gift; no ·principle, however glorious, may justify the taking of it. I beg you, woman, prevail upon your husband to confess. Let him give his lie. Quail not before God's judgement in this, for it may well be God damns a liar less than he that throws his life away for pride.[23]

To her reply that his argument sounds like the Devil's, Hale counters with a final desperate plea.

'Woman, before the laws of God we are as swine!' he exclaims, 'We cannot read His will!'

Thus has the minister fallen from high idealism to mordant disillusionment, from a shining belief in human potential to the bleakest despair at human frailty. It is ironically appropriate that Hale should live while Proctor perishes, because in his case death can neither affirm nor atone. The churchman lives in the comprehension of his unworthiness; the farmer dies in the awareness of his value.

One of the notable alternations Miller made in *The Crucible* involved Proctor's final speech. In the original production it consisted simply of his harsh command to Elizabeth not to show any weakness before their enemies.

'Give them no tear!' he admonished her. 'Show a stony heart and sink them with it!'

In the revision, Proctor tears up his confession and answers Hale's final warning that he will hang for his obstinacy, with the following exclamation:

[his eyes full of tears] I can. And there's your first marvel, that I can. You have made your magic now, for now I do think I see some shred of goodness in John Proctor. Not enough to weave a banner with, but white enough to keep it from such dogs. [Elizabeth in a burst of terror rushes to him and weeps against his hand] Give them no tear! Tears pleasure them! Show honour now, show a stony heart and

[23] Miller, 'The Crucible,' *Collected Plays*, pp.319–320.

sink them with it! [He has lifted her, and kisses her now with great passion].[24]

Proctor has found his worth, and finding himself through a torturous process, he will not qualify his discovery in false piety or sentiment. If he must die, he does not intend for one moment to make the task any easier for his executioners, and he turns his cheek only to spit at them. Giles Corey is not the only 'fearsome man' in *The Crucible*.

Structurally, the play is a marked departure from *Death of a Salesman*. Omitting the complex time structure of the latter, as well as its lyric mood, it follows instead the tradition of the well-made play, beginning slowly, establishing scene and tone, and then building with rapidly gathering force to a dramatic crescendo. Each act closes on a strong climax, with each succeeding climax more powerful than the previous one, so that the dramatic action beautifully manifests its thematic development.

While *Death of a Salesman* is ultimately concerned with the complex and intriguing creation of a multifaceted human being, *The Crucible*'s central interest is directed toward a man's actions as well as his composition. In an excellent critical essay, Robert Hogan stated the difference between the two plays succinctly and perceptively:

> The plots of *Death of a Salesman* are not the centre of the play, but in *The Crucible* the action is the play's very basis, its consuming centre. One watches *Death of a Salesman* to discover what a man is like, but one watches *The Crucible* to discover what a man does. . . . In the life of John Proctor, one single action is decisive, dominating, and totally pertinent, and this action, this moment of decision and commitment, is that climax toward which every incident in the play tends.[25]

It is a fact rather than a value judgment that *The Crucible* has a much stronger centrality of plot and clarity of theme than *Death of a Salesman*. If the story of John Proctor lacks the haunting compassion of Willy Loman's life and death, it counters with a greater dramatic impact, and exhibits more clearly the possibility of high tragedy.

[24] *Ibid.*, p.238.
[25] Robert Hogan, *Arthur Miller*, University of Minnesota Pamphlets on American Writers, p.28.

In Proctor's drama, three fundamentals of tragedy are fulfilled. First, through a torturous process of self-examination an individual arrives at a new realization of himself and his relationship to the world at large. Secondly, the individual discovers in the necessity of making a choice the power of his will, even in the face of seemingly insurmountable odds. Thirdly, although the movement toward self-recognition leads to destruction, an affirmation of life is ultimately propounded.

If Willy Loman is a tragic figure, his tragedy is necessarily and unmistakably laced with pathos. There is nothing false about this because the pathos is genuine and moving. Proctor's tragedy lacks this pathos because he is a character of much greater consciousness than Willy. He is able to stand outside himself while Willy is not; therefore his drama is considerably removed from the anguished subjectivity of *Death of a Salesman*.

Consequently it is superficially ripe for the kind of critical comment made by Walter Kerr when in defining the play as 'a mechanical parable,' he claimed that 'it is better to make a man than to make a point.'[26] It is better still to make both, and in *The Crucible* Miller does. If the drama's emotional charge seems weaker than *Death of a Salesman*'s, perhaps the difference has less to do with degree of emotion than with kind.*

John Proctor suffers, but he simultaneously examines and comes to understand the causes, meaning, and consequences of his travail. Willy Loman also suffers, but because of his limited critical and intellectual faculties, some of the meaning and ironies of his situation escape him. And because he does not complicate our responses by becoming his own critic, we can more easily sympathize with and pity him. However, if Proctor does not elicit our pity, he does arouse our admiration, even our awe.

At the core of Willy's suicide there is a mystery, which is lyrically and movingly evoked in the concluding elegy of the Requiem. At

---

[26] Walter Kerr, *New York Herald Tribune*, January 23, 1953.

* It is interesting that Kerr's complaint that in *The Crucible* Miller had sacrificed emotion to polemics was countered by Richard Watts's observation in the *New York Post* that although the play was emotionally effective, it lacked intellectual depth. Equally interesting is Watts's increasing admiration for the drama. '*The Crucible* is that rarity in the American theatre,' he wrote in an introduction to the Bantam edition of the play (New York, 1959), 'a play which seems finer and more alive today than when it was first produced.'

the core of Proctor's death there is a clarification. Since he ultimately knows the whys and wherefores of his life, there is nothing
equivocal about his death. It is more than coincidental therefore
that *Death of a Salesman* closes on a darkening twilight stage, while
The Crucible's curtain descends on a new sun pouring its light on
the place where John Proctor of Salem has just stood.

13

'My objection is, he refuses to repent'

The Crucible opened on the evening of January 22, 1953, under the production of Kermit Bloomgarden and the direction of Jed Harris. With Arthur Kennedy and Beatrice Straight as John and Elizabeth Proctor, E. G. Marshall as the Reverend Hale, Walter Hampden as Danforth, and Madeleine Sherwood as Abigail Williams, the play managed a respectable run of 197 performances and won both the Antoinette Perry and Donaldson awards as the most distinguished American drama of the year.

A subsequent off-Broadway production five years later, which elicited high critical acclaim, plus three London productions in 1954, 1956, and 1965—the latter produced by Laurence Olivier for the National Theatre and termed by Miller the best staging of the play he had seen to date—greatly substantiated the playwright's faith in the validity of his drama.*

A little over two and a half years after the New York premiere of *The Crucible,* two new Miller plays, *A Memory of Two Mondays* and *A View from the Bridge,* opened as a double bill at the Coronet Theatre on Broadway. Because of the poor production and performance of *A Memory of Two Mondays* and Miller's inadequate conception and structuring of *A View from the Bridge,* the event was disappointing, and the plays subsequently limped off with the poorest run (149 performances) and bleakest critical

* On May 4, 1967, a Xerox Corporation-sponsored television production of the play on the Columbia Broadcasting System received further acclaim. In that dramatization, which was specially adapted by Miller for the medium, George C. Scott and Colleen Dewhurst turned in the finest portrayals of John and Elizabeth Proctor I have seen.

reaction to an original Miller effort since the debut of the ill-fated *Man Who Had All the Luck*.

Although he was disheartened by the reception accorded his latest dramas, the playwright's aesthetic and financial problems in the autumn of 1955 were slight by comparison to the personal and political conflicts in which he was rapidly becoming embroiled in those same hectic days. From the spring of 1955 to the autumn of 1957, Miller found himself the protagonist of three separate but interrelated dramas, each of which could have conceivably been termed absurdist.

The first began quite inauspiciously in the spring of 1955 when a small television producing firm called Combined Artists reached a tentative agreement with the Youth Board of New York City to produce a feature-length film based upon the Board's work with juvenile gangs in New York.

According to the agreement, the Board would make its files and techniques available to the producers and writers, in return for which the City would receive five percent of the film's profits. With accord reached and big-name screen personalities planned for the starring roles, Combined Artists then offered the vital job of scriptwriting to Arthur Miller. Although he was immediately interested in the project, the playwright withheld any confirmation until he could get a firsthand look at the situation. Consequently, for a little over a week in the middle of June, he set out to learn personally what his projected screenplay would be all about.

Accompanying Youth Board workers on their rounds, he watched and listened to them cope with the kids on the streets, noted and felt their frustrations and disappointments, and shared their rare occasional triumphs when a youngster was 'reached,' even momentarily. And as he became increasingly involved with them, he marveled at the stamina and dedication of these young men and women who often worked 'forty-two hour stretches to head off a gang fight; no time to eat, to sleep, to shave, shot at, stabbed, beaten, arrested, degraded; ending up with broken heads and ulcers . . . for $3000 a year.'[1]

Despite the grimness of the overall situation, for Miller the experience was as exhilarating as it was challenging. Not since the days when he roamed army camps searching for the spine to

[1] Arthur Miller, quoted in Walter Goodman, 'How Not to Produce a Film,' *The New Republic*, 133 (December 26, 1955), p.12.

The Story of G.I. Joe had he felt the excitement of tracking down a potential drama that he knew needed telling. As his initiation into the projected film drew to an end, he made up his mind and enthusiastically agreed to do the script.

For the next month and a half the writer spent his mornings casting *A Memory of Two Mondays* and *A View from the Bridge* and his evenings on the streets with the Youth Board workers. He watched them in action, and took notes. He spoke to the gang members, and added more notes. His notebooks began to bulge with jottings, bits of dialogue, scene sketches, and characterizations. As the summer grew sultrier he fused his observations and ideas into a twenty-five page scenario that he called 'Bridge to a Savage World.' It was hardly coincidental that the title was so similar to that of his latest drama. Both works dealt in part with the relationship of savagery to civilization, and each stressed the need for communication as a vital means of humanizing the fang and claw world on the other side of the tenuous bridge. In his opening remarks, Miller delineated the basic theme of the film:

> In this picture we shall meet boys who, before they are reached, could fit comfortably into the behavior pattern of the early hordes that roamed the virgin forests. There are elements in the gang codes today which are more primitive than those that governed the earliest clan societies. When a Youth Board worker descends into the streets he is going back into human history a distance of thousands of years. Thus it is fruitless merely to say that the delinquents must be given love and care—or the birch rod. What is involved here is a profound conflict of man's most subtle values. The deeper into their lives the Youth Board worker goes, the more apparent is becomes that they are essentially boys who have never made contact with civilized values: boys without a concept of the father, as the father is normally conceived, boys without an inkling of the idea of social obligation, personal duty or even rudimentary honor. To save one of these is obviously a great piece of work . . . what is involved is a deep spiritual transformation which, among other things, makes for the highest drama.[2]

The civilizing process, the 'reaching' of these boys, was to be

[2] Miller, 'Bridge to a Savage World,' *Esquire* (October, 1958), p.185.

the primary action of the film, and the Youth Board worker, Jerry Bone, who would serve as both catalyst and protagonist, would initiate and propel this action. His function would be twofold: to get through to the boys, and—as a prerequisite for establishing contact with them—to attain a kind of self-awareness as well.

'Bone himself will become aware as he sets forth these values . . . that what he is teaching them he must first teach himself. Thus, we shall witness the maturation of Jerry Bone even as he is helping these dangerous boys to grow up.'

The process would be painful, even searing, and victory would be anything but total, but eventually some form of connection would be made. Unable to reach them all, Bone would communicate with some of the gang members, strongly influencing one in particular, so that at the end there would be a sense of affirmation, not glib, yet evident. Ultimately the film would emphasize the element at the core of every Miller drama: the fundamental worth of the individual in his continual struggle for reassertion against the forces that erode and undermine him. The scenario concluded with the dramatist's emphasis on the quality some of the gang members would gain from their experiences.

> What they must have in exchange for peace, however, is a shred of dignity. These are children who have never known life excepting as a worthless thing. They have been told from birth that they are nothing, that their parents are nothing, that their hopes are nothing. The group in this picture will end, by and large, with a discovery of their innate worth.[3]

An ending not very different thematically from *Focus, All My Sons, Death of a Salesman,* and *The Crucible.* But in this instance a conclusion that would never be realized.

At approximately the same time that Miller presented his scenario to Combined Artists, Scripps-Howard reporter Frederick Woltman wrote a stinging column in the *New York World-Telegram* charging the playwright with left-wing activities. Within the week the newspaper came out with a lead editorial staunchly supporting its reporter's charges and demanding that New York City break off all agreements it had made with the dramatist. The *World-Telegram*'s sudden campaign to protect eight million unwary and innocent citizens from the poisonous pen of Arthur Miller coincided intriguingly with the arrival in New York of the House Un-American Activities Committee on one of its typical searches for subversives in the entertainment industry.

Despite a flurry of rumors, Miller was not subpoenaed to testify before the organization, but a Committee member did contact the Youth Board and demand that it curtail its relationship with the dramatist. The Board responded by unanimously voting to support both Miller and the film project.

Unfortunately, the story does not end on this idealistic note of communal courage. Like Ibsen's Doctor Stockmann, Miller was soon to witness the shoddy spectacle of his backers' convictions crumbling like the celebrated Maginot Line before a juggernaut of pressure and panic.

The first chink in the defense appeared when Mayor Robert Wagner qualified the Youth Board's vote of confidence by asking for a discreet check of Miller's background. Emphatically denying that he was engaged in any kind of 'witch hunt,' the mayor explained that he personally had no desire to deprive anyone of the right to make a living, but that he felt, in the light of the project's publicity, that an investigation was justified, and he assigned the task to Investigation Commissioner Charles H. Tenney.

Tenney discovered nothing very subversive or even startling in Miller's past activities. As a young man Miller had been attracted to Marxism in the 1930s and continued to lean to the left of the mythical center in the 40s. In 1947 Miller had attended several meetings of Communist writers in New York, and that same year was listed as a sponsor of a world youth festival in Prague. He had also signed a statement protesting the outlawing of the Communist party. In 1954, when he applied for a passport to go to Brussels for the opening of *The Crucible,* his request was denied by the State Department under regulations refusing passports to persons believed to be supporting the Communist movement, regardless of whether they were actually members of the Party. This, in sum, was the portrait of the Enemy of the People contained in the report Commissioner Tenney presented to Mayor Wagner.

Publicly stating that the investigation had turned up nothing derogatory to Miller, the mayor added that although the dramatist's previous public activities indicated some leftist sympathy, no evidence of current left-wing associations had been found.

Wagner optimistically concluded by expressing his belief that the New York Board of Estimate, which had to approve the City's contract with Combined Artists before the film could begin, would rule favorably on the project and its author.

But the mayor's prognostication was already being undermined by three powerful members of the Board of Estimate, Brooklyn Borough President John Cashmore, Bronx Borough President James J. Lyons, and City Comptroller Lawrence E. Gerosa, each of whom let it be known that he was flatly against any association with Miller.

The Board of Estimate did not veto the contract; characteristically the members began to volleyball it to oblivion. On the twenty-ninth of November, Mayor Wagner announced that on the 'informal opinion' of Corporation Counsel Peter C. Brown, he and the Board of Estimate were sending the contract back to the Youth Board to make a final decision. To a reporter's suggestion that this might be a ploy to get both City Hall and the Board of Estimate out of a tight spot, the mayor made a vehement denial.

The members of the Youth Board meanwhile were something less than ecstatic at having the political hand grenade lobbed back into their collective laps, and their subsequent actions contrasted vividly with their initial vote of confidence. Reverting to the favorite pastime of bureaucracies, they appointed by a squeakingly narrow nine to eight vote, a subcommittee to further investigate the material contained in Tenney's report. The subcommittee met with Miller during the first week of December and made a tenuous attempt to convince him to compromise with the Board of Estimate and the readers of the *World-Telegram* by making some kind of public apology for past relationships. When he heard the proposal, the playwright did not even try to conceal his disgust and anger.

> I told the Board that I was not going to genuflect to any newspapermen or howling mob. My attitudes on dictatorship, Nazi and Communist, had been established by many essays. I'd signed the customary loyalty oath when obtaining my passport. I was not going to submit myself to any political means test to practice the profession of letters in the United States.[4]

[4] Miller, quoted in Goodman, *The New Republic,* p.13.

The subcommittee must have been impressed with Miller's stand, for they voted five to one to support him and uphold the contract. But the gesture was the final surfacing of a drowning man, and even as they repeated their confidence, the political waves were being lashed into tidal fury. The American Legion, the Catholic War Veterans, and a superpatriotic vigilante organization with the pompously portentous name of AWARE were now howling for Miller's scalp.

On the sixth of December, J. Addington Wagner, the national commander of the American Legion, announced that his organization had data pertinent to Miller's association with suspect organizations, and then tartly rebuked the City for its handling of the situation.

'This proposition has apparently been handed around among various city officials who finally turned it back to a small committee of citizens who approved it,' he snorted derisively.[5]

Under the combined pressure of the various groups, the Youth Board finally capitulated. On the seventh of December, the same individuals who only days before had unanimously voted Arthur Miller their confidence and support, now commemorated the anniversary of Pearl Harbor by torpedoing the writer and the film. At the end of almost two hours of heated argument, the Board voted eleven to nine to override the wishes of its own subcommittee and drop its association with Combined Artists. After its decision it issued the following statement:

> The Youth Board is a city agency representing the total community of New York City, and we cannot make any decision which would assure us of less than one hundred per cent cooperation from all of the people in the city of New York. In view of this fact, the Youth Board voted in a divided vote not to go ahead with the contract with Combined Artists, Inc. We wish to make it entirely clear that by this decision we are not passing judgment on Mr Miller's loyalty as a citizen or on his merits as a great artist.[6]

[5] J. Addington Wagner, quoted in *New York Herald Tribune*, December 7, 1955.

[6] Youth Board of New York, quoted in *New York Herald Tribune*, December 8, 1955.

The *New York World-Telegram* did not have to pussyfoot around the basic reasons for the playwright's dismissal, and in its lead editorial of December 8, it cut beneath the limp rhetoric of the Youth Board and City Hall by smugly declaring that

> the question was not whether Mr Miller is talented—or whether he could write an unbiased script on the work of the Youth Board. It was simply whether the city should enhance the playwright's prestige and diminish its own by indirectly hiring a man with such a questionable political background.[7]

A day after thousands of New Yorkers were reading about their narrow escape from contamination, the alleged contaminator made his own statement.

> I salute the minority members of the Youth Board, not only for their courage in a tough moment but for their devotion to the youth of this city which their vote dramatizes. I salute the street workers of the Youth Board who, without commissioner, limousines, and at miserable pay, are taking their lives in their hands and working for as long as thirty hours at a stretch in the rain and snow, in the day and night, striving to open the minds of this city's kids to a glimmer of humane values.
>
> My hope was to show this process in the film, to show how a boy was saved, and how ten thousand more might be saved. I salute above all the boys and girls themselves, the legions of bewildered kids roaming the avenues of the world's wealthiest city, looking for a little human warmth, a hope in life, a symbol of some kind in which they might believe and through that belief reconstruct their broken hearts and shattered souls. I had wanted to speak for these children and to them. I had wanted to raise up into the light of day the wondrous creativity that lies imprisoned in their frustrated and furious minds. I wanted to turn the face of this city into the mirror which is its youth so that more people might feel the reality that when a boy kills a boy, in truth our great buildings shake and on the hands of every man and woman living there is a spot of blood.
>
> I had hoped, in short, to tell the truth, the unvarnished facts about delinquency, the facts seen and the facts unseen. *I had*

[7] *New York World-Telegram*, December 8, 1955.

hoped to make not merely a drama but a civilizing work of art.

The majority of the Youth Board has now decided that this picture shall not be made. So be it. Now let us see whether fanaticism can do what it never could do in the history of the world; let it perform a creative act, let it take its club in hand and write what it has just destroyed.[8]

The statement's tone and meaning provided clear and eloquent testimony to the complaint made by one of the Youth Board members who had cast his vote against the playwright.

'I'm not calling him a Communist,' he remarked with bullish candor. 'My objection is that he refuses to repent.'

If Miller was disappointed and angered at the outcome of his skirmish with the City of New York, he did not yet know on that December day of 1955 how stern a test his 'refusal to repent' would finally face.

June and July of the following year were two of the most hectic months in the dramatist's life. In the space of six weeks he found himself divorced, remarried, and cited for contempt of Congress. He became front-page news across the country as the House Un-American Activities Committee and Marilyn Monroe combined in spectacularly dissimilar ways to make a glaringly public figure out of a man who had always placed a high premium on his privacy.

On the twelfth of June, 1956, Miller's marriage to Mary Slattery, which had been floundering for some time, finally ended in a Reno divorce court. Seventeen days later the playwright married Marilyn Monroe, the most celebrated star of her time. They had met in Hollywood in 1951, but their relationship did not become intense until she moved to New York in 1955. They were married in a civil ceremony in White Plains, New York, on June 29, and again in a Jewish service on the first of July.

The wedding, which came in the midst of Miller's difficulties with the House Un-American Activities Committee, surprised friends and public alike. It was not so much the apparent swiftness of the move, but the tremendous contrast of the personalities involved that stunned not only the general public but many persons

---

[8] Miller, quoted in *New York Herald Tribune*. December 9, 1955. Italics my own.

close to both the bride and the groom. The newspapers and magazines had a veritable field day with headlines and feature articles.

Most people who knew the Millers—and just about everyone who did not—quickly predicted the marriage would not last. Perhaps only the playwright and his bride believed from the very beginning that they could give each other the kind of love and attention they needed. It is mordantly ironic that while the public façade of the marriage contradicted general expectations for the next four years, the personal relationship rapidly and harrowingly validated them.

But the inferno came later. In those initial days and weeks, his new marriage provided Miller with the one blissful interlude in an otherwise hectic and harassing summer. The events of the season began casually enough when he applied for a passport to travel to England with his bride-to-be. He was going to arrange for a London production of *A View from the Bridge,* and she was on her way to co-star with Laurence Olivier in *The Prince and the Showgirl,* a film version of Terrence Rattigan's popular play. Again the State Department delayed action on granting the passport because, in the words of one of its spokesmen, it had some 'derogatory information' about Miller that first had to be 'answered by an affidavit.'[9]

While this was pending, the playwright was subpoenaed by the House Un-American Activities Committee, which—under the chairmanship of Representative Francis E. Walter of Pennsylvania—was currently investigating the unauthorized use of United States passports. Miller was called with reference to two previous passport applications, one in 1947, which was granted, and the 1954 application, which was not, as well as to the one currently before the State Department.

On a warm twenty-first of June, the dramatist, accompanied by his counsel, Joseph Rauh, Jr, went before the House Committee in Washington, D.C. The inquiry was relatively brief, for the most part polite and decorous, and Miller did not resort to the protective Fifth Amendment as he answered a number of questions dealing with his opinions on a variety of topics ranging from the Communist Party, Red China, the Smith Act, and Congressional

[9] *New York Times,* June 22, 1956, pp.1, 9.

Committees, to specific playwrights and novelists, his own work, and the position of the writer in America.

He spoke seriously and capably of leftist causes he had supported in the 1940s, and of his problems with the Youth Board of New York City the previous year. He also discussed his protests against the entertainment industry's blacklisting of suspected Communists, his defense of the leftist writer Howard Fast, and his ruptured friendship with Elia Kazan and others who had named names in previous HUAC hearings. In a long exchange with Congressman Scherer over the validity of the Smith Act, he lucidly voiced his opposition to it.

'I am opposed to the Smith Act and I am still opposed to anyone being penalized for advocating anything,' he stated frankly, 'and I say that because of a very simple reason. I don't believe that in the history of letters there are many great books or great plays that don't advocate. That doesn't mean that a man is a propagandist. It is in the nature of life and it is the nature of literature that the passions of an author congeal around literature. You can go from *War and Peace* through all the great novels of our time and they are all advocating something. Therefore, when I heard that the United States Government wanted to pass a law against the advocacy without any overt action, I was alarmed because I am not here defending Communists. I am here defending the right of an author to advocate, to write.'*

When Scherer asked him if this included advocating the overthrow of the American government by force and violence, Miller replied: 'I am now speaking, sir, of creative literature. There are risks and balances of risks.'

Challenged further on the issue of advocacy, he continued.

'I think that a work of art—' he paused for a minute, trying to formulate his thoughts.

'My point,' he began again, 'is very simple. I think that, once you start to cut away, there is a certain common sense in mankind which makes these limits automatic. There are risks which are balanced. The Constitution is full of those risks. We have rights,

* The dialogue throughout this re-creation of Miller's appearance before the House Committee is taken verbatim from 'The Testimony of Arthur Miller, accompanied by Counsel, Joseph L. Rauh, Jr' from Part 4 of the House Committee on Un-American Activities' *Investigation of the Unauthorized Use of United States Passports*, 84th Congress, pp.4660–4690.

which, if they are violated, or rather used in an irresponsible way, can do damage. Yet they are there and the common sense of the people of the United States has kept this in sort of a balance.'

He then drove the point home quietly but firmly.

'I would prefer any day to say, "Yes, there should be no limit set upon the literary freedom," than to say, "You can go up this far and no further," because then you are getting into an area where people are going to say, "I think that this goes over the line," and then you are in an area where there is no limit to the censorship that can take place.'

When this and additional comments on the relationship of the writer to his society prompted another committee member to observe that Miller was 'putting the artist and literature in a preferred class,' the playwright smiled for a moment, and then replied.

'I thought we were going to get this,' he said, 'and it places me in a slightly impossible position, and I would be lying to you if I said that I didn't think the artist was, to a certain degree, in a special class. . . . The artist is a peculiar man in one respect. Therefore he has got a peculiar mandate in the history of civilization from people, and that is he has a mandate not only in his literature but in the way he behaves and the way he lives. . . . Most of us have an opinion. We . . . may have a view of life which on a rare occasion we have time to speak of. That is the artist's line of work. That is what he does all day long and, consequently, he is particularly sensitive to its limitations.'

'In other words,' came the rejoinder, 'your thought as I get it is that the artist lives in a different world from anyone else.'

Again Miller hesitated. 'No he doesn't,' he replied, 'but there is a conflict, I admit.'

He looked around the room for a moment as he searched for an analogy.

'I think there is an old conflict that goes back to Socrates,' he continued, 'between the man who is involved with ideal things and the man who has the terrible responsibility of keeping things going as they are and protecting the state and keeping an army and getting people fed.'

Throughout the first half of the testimony Miller kept relating his social and political life to his art, sometimes at the behest of a committee member, but more often to the polite exasperation of the committee. What they did not understand that day, or perhaps ever, was the primary truth of Miller's belief in the artist's total involvement with his social context. He was attempting to communicate to them as best he knew how what his chosen vocation meant to him, and by implication, what it should perhaps mean to them.

Then the almost casual tone of the hearing ended as Committee counsel Richard Arens took over and turned the questioning from the theoretical to the biographical. He zeroed in on Miller's past affiliations with Communist organizations, including his 1947 sponsorship of the Prague world youth festival and various signatures on statements protesting the outlawing of the Communist party and defending Communist official Gerhard Eisler. In response, the writer claimed he had little memory of the signatures to which Arens referred, but that would not deny them.

'In those days I did sign a lot of things,' he said, but in recent years '[I] ceased issuing statements right and left except where I was personally involved. I found I was getting tangled up in too many things I didn't want to defend one hundred per cent.'

When Arens reminded him of his statements and essays attacking the very committee before which he was now testifying, Miller again made no denials. He had always been bitterly opposed to the House Investigating Committee, which he viewed as another manifestation of the public manipulation of private conscience that he had examined in *The Crucible*. In fact, in 1954, shortly after he was refused a passport, he laced into the rationale behind such investigative bodies in a scathing satire published in the July 3 issue of *The Nation*.

Entitled 'A Modest Proposal For Pacifying The Public Temper,' the article proposed that on his eighteenth birthday and every two years thereafter, each American citizen surrender himself for Patriotic Arrest, to be investigated and classified as to his degree of allegiance to his country. There would be two basic classifications: Conceptual Traitor and Action Traitor.

The first would include any person who either indulged in actions 'Not Positively Conducive to the Defense of the Nation against the Enemy,' or 'failed to demonstrate a lively, viable or audible resentment' against such actions. As punishment the Conceptual Traitor would be forced to wear a CT identity card and to display the CT brand on all his work and correspondence.

Employers of Conceptual Traitors would have to display
their Conceptual Traitor's Employment Permits and show a
WECT (We Employ a Conceptual Traitor) mark on all their
stationery.

The second category, Action Traitor, would refer to any individual who either attended meetings of blacklisted groups, spoke in
praise of such organizations, or was called before any committee
of Congress and did not satisfy that august body or any *two*
members on it. His penalty would simply and bluntly consist of
a two thousand dollar fine and five to eight years in a federal
penitentiary.

Then, with a precision and irony that would have delighted
Dean Swift, Miller defined still another division of citizens under
the category Unclassified. This group, which would be delineated
by a large 'U' to differentiate them from the contaminated CT's
and AT's, would include the following persons: any individual
who could not speak or understand English, anyone committed to
a home for the aged or an insane asylum, all members of the FBI,
all members of the Congressional Investigating Committee, officers
of the United States Chamber of Commerce, persons who had not
registered in public libraries, veterans of the Civil War, donators
to the Winchell-Runyon Cancer Fund, anyone garnering favorable
mention in Ed Sullivan's column, and *most* children.*

Having outlined his proposal, Miller than blandly dealt with any
possible objections to it by reminding his reader that since each
American would willingly surrender himself 'with Love in his
Heart, with the burning desire to Prove to all his fellow-citizens
that he Is an American and is eager to let everybody know every
Action of his Life and its Patriotic Significance,' no one would
really be losing his liberty.[10] On the contrary, Patriotic Arrest
would become a kind of 'proud Initiation for the Young
American,' of which it could be justly said that 'if an American
boy is good enough to fight he is good enough to go to jail for the

---

* Some children in the 1950s could not even have received a 'U' from
AWARE unless it stood for Unacceptable. In situations where the border
between lunacy and rationality was as firm as a campaign promise, a few
child actors and juvenile performers were blacklisted by the vigilante
organization because of leftist associations either through their parents or
as a consequence of their own precocity.

[10] Miller, 'A Modest Proposal for Pacifying the Public Temper,' *The
Nation*, 179 (July 3, 1954), p.7.

peace of mind of his Country.' A coming-out party could even be held on his release.

Consequently, every American would be granted his chance for public confession, and every citizen, not just the fortunate traitors, would have the glorious opportunity to Open his Heart. Since our society inspects and 'clears' elevators, dogs, foodstuffs, and automobiles beforehand, why should it not do the same for its citizens? Then everyone would be able to know where everyone else stands, acts, and thinks. 'A sense of Confidence and Mutual Trust will once more flow into the Land.'

The author of 'A Modest Proposal For Pacifying The Public Temper' could not easily deny that his opinion of the Committee before which he was currently sitting was something less than reverent.

Having established Miller's antipathy to HUAC, Arens returned to his associations with Communist front activities.

'Do you know a person by the name of Sue Warren?' he asked, and the writer replied that he could not recall at that moment. Arens did not hesitate.

'Do you know or have you known a person by the name of Arnaud D'Usseau?'

He paused dramatically, eyed the playwright closely, and, emphasizing each letter, spelled out the name of the co-author of *Tomorrow the World*, one of the notable dramas of the 1943 Broadway season. Arens' intent was crystal clear now, and Miller could sense the tension in and around him as he waited for the question that he knew was inevitable.

'I have met him,' he answered.

'What was the nature of your activity in connection with Arnaud D'Usseau?'

'Just what is the point?' The writer was biding time; he knew what the point was.

'Have you been in any Communist party sessions with Arnaud D'Usseau?'

'I was present at meetings of Communist party writers in 1947,' Miller replied, 'about five or six meetings.'

'Where were those meetings held?'

'They were held in someone's apartment. I don't know who it was.'

'Were those closed party meetings?'

'I wouldn't be able to tell you that.'

'Was anyone there who, to your knowledge, was not a Communist?'

'I wouldn't know that,' the playwright answered as he readied himself for the next question.

'Have you ever made application for membership in the Communist party?'

Although his face remained impassive, Miller was surprised. Arens had let it go by. As he tried to analyze the counsel's reasoning, he replied to the question.

'In 1939 I believe it was, or in 1940, I went to attend a Marxist study course in the vacant store open to the street in my neighborhood in Brooklyn. I there signed some form or another.'

Arens was persistent. 'That was an application for membership in the Communist Party, was it not?'

'I would not say that.' Then, realizing the evasiveness of his rejoinder, Miller added: 'I am here to tell you what I know.'

Arens did not attempt to conceal the exasperation in his voice. 'Tell us what you know,' he said impatiently.

'This is now sixteen years ago. That is half a lifetime away. I don't recall and I haven't been able to recall, and, if I could, I would tell you the exact nature of that application. I understood then that this was to be, as I have said, a study course. I was there for about three or four times perhaps. It was of no interest to me and I didn't return.'

'Who invited you to attend?'

'I wouldn't remember. It was a long time ago.'

Now the playwright could sense the warning alarm again. He was not surprised when Arens shifted the topic back to the meetings of Communist party writers in 1947.

'I was by then a well-known writer,' Miller explained. 'I had written *All My Sons*, a novel, *Focus*, and a book of reportage about Ernie Pyle and my work with him on attempting to make the picture *The Story of G.I. Joe*. I did the research for that, so that by the time I was quite well known, and I attended these meetings in order to locate my ideas in relation to Marxism because I had been assailed for years by all kinds of interpretations of what Communism was, what Marxism was, and I went there to discover where I stood finally and completely, and I listened and said very little, I think, the four or five times—'

Arens cut in. 'Could I just interject this question so that we have it in the proper chronology? What occasioned your presence? Who invited you there?'

'I couldn't tell you. I don't know.' But even as he replied Miller knew what the next question would be. This time there was no mistaking it.

Arens faced the tall, lean man before him. 'Can you tell us,' he inquired almost casually, 'who was there when you walked into the room?'

The Committee Room was very quiet. Miller let the meaning of the question soak in; then he turned to Chairman Walter.

'Mr Chairman,' he began, 'I understand the philosophy behind this question and I want you to understand mine. When I say this I want you to understand that I am not protecting the Communists or the Communist party. I am trying to and I will protect my sense of myself. I could not use the name of another person and bring trouble on him.'

He paused for only a moment.

'These were writers, poets, as far as I could see, and the life of a writer, despite what it sometimes seems, is pretty tough. I wouldn't make it tougher for anybody.'

Even as he spoke, anyone in the chamber familiar with *The Crucible* was aware of the irony of a situation in which life was reversing the standard procedure by imitating art. All the dramatist needed to add was Proctor's line: 'I like not to spoil their names.' Instead, he chose his final words carefully.

'I ask you not to ask me that question,' he concluded.

But the question had already been asked, and Miller was quite aware of it. He turned to confer with Joseph Rauh, then turned back to the Committee.

'I will tell you anything about myself, as I have,' he reiterated.

However Arens would not be denied. 'These were Communist party meeetings, were they not?' he asked sharply.

'I will be perfectly frank with you about anything relating to my activities,' Miller replied. 'I take the responsibility for everything I have ever done, but I cannot take responsibility for another human being.'

Arens bored in again. 'This record shows, does it not, Mr Miller, that these were Communist party meetings?'

After a second conference with his counsel, the playwright stated that he understood the participants to be Communist writers who were meeting regularly.

But Arens was growing impatient with the duel in semantics, and asked Representative Walter to direct the witness to reply to the question concerning whom he saw at the meetings. His request was immediately supported by Representative Donald Jackson of California, who cut in before the Chairman could reply.

'May I say,' he exclaimed, 'that moral scruples, however laudable, do not constitute legal reason for refusing to answer the question. I certainly endorse the request for direction.'

Walter then directed Miller to answer Arens' question, but after again conferring with Rauh, the playwright asked the Chairman to postpone it until the rest of the testimony was completed and he could gauge its relevance.

'Of course, you can do that,' Representative Walter replied. 'but I understand that this is about the end of the hearing.'

It was. Arens asked another question about Miller's knowledge of D'Usseau's chairmanship of the meetings they had attended, and the writer again refused to answer. The Committee counsel then made a few more inquiries, as did Representatives Scherer and Doyle, and Miller briefly reiterated his literary relationship to Marxism. Finally the session concluded with a wish and a warning. The wish came from Representative Doyle who asked the playwright why he did not 'direct some of that magnificent ability . . . to fighting against well-known Communist subversive conspiracies in our country and in the world,' and why he did not channel his 'magnificent talents to that, in part . . . more positively.'

Miller replied that he 'would like more than anything else in the world to make positive my plays, and I intend to do so before I finish.' But, he noted, the effort would have to be made 'on the basis of reality.'

The warning came from Chairman Walter, who advised the dramatist that he risked a possible contempt citation for refusing to answer counsel Arens' questions. The meeting was then adjourned.

Six days later the Committee voted to allow Miller ten days in which to answer the questions concerning the presence of Arnaud D'Usseau and others at the Communist party meetings the playwright had attended, or face citation for contempt of Congress. Ten days after the ultimatum, Miller married Marilyn Monroe, and on July 6 was finally issued the controversial passport. Before he and his wife left for London, he sent the following letter to Chairman Walter:

I know myself to be a person devoted to democratic institutions and opposed to totalitarianism. The meetings in question occurred nearly ten years ago. At that time the Communist Party, as far as I was aware, had not been declared a conspiracy, but was legally recognized and accorded the privileges of a political party. . . . On the ground of their participating in illegal actions, therefore, I cannot justify myself in naming these people. But in addition, the five or six whose names I know are, to my knowledge, as they were at the time, free-lance writers or minor figures in the theatrical world and they have had no governmental or industrial function.[11]

Walter's reply was brief and to the point:
'If that's his answer to the opportunity offered by the committee to avoid contempt then it seems to me he is inviting it.'

On the tenth of July, in closed session the Committee voted unanimously to cite Miller for contempt of Congress, and sent its recommendation to the House of Representatives, where it evoked some spirited albeit vain debate. Emanuel Celler, Democratic Representative from New York, made the most impassioned plea in behalf of the playwright when he warned his colleagues that 'we seriously indict ourselves if we pass this bill of indictment. . . . A Miller is not born every day. A Miller comes rarely. Do we foster talent, the type he has, by way of jail?'

Apparently the majority of the House either felt jail would be a character-building experience or were simply in no mood to play patron to the arts. The contempt citation was ratified by a lopsided vote of 373 to 9 and sent on to the Justice Department for probable prosecution. The wheels of the Justice Department ground slowly but exceedingly fine, and on the eighteenth of February, 1957, Miller was indicted on two charges of contempt: refusing to acknowledge whether Arnaud D'Usseau was chairman of the meetings of the Communist party sessions Miller had attended, and refusing to name other individuals who were present at those meetings.

[11] Miller, quoted in *New York Times*, July 11, 1956.

With his trial scheduled for May 14, the dramatist still refused to repent. On the seventh of May he addressed the National Assembly of the Author's League of America and promptly scored the State Department bans on communication between artists and scholars of nations ideologically at odds with each other.

I believe that once we assent to the idea that high policy alone is sacred, and that every other value can easily be sacrificed to it, we shall have abdicated our independence as writers and citizens. I believe we have by silence given this consent, and by silence helped to raise the state to a kind of power over all of us which it cannot have without crippling the soul of art and the people themselves. The mission of the written word is not to buttress high policy but to proclaim the truth, the truth for whose lack we must surely die; it is a mission not lightly to be cast aside for temporary advantage.[12]

Although such statements showed the playwright ready and willing to go to court, in the light of the publicity surrounding it Miller's trial was decidedly anticlimactic. The highly advertised drama opened with great expectations that the new Mrs Miller would be in attendance, and newspapers and magazines sent extra reporters, feature writers, and sketch artists to Federal District Court in Washington, D.C. in open-mouthed anticipation of the beautiful star and the garish human interest articles she would evoke. But Marilyn Monroe did not appear, and, as the *New York Times* sadly reported, 'instead of seeing a glamorous actress, the spectators listened to arid discussions of legal issues.'[13]

The trial was presided over by Judge Charles F. McLaughlin, with Joseph L. Rauh, Jr, representing the defendant, and Assistant United States District Attorney William Hitz, the prosecution. No jury was empaneled because McLaughlin had ruled in pretrial motions that the sole issue involved was a question of law for the courts to decide, rather than of fact for submission to a jury.

The trial turned out to be strictly a lawyers' show. This was to be a matter of interpretation, without a jury, and as was generally the rule in such cases, Miller would not be called to testify. And whichever side won, the other was certain to appeal the verdict

[12] Miller, quoted in *New York Times*, May 8, 1957.
[13] *New York Times*, May 15, 1957.

to a higher court. So while the attorneys fenced over Constitutional fine points, admission of documents into evidence, and the defendant's prior testimony, Miller coolly watched the proceedings.

Dressed in a black silk suit and white shirt, he reclined his long frame in a small green leather swivel chair, with his chin cradled in his left hand and his forefinger pressed against his cheek. His face was impassive and his manner remote, as if he were sitting in a darkened theater, judging an amateur theatrical. Even when Rauh eloquently and passionately read Miller's reply to the Committee question as to why his plays were so gloomy and depressing— 'I reflect what my heart tells me from the society around me. We are living in a time when there is great uncertainty in this country. It is not a Communist idea. . . . I love this country, I think, as much as any man, and it is because I see things that I think traduce certainly the values that have been in this country, that I speak'—the playwright's visage remained inscrutable. Only during a recess did he open up and apprise Rauh of his performance.

'Pretty hammy,' he grinned.

During the breaks, Miller paced alone in the corridor and smoked; and significantly, the reporters who were assigned to the trial stood at a distance. No one approached him for interviews or even passing comments, as if each respected his right to privacy, perhaps realizing that after all it was precisely this right that was at the core of the particular drama he was witnessing.

Pertinency was the major issue over which the attorneys clashed. Rauh contended that it was clearly lacking since there was no evidence that the persons who had been present at the meetings attended by Miller had been involved in misuse of passports or in obtaining them by misrepresentation. He contended that in calling the playwright as a witness, the Committee wanted essentially to punish Miller for his past criticisms of it. Hitz claimed pertinency, contending that the Committee had the power to determine the extent, nature, and scope of the Communist movement, and was thus properly investigating misuse of passports when Miller had testified.

Judge McLaughlin agreed with the Assistant United States District Attorney. After concluding the trial on May 23, he handed down his decision a week later and found the writer guilty of contempt of Congress on both counts stipulated in the indictment.

As the basis for his decision he ruled that the Committee had met the requirement of having valid legislative purpose for its hearing.

'Since the Congress has power to legislate concerning passports,' the Judge affirmed, 'it is evident that Congress had the right to investigate the subject of passports.'

He further stated that Communist sympathizers had used passports unlawfully, that Miller had held a passport in 1947, that he had been denied one in 1954, and that one was pending for him at the time of the hearing. Thus, 'in the circumstances, an inquiry directed to the defendant as to the identity of the Communist party writers with whom he foregathered for discussions of the works of Communist writers would seem to be one logically calculated to produce information which could be of assistance to the committee in connection with its investigation of communistic passport activities in relation to the aforementioned matter of legislative concern.'

Referring to Miller's reason for refusing to answer, the Judge noted that 'however commendable may be regarded the motive of the defendant in refusing to disclose the identity or the official position of another with whom he was in association, lest said disclosure might bring trouble on him, that motive and that refusal have been removed from this court's consideration.'[14]

But even before the playwright received his sentence, the machinery that would eventually overrule it was already in motion. On the seventeenth of June, the United States Supreme Court ruled that the conviction on contempt of Congress charges of one John T. Watkins, a labor leader, for refusal to answer Investigating Committee questions about his former associates, be set aside. The Court's decision stated that Congress had not been specific enough in outlining the jurisdiction of the Committee, and further held that a witness before a Congressional committee had a right to know why the questions put to him were pertinent.

On the basis of the new ruling, Rauh promptly moved for dismissal of the charges against his client. Asserting that the decision 'fits the Miller case like a glove . . . even more clearly than it fits the Watkins case,' Rauh filed a memorandum in which he stated that 'the Supreme Court has now made it unmistakably clear

[14] Judge Charles F. McLaughlin, quoted in *New York Times*, June 1, 1957.

that a witness before a Congressional committee does not have to plead the Fifth Amendment to avoid informing on others. . . . In accommodating the "protected freedoms" under the Bill of Rights with the Congressional need for legislative information, the First Amendment rights of speech, press, and association have once again regained their preferred status. To force [Miller] into additional legal proceedings to clear himself would be to harass him further for exercising the very rights expressly recognized yesterday by the Supreme Court of the United States.'[15]

Confronted by Rauh's appeal, Judge McLaughlin reaffirmed his conviction of the dramatist, but reversed himself on the second of the two counts on which he had previously found Miller guilty. Upholding his ruling on the playwright's refusal to name names, the Judge noted that Miller had not raised the issue of pertinency but instead gave reasons of conscience for not replying.

'Under the circumstances,' McLaughlin observed, 'the committee was under no requirement to state to the defendant the manner in which the propounded question was pertinent to the subject under inquiry at the time.'

Reversing the second count, the Judge ruled that Miller had challenged the committee specifically on the point when asked if Arnaud D'Usseau had been chairman of the meetings he attended.

'Objection was made by the defendant that the question asked by the committee was not pertinent to the inquiry as to whether defendant should have a passport. . . . The subcommittee did not, thereupon, comply with the requirement laid down in Watkins by stating to the defendant the manner in which the propounded question was pertinent to the subject under inquiry.'[16]

On the nineteenth of July, Miller was fined $500 and given a suspended one-month jail sentence. Although this was a considerable reduction from the maximum penalty of $1000 and one year in jail, it made no difference to him. He was not interested in the money or the time. His concern was the verdict. That was at the core of the issue, and he wanted nothing less than its complete reversal.

A year later he got it. The nine-man Court of Appeals unani-

---

[15] Joseph L. Rauh, Jr, as quoted in *New York Herald Tribune,* June 19, 1957.

[16] McLaughlin, quoted in *New York Times,* June 29, 1957.

mously held that the House Committee on Un-American Activities had not sufficiently warned the playwright of the risk of contempt if he refused to answer its questions. On the eighth of April, 1958, the day of his acquittal, Miller made a formal statement to the press:

> The decision has made the long struggle of the past few years fully worth while. . . . I can only hope that the decision will make some small contribution toward eliminating the excesses of Congressional committees, and particularly toward stopping the inhuman practice of making witnesses inform on long past friends and acquaintances.[17]

However, even as he issued the comment, Miller knew that the decision, gratifying as it was, did not really cut to the heart of the matter for him. He had been acquitted on a matter of legal procedure because he had not been sufficiently forewarned of the penalty for refusing to answer the questions. But he had known of the penalties even before he stepped into the Committee chambers. And knowing, he had decided from the beginning that he would never inform.

> Nobody wants to be a hero . . . but in every man there is something he cannot give up and still remain himself—a core, an identity, a thing that is summed up for him by the sound of his own name on his own ears. If he gives that up, he becomes a different man, not himself.

In a time when men and women were being enticed and coerced into giving up their cores and identities, the author of *The Crucible* remained himself. It was a knowledge and a victory that reached far beyond any court decision.

[17] Miller, quoted in *New York Times*, August 8, 1958.

14

'I'll come back sometime.

I'll visit you'

'The play is memory.'

So says Tom Wingfield of the story he is about to unfold in Tennessee Williams' *The Glass Menagerie*. So, too, might Bert say of the tale he tells in *A Memory of Two Mondays*. The similarity between the two dramas is striking. In both plays the characters are caught in the most ordinary and awful of human situations: attempting to exist meaningfully in a world which allows them no sensible reason for either existence or meaning.

Each play is about hope attempted and deferred, and in each, one character manages, however dubiously, to break out of the trap of deadening routine. But the break is neither conclusive nor complete, and both escapees, Tom Wingfield and Bert, carry their memories with them, more faithful—as Tom reminds himself— than they thought they would be. Each returns to his past in memoriam and with love, and each offers a final, mournful salute, as Tom's sister Laura blows out her candles and Bert's friend Kenneth concludes his song.

Moreover, each narrator speaks in great part for his author. Although Bert is no more an unerring autobiographical portrait of Miller than Tom is of Williams, both characters recall events based upon the playwrights' lives. Tom Wingfield remembers a family conflict similar to Williams' in St Louis during the Depression, and Bert evokes the memory of the year and a half Miller worked in an automobile parts warehouse in Manhattan during the same bleak decade.

Like Miller, Bert is working in the warehouse to earn enough money to get to college. Like Miller, he becomes attached to the people with whom he works, gradually coming to know them and sharing their troubles, joys, hopes, and disillusionments. And then, following his author's footsteps, he leaves. On the morning of his departure he expects some kind of significant moment, a sign perhaps that his presence has meant something to his friends; but lost in their personal problems and the deadening morass of routine, they barely notice him. Bert steps out of one existence and into another without a single clarion call heralding the momentous event. And the play is over.

Because *A Memory of Two Mondays* is shaped by Bert's memory, the play is not wholly realistic. The recollections of the warehouse and its inhabitants are not as feverishly subjective as those which flicker through Willy Loman's distraught mind, but characters and incidents are dramatized as they are impressed upon Bert's consciousness; and when he chooses to stop the flow of memory and comment upon it, he simply does so, once in the middle of the play, as an interlude between the two Mondays he is recalling, and again toward the end of the drama, as a kind of premature coda. And since the play is memory, it advances less by plot than by a series of seemingly random incidents and casual relationships. But its apparently loose form is deceptive. *A Memory of Two Mondays* is no more an arbitrary collection of characters and events than are *Uncle Vanya* and *The Cherry Orchard*.* Beneath the outward aimlessness of its action is a tight, carefully conceived structure.

Although the first Monday is set in midsummer and the second in winter, their chronology is blurred. We do not know if the winter belongs to the same year as the preceding summer or to the following year. The two days are structured laterally, set parallel to each other like two railroad tracks, never touching yet integrally related as they move off toward eternity. The time sequence between them is not measured in hours or weeks but in the period it has taken Bert to earn his first semester's tuition at college. The transition is made as the first Monday draws to a close.

Bert and Kenneth decide to wash the incredibly filthy windows

---

* *A Memory of Two Mondays* is the most Chekhovian of Miller's plays. In its arrival-departure structure it is quite similar to the time pattern of Chekhov's dramas. And even more significantly, in its consideration of human attrition in the ceaseless ebb and flow of time it strikes a thematic chord that reverberates in all four of Chekhov's major plays.

of the warehouse. As they do, summer light flows into the room, followed gradually by the harder and colder light of winter. While Kenneth continues to wipe the windows, Bert moves out of the action for a moment and soliloquizes about the awesome eternality of the lives that surround and affect his:

> There's something so terrible here!
> There always was, and I don't know what.
> Gus, and Agnes, and Tommy and Larry, Jim and Patricia—
> Why does it make me so sad to see them every morning?
> It's like the subway;
> Every day I see the same people getting on
> And the same people getting off,
> And all that happens is that they get older. God!
> Sometimes it scares me; like all of us in the world
> Were riding back and forth across a great big room,
> From wall to wall and back again,
> And no end ever! Just no end![1]

Bert's lyrical contemplation signals the interlude between the two Mondays, and also provides the central image of the play while illuminating its meaning. Much less pertinent is the young man's second verse soliloquy toward the end. Although it exhibits Bert's adolescent self-consciousness ('Gee, it's peculiar to leave a place, forever! . . . They'll forget my name, and mix me up with another boy who worked here once, and went. Gee, it's a mystery!'), it too bluntly reemphasizes what the entire movement of the drama has already clarified. Like Linda Loman's little-men-also-suffer speech, it is sentimental but superfluous.

If, at the conclusion, Bert's departure remains unheralded, it is nevertheless the most positive action in the drama. It is both an escape from calcification and a movement toward an objective. From the beginning of the play, Bert is differentiated from the others by his youthful aspirations and his unassuming persistence in seeing them realized. Kenneth points to these differences when he conjectures that Bert must have 'some strong idea in his mind.'

'That's the thing, y'know,' he affirms in the poignant awareness of his own weakness. 'I often conceive them myself, but I'm all the

---

[1] Miller, 'A Memory of Two Mondays,' *Collected Plays*, p.358.

time losin' them, though. It's the holdin' on—that's what does it. You can almost see it in him, y'know? He's holdin' on to something.'[2]

Unobtrusively, even shyly, Bert is doing just that. He is stronger than the rest of them. He has his goal, and the play traces his approach toward it by contrasting him with the others who 'often conceive' goals, but are 'all the time losin' them.'

In one respect Bert resembles other Miller protagonists: he is on a quest for knowledge. Its literal manifestation is the college education for which he is working, but his instruction has already begun in the warehouse to which he has become so ambivalently attached. Bert's is the story of a boy's initiation into maturity, the bumpy voyage from the deceptive surety of innocence to the doubt and anguish bred of experience.

In another respect, Bert is markedly dissimilar to the usual Miller hero. The knowledge he gains is not so much an understanding of himself as it is the most tentative kind of intuition into the lives of the people with whom he has spent the past year. It is entirely fitting that at the end of the play Bert should come to no conclusions or resolutions about life, other than the realization that it is indeed a mystery. He leaves appropriately bewildered, and yet in his confusion he has quietly but emphatically taken the first important step in his education.

Interestingly, Miller has expressed astonishment that *A Memory of Two Mondays* was interpreted by many viewers as 'something utterly sad and hopeless as a comment on life.' Although he acknowledged the raucous despair of most of Bert's co-workers, the playwright nevertheless pointed to his protagonist as a manifestation of the affirmative in man.

' After all, from this endless, timeless, will-less environment,' he argued, 'a boy emerges who will not accept its defeat or its mood as final, and literally takes himself off on a quest for a higher gratification.'[3]

Even though Miller's point about Bert is well taken, with respect to the play as a whole it is somewhat misleading. He may want us to focus our attention on Bert, but it is difficult to do so. The shyness, unobtrusiveness, and bewilderment which render the boy

[2] *Ibid.*, p.341.

[3] Miller, 'Introduction,' *Collected Plays*, p.49.

such a perfect evocation of youth on the verge of maturity, simultaneously mitigate his dynamism as the protagonist. For all his genuine strength and promise, he is dramatically the most passive character in the play.

Consequently, it is not so much the affirmation implied in Bert's escape which remains imprinted on the audience's memory, as it is 'the endless, timeless, will-less environment' and the despair of those frustrated souls who stumble through it. We remember the departing Bert, but we recall even more clearly and poignantly those who stay behind: Gus and Larry and Kenneth and Tommy and Agnes and Jimmy and Patricia and Raymond.* Together, like the denizens of *The Lower Depths*, they are the protagonists of *A Memory of Two Mondays*, and through them the play speaks sadly and humorously of change and inertia, hope and despair, life and death—all the aspects of the supreme mystery that Bert is only beginning to comprehend.

The two Mondays which the young man remembers are deceptively similar. The same characters are at the same jobs; their conversations are dotted with the same bits and pieces of repetitious dialogue; some of their jokes and most of their complaints are unchanged; even their wariness of the employer who comes to check on them each of these Mondays has not abated. Nevertheless, changes have taken place, and in two of the relationships they are readily recognizable.

The relationship between Kenneth and Tom Kelly almost completely reverses itself between the two Mondays. Kenneth, the sensitive, poetic young Irishman of the first scene, has begun to deteriorate in the second. He is still sensitive, compassionate, and appealing; but he is now slipping into alcoholism. It is not a marked dissipation, but his constant complaint that he can no longer remember the snatches of poetry which he formerly delighted in reciting is a painful indication of his slow but remorseless descent.

On the other hand, Tom Kelly has risen. The seemingly hopeless drunk of the first scene, teetering on the brink of expulsion from

* Tom Wingfield of *The Glass Menagerie* parallels Bert on this score, too. Although he is the narrator and the individual who has at least literally escaped from the trap his home has become, Tom is etched less clearly in the viewer's memory than the defeated mother and sister who remain eternally behind.

his job, has by some incredible exertion of will pulled himself together and become a respectable teetotaler. There is no precise correlation between the changes in the two men. They are not particularly close friends and there is no indication that they have influenced each other. Nonetheless, emerging out of their reversals is the element that defines each of them and most of their co-workers: a sense of loss.

Kenneth's charm and spontaneity have all but dissolved in a drunken torpor, and Tom, although he has apparently straightened himself out, has become somewhat unbearable, puffed up with an unattractive self-righteousness that contrasts ironically with the inebriate affability of his former self. Larry cuts to the heart of the change when he reminds Tom that he liked him better as an alcoholic.

'I mean it,' he asserts. 'Before, we only had to pick you up all the time; now you got opinions about everything.'

Larry is also a study in loss, and his relationship with Patricia, the girl who works in the outer office, again emphasizes this motif and mood. On the first Monday Larry has just rebelled against his claustrophobic existence by buying a car he cannot afford. He has done so as an act of self-assertion over the protests of his wife, and his brother and sister who are both in debt to him but who never hesitate to remind him of his responsibilities. His casual invitation to Patricia to go driving is a further attempt to reassert his independence, and this new feeling of assurance reaches a peak when Larry rises majestically to the greatest challenge existence in the warehouse has to offer: finding a replacement for an obsolete truck part.

Locating the piece of machinery becomes a mock-heroic quest, and as Larry tells Bert how to find it, the rest of the workers group around him in open-mouthed wonder and respect. For a brief moment, man has chosen to do battle with the mechanized, deterministic jungle around him, to assert his will and conquer the forces that have victimized him.

> Bert. Get the key to the third floor from Miss Molloy. Go up there, and when you open the door you'll see those Model-T mufflers stacked up. . . . Well, go past the mufflers and you'll see a lot of bins going up to the ceiling. They're full of Marmon valves and ignition stuff . . . . Go past them and you'll come to a little corridor, see? At the end of the corridor

is a pile of crates—I think there's some Maxwell differentials in there. Climb over the crates, but don't keep goin', see. Stand on top of the crates and turn right. Then bend down, and there's a bin— No, I tell you, get off the crates, and you can reach behind them, but to the right, and reach into that bin. There's a lot of Locomobile headnuts in there, but way back—you gotta stick your hand way in, see, and you'll find one of these.[4]

This is part search for the Holy Grail, part voyage into the Heart of Darkness, and part descent into Jack Benny's vault. In recent drama its closest parallel is Willy Faroughli's ecstatic triumph over that glittering symbol of modern, mechanized society, the pinball machine, in Saroyan's *The Time of Your Life*. It is Larry's victory over necessity, and the moment is shiningly his.

On the second Monday he is confronted only with defeat. The car has been sold, an affair with Patricia is sputtering to a dismal conclusion, and he is once more between the pincers.

Larry's defeat is also Patricia's. The bright, brassy girl of the first Monday has hardened; the brass has begun to tarnish. There will be more Larrys for her, but without his sincerity. Like Kenneth and Tom, Patricia and Larry have lost some charm, some warmth, and some belief.

The other characters in the play do not change perceptibly. They act on the second Monday as they did on the first. Raymond, the manager, dourly attempts to keep the operation running smoothly; Gus lecherously teases Patricia; Agnes continues her spinsterly giggles and blushes; Jerry and Willy still display their crude efforts at sophistication; Frank the truckdriver still arranges his route so he can stop over with various girl friends strategically interspersed throughout the five boroughs of New York; and Jim loyally and quietly looks after his friend Gus.

But even for those to whom the second Monday is a carbon copy of the first, some measure of defeat is evident. Like a carbon, the second day lacks a freshness and spontaneity, a vitality which marks Bert's first recollections. And although the workers have not undergone marked alterations, they have still experienced loss. They have all grown older, wearier, and more disillusioned. We see them finally by winter light.

[4] Miller, 'A Memory of Two Mondays,' *Collected Plays*, p.351.

Kenneth has cleaned the windows to better view the sky, but instead he has opened onto a neighboring brothel. No one objects to the new vista but Kenneth, and when he complains to his employer about the morally dispiriting effects of such a spectacle, he is told quite matter-of-factly that perhaps he should not have washed the windows. The alternatives in this situation clearly mirror the choices for most of the characters: they must either accustom themselves to the darkness or be prepared to confront the reversals that letting in any light might entail. The majority have already acclimated themselves to the darkness.

Miller has termed *A Memory of Two Mondays* a 'pathetic comedy.' Certainly the strongest effect of the play is the genuine sympathy it evokes for all those who remain behind after Bert's departure. But the pathos of the drama never degenerates into sentimentality. One of the compelling reasons we feel compassion for these people is because they do not ask for it; they do not feel sorry for themselves. Loudly and actively they affirm their existences in that musty community, laughing, crying, even sporadically raging against their woefully circumscribed destinies. And nowhere is this phenomenon more graphically personified than in the character and situation of Gus, the coarse, indomitable old lecher whose vigor and defiance attain almost heroic dimensions.

Gus is actually the man hit hardest by adversity. In the first scene, while he is carousing away a drunken weekend with his friend Jim, his ailing wife dies. In the second scene, although he still makes obscene remarks, chases the girls, and growls defiance at his employer, he is a changed man, racked by the guilt he feels for his wife's death. But although Gus is finally destroyed, he goes down riotously and uncompromisingly on a monumental spree of drunken self-assertion.

He begins by intending to visit his wife's grave, but he never gets there. Instead he buys two fenders to put on an old wreck of a Ford he has picked up somewhere, and he spends the whole weekend lugging them around, until he finally brings them to the warehouse. Then he lashes out in a final rebellion against the accumulated monotony of his life, and stalks out. Drawing all his money out of the bank, he goes on one last great bender, purchasing new clothes, picking up some girls, hiring three taxis (one for himself, one for Jim, and the other to bring up the rear in case of emergency), and making a rum-sodden pilgrimage to every bar he can find. He finally dies in his taxi, amid his girls, in a rather bizarre approximation of Oriental splendor.

However, for all his vitality, bravado, and rebelliousness, Gus is crushed by the tonnage of twenty-two years in the warehouse. His valedictory speech, in which he traces those years in the cars he has serviced, beautifully illuminates his character and the themes of the play. Referring to his boss, he calls out to Bert and the others:

> When Mr Eagle was in high school I was already here. When there was Winston Six I was here. When was Minerva car I was here. When was Stanley Steamer I was here, and Stearns Knight, and Marmon was good car; I was here all them times. I was here first day Raymond come; he was young boy; work hard be manager. When Agnes still think she was gonna get married I was here. When was Locomobile, and Model K Ford and Model N Ford—all them different Fords, and Franklin was good car, Jordan car, Reo car, Pierce Arrow, Cleveland car—all them was good cars. All them times I was here.[5]

'I know,' Bert says sympathetically, and Gus replies, 'You don't know nothing.'

To a great extent he is right. Bert cannot fully comprehend the terrible obsolescence the older man has described. He does not even know why he should be the one fortunate enough to escape Gus's grim inventory.

For all its flamboyance, Gus's death symbolizes the defeat of those who remain; and by contrast to his final blaze of defiance, their corporate demise is marked by its implacable ordinariness. Just as Bert's achievement is unheralded, so is their failure. And it is ironically apropos that their reactions to the young man's departure are even more dulled by the news of Gus's death.

At the end, Bert walks, slowly, almost unwillingly toward the door, while around him there is constant activity. Willy snatches an order slip from the hook; Kenneth wraps a package; Jerry enters, picks up a parcel, and leaves; Jim arrives, drops some goods on the table, and exits; Larry comes in with a container of coffee and checks through some orders; Patricia enters and ambles past Bert to get some fresh air at the window; and Tom bumbles through a pile of goods on the table, checking a package against the order slip in his hand.

Arrivals. Departures. Perpetual motion. And yet the overwhelming staisis as time and circumstance combine to make a mockery of all this effort. Things are sent out, things are received—but nothing is really accomplished, and as the activity continues, time slips away, slowly and imperceptibly narrowing the circumferences of the lives that comprise the existence of that large, pallid room. Only the boy, edging hesitantly and disappointedly toward the door, makes a movement that is not circular and self-defeating.

A Memory of Two Mondays does not fit into any plan that neatly traces the thematic development of Arthur Miller. An almost flawlessly structured play, it shows the dramatist in complete control of his form, but basically departing from the major themes and conflicts that had interested him in the past and would again preoccupy him in future endeavors. The play does not deal with ethical problems; it contains no strong moral conflicts nor does it present the need for self-recognition, free choice, or commitment. It is not about family strife; and it does not pattern itself after a court of inquiry or a trial. It does not advocate, condemn, polemicize, or even judge.

It is elegiac in both form and mood, evoking a tragicomic portrait of human existence as it vacillates between the interrelated poles of death and rebirth. At the conclusion a man dies and a boy sets out on a new life, while in the balance a dozen lives are suspended in a limbo of attrition. But ultimately Bert is not the only one who is resurrected. He promises Kenneth that he will return.

'I'll come back sometime,' he vows. 'I'll visit you.'

The play is the fulfillment of that promise. Bert returns, in love and in sorrow, in respect, and with a certain wonder, with a hail and a farewell. And by so doing, resurrects them all.

'Nothing in this book,' wrote Miller in the Introduction to his *Collected Plays*, 'was written with greater love, and for myself I love nothing printed here better than this play.'

Obviously.

15

'And yet it is better to settle for half,
it must be!'

Audiences settling back in their seats after *A Memory of Two Mondays* were stunningly jolted out of any reveries they may have been indulging when *A View from the Bridge* exploded on them as the second play of the double bill that premiered on the evening of September 29, 1955. Moving at juggernaut speed, the stark and gripping tale of a man propelled to destruction by a passion he can barely comprehend proved to be a sharp contrast to the elegiac memory play that had just preceded it.

The story concerns Eddie Carbone, an Italian-American longshoreman living in the Red Hook section of Brooklyn with his wife Beatrice and his niece Catherine. He has raised the girl from childhood, and now that she is a young woman he is reluctant to part with her. Caught between an overt paternal protectiveness and a covert sexual desire, Eddie twists his life into a perverse knot which soon threatens to strangle Catherine, Beatrice, and two other individuals who are drawn into its loop.

When he shelters Marco and Rodolpho, relatives of Beatrice who have entered the country illegally, Eddie unknowingly pulls the noose tighter. Catherine and Rodolpho fall in love, and Eddie bullishly attempts to destroy their relationship. Finally, when his increasingly frantic efforts to separate them only succeed in driving the boy and girl closer together, he informs on Rodolpho and Marco to the immigration authorities. Denounced by Marco to the neighborhood for dishonoring one of the most inviolable codes of the community, Eddie tries to regain his integrity by challenging his accuser to a fight. In the ensuing combat, he is killed by Marco, and the play slams to its conclusion.

The tale of Eddie Carbone's destruction was initially dramatized in a single act of free verse, with a sharp and clean story line shorn of any material incidental to the central movement. To emphasize this subordination of characterization to action, Miller employed a narrator, a lawyer named Alfieri, whose comments were aimed at defining and clarifying the story. Even the stage setting was conceived with this economy in mind. It consisted of an abstractly austere house, with a platform containing the living room, and a Grecian pediment overhanging the doorway.

Miller has explicitly commented on his reasons for this skeletal form and characterization.

'This version was in one act,' he wrote in the Introduction to his *Collected Plays*, 'because it had seemed to me that the essentials of the dilemma were all that was required, for I wished it to be kept distant from the empathic flood which a realistic portrayal of the same tale and characters might unloose.'[1]

In his introductory essay to the original version of the play, he elaborated further:

I saw the characters purely in terms of action . . . they are a kind of people who, when inactive, have no new significant definition as people. The form of the play, finally, had a special attraction for me because once the decision was made to tell it without an excess line, the play took a harder, more objective shape. In effect, the form announces in the first moments of the play that only that will be told which is cogent, and that this story is the only part of Eddie Carbone's life worth our notice and therefore no effort will be made to draw in elements of his life that are beneath these, the most tense and meaningful of his hours.[2]

And what do the important hours in this life manifest?

The awesomeness of a passion which, despite its contradicting the self-interest of the individual it inhabits, despite every kind of warning, despite even its destruction of the moral beliefs of the individual, proceeds to magnify its power over him until it destroys him.[3]

[1] Miller, 'Introduction,' *Collected Plays,* p.50.

[2] Miller, 'On Social Plays,' *A View from the Bridge* (New York: Viking, 1955), p.18.

[3] Miller, 'Introduction,' *Collected Plays,* p.48.

The intention was bold but the result was botched.

Stripped bare of all dramatic accessories, Eddie Carbone did not so much emerge as his author's 'awesome fact of existence' as he did a kind of dramatic curiosity, whipping himself into a frothing fury, but in a context so rarefied that the froth seemed to be elicited less by the interaction of character and situation than by the playwright's neo-Grecian bubble machine. Attempting to free his hero from the burden of psychosexual realism, Miller came perilously close to liberating him from the human race entirely; and trying to prevent the play from generating the wrong kind of warmth ('the tender emotions, I felt, were being overworked'), he succeeded in frosting it with manufactured ice. Consequently the play had the impact of a speeding iceberg. And the plausibility. After a disappointing New York run, the dramatist revised *A View from the Bridge* for a London production scheduled for the following year. This was the version ultimately included in his *Collected Plays*.

Miller added more realistic detail to the play by fleshing out the Red Hook environment of the Carbones and rewrote most of the dialogue as prose. He developed Eddie's character and drew both Beatrice and Catherine more integrally into their relationships with him. Miller appropriately rendered the Carbones childless and focused with sharper intensity on their triangular involvement with Catherine.

Alfieri's speeches were shortened, toned down, and made more prosaic and personal as the character was drawn more pertinently into the action. Finally, the one-act structure was lengthened and divided into two, with the break coming after Eddie humiliates Rodolpho in a mock boxing lesson, and is subsequently challenged and warned by Marco, who bests him in a chair-lifting contest. The sequence where Marco holds the chair victoriously and menacingly above Eddie's head is a perfect spot to divide the acts. It closes the scene on a wordless but intensely powerful tableau that is both a fitting climax to the first act and a preview of the final scene of the second, in which a knife is substituted for the chair, and one man's triumph becomes the other's destruction.

Most observers found the play improved by the revisions, but a few complained that in its new version, *A View from the Bridge* had lost a purity of form, that 'clear, clean line of Eddie's catastrophe,' which Miller envisioned as the first and dominant image of the drama. One critic, in fact, saw the revised play as a disaster 'blurred by details,' its austerity crumbling into melodrama, and the 'myth' made 'ordinary.'

'And what of that carved structure, majestic in simplicity?' mourned Sheila Huftel in her study, *Arthur Miller: The Burning Glass*, '. . . the focus was destroyed and the rewriting laid the play open to that "empathic flood" from which [Miller] had tried to protect the original. Its proportion was shattered.'[4]

Austerity, however, is not a self-contained virtue. The austerity of *The Crucible* is entirely in keeping with the artistic integrity of the Salem drama. In the initial version of *A View from the Bridge* it was not. Rather than serving as an integral element in the drama's composition, it was an unnecessarily stringent straitjacket forced over it. Inherent in Eddie's story is a strong emotional quality that could plunge the play into lurid melodrama if not skillfully modulated. Undoubtedly a certain amount of distancing between the onstage events and the audience's involvement in them is important for a proper grasp of the play's intentions. But that distance is amply provided by the narrator, Alfieri. To further lengthen the emotional span between drama and spectator is to prevent an empathic flood by drying up the whole river.

From the reaction to the stunning 1965–1966 off-Broadway production of the play, it is safe to say that an audience is still not going to dissolve in sentiment over the remodeled Eddie Carbone. But it does stand a better chance of comprehending him and the meaning of his catastrophe, a meaning that was subverted by the alleged mythical grandeur of the initial drama.

Unfortunately, it is rather simple to confuse mythic pretentiousness with mythic purity. As he began his play, Miller obviously saw himself striving for the latter.

> When I heard this tale first it seemed to me that I had heard it before, very long ago. After a time I thought that it must be some re-enactment of a Greek myth which was ringing a long-buried bell in my own subconscious mind. I have not been able to find such a myth and yet the conviction persists, and for that reason I wished not to interfere with the myth-like march of the tale.[5]

[4] Sheila Huftel, *Arthur Miller: The Burning Glass* (New York: Citadel, 1965), p.158.

[5] Miller, 'On Social Plays,' *A View from the Bridge*, p.17.

There is nothing inherently wrong with a mythlike march as long as the playwright doesn't allow it to become a strut. The original version of *A View from the Bridge* was not only strutting, but with its garish employment of free verse and stage settings that might tolerantly be termed early Greek abstract, it was high-kicking its gilt-edged universality down its audience's collective throat.

Miller's zeal to reenact Euripides in Red Hook was not the only reason for this misguided effort. When the story was first told to him by a longshoreman who had known Eddie Carbone's prototype, its relevance eluded him.

'I could not fit it into myself,' he recalled. 'It existed apart from me and seemed not to express anything within me. Yet it refused to disappear. I wrote it in a mood of experiment—to see what it might mean.'[6]

Not until he saw the play a few times during its initial New York run did the writer begin to perceive its attraction for him. He realized that his fascination with the plight of Carbone was not just due to the purity and mythlike clarity of the action, but to the meaning inherent in it. Finally fitting the play into himself, he recognized that although it was about 'the awesomeness of a passion,' it was no less concerned with the effects of that passion on the mutually interacting relationship between the individual and his society.

> The mind of Eddie Carbone is not comprehensible apart from its relation to his neighborhood, his fellow workers, his social situation. His self-esteem depends upon their estimate of him, and his value is created largely by his fidelity to the code of his culture.[7]

The revised play evolved out of this awareness.

'Once Eddie had been placed squarely in his social context, among his people,' Miller reflected, 'the mythlike feeling of the story emerged of itself, and he could be made more human and less a figure, a force.'[8]

There is still nothing commonplace about Eddie Carbone. He is

[6] Miller, Introduction to Bantam edition of *A View from the Bridge* (New York, 1961), p.vii.

[7] *Ibid.*, p.viii.

[8] *Ibid.*, p.ix.

about as average a longshoreman as Willy Loman is a salesman
or John Proctor a farmer. Without the facts of ordinary life to help
define him, he was little more than a grotesque; with them, his
singularity is not dissipated, but graphically delineated against a
recognizable environment.

The revised drama follows the same arc of Eddie's catastrophe
that the original did. However, the meaning of the play is now not
just rooted in an abstraction, but in an individual and a community.
Alfieri makes this point most cogently in both versions when he
places Eddie in a communal context that is pungently physical and
profoundly moral.

'The fish is in the water,' Miller once remarked of the relationship between man and his social environment, 'and the water is in
the fish.'

The implications of this statement are as pertinent to *A View
from the Bridge* as they are to any of his other plays. To emphasize
the moral environment without creating a physical one is to yank
the fish out of the water and leave him flopping helplessly and
purposelessly on an arid beach. In placing Carbone's story in a
realistic context, Miller did not sidetrack or encumber the action;
he clarified and deepened it.

Because of the violent psychosexual nature of its story, *A View
from the Bridge* has been termed a radical departure from Miller's
dramatic canon. Certainly Eddie Carbone's semiconscious desire
for his niece, his frigidity toward his wife, and the possibility of
his latent homosexuality (his obsession with Rodolpho's 'queer-
ness,' which he attempts to substantiate by humiliating the boy
with a savage kiss, obviously reveals more about Eddie than about
Rodolpho) give greater emphasis to the psychosexual factors than
any previous Miller drama. Nonetheless, it does not make any
sharp thematic digression from *All My Sons, Death of a Salesman,*
and *The Crucible*. Like those of preceding protagonists, Eddie
Carbone's inner crisis does not exist in a psychological vacuum
but is irrevocably welded to his communal being.

In sinning against his society, Eddie resembles Joe Keller. Keller,
however, is much more conscious of why he has sinned, and his
transgression is not directed against his immediate community—
whose morality has helped foster it—but rather toward a more
abstract concept of community implied in the title of his play.
Eddie, on the other hand, breaks a precise and identifiable com-

munal code. But even though he is almost totally unaware of his motivations, his rationalization for his deed is similar to Keller's: each man believes he has acted out of family loyalty.

Nevertheless, because they break unwritten laws embodying values greater than this loyalty, their attempts to retain familial solidarity only succeed in smashing their families to bits. Like Joe Keller, Eddie Carbone ultimately dies for his transgression, but significantly without the illumination that Keller experiences. Although he loses his identity, Eddie does not gain any new consciousness or awareness. In contrast to Joe's final realization that 'they were all my sons,' Eddie can only ask dazedly, 'Why?'

That final question has been cited as proof of Eddie's limited comprehension of the situation he has wrought. To an extent this is true. His inability to perceive the nature of his dilemma is pertinent to Eddie's catastrophe. But the play also hammers home the equally important fact that he gains no new illumination, not just because he is obtuse, but *because there is nothing more for him to learn about his place in his community*. Eddie Carbone has always known the principles of his society and they have always been sacred to him. In the very beginning of the play he shows how deeply these codes are ingrained when he tells Beatrice and Catherine how he feels about sheltering Marco and Rodolpho:

It's an honor, B. I mean it. I was just thinkin' before, comin' home, suppose my father didn't come to this country and I was starvin' like them over there . . . and I had people in America could keep me a couple of months? The man would be honored to lend me a place to sleep.[9]

And he is fully aware of the consequences for breaking these codes. Cautioning Catherine against letting any information leak out about Marco and Rodolpho, he urges Beatrice to tell her about a boy named Vinny Bolzano who informed on one of his relatives.

'Oh it was terrible,' Beatrice recalls. 'He had five brothers and the old father. And they grabbed him in the kitchen and pulled him down the stairs—three flights his head was bouncin' like a coconut. And they spit on him in the street, his own father and his brothers. The whole neighborhood was cryin'.'[10]

[9] Miller, 'A View from the Bridge,' *Collected Plays*, p.383.
[10] *Ibid.*, p.389.

Eddie drives home the moral of the incident when he passes his final judgment on Vinny:

Him? You'll never see him no more, a guy do a thing like that? How's he gonna' show his face? Just remember, kid, you can quicker get back a million dollars that was stole than a word that you gave away.[11]

The ultimate horror of *A View from the Bridge* rises out of the fact that although Eddie understands and fervently accepts the ethics of his community, he still outrages them; and it is to this end that Miller stresses the blind passions that drive the longshoreman to the act of informing—the supreme manifestation of betrayal that strikes at the heart of his society's moral code. Nothing less than an incomprehensible and monstrous force could turn him against a code of behavior with which he has previously identified himself. Thus his betrayal of Rodolpho and Marco does not just prevent them from helping their family in Italy, a grim enough consequence, but even more terrible and central to the meaning of the play, it isolates Eddie from his society, which holds as one of its basic tenets the deep trust and interdependence of its members.*

---

[11] *Ibid.*, p.389.

* In the winter of 1949–50, while *Death of a Salesman* was in the midst of its Broadway run, Miller wrote a film script about longshoremen on the Brooklyn waterfront, a story with 'definite social implications,' which he tentatively titled *The Hook* and readied for production by an independent film company he intended to form with director Elia Kazan and producer Kermit Bloomgarden. But the project bogged down. Miller abandoned the screenplay to adapt *An Enemy of the People*, and his friendship with Kazan was severed when the director testified before the House Committee on Un-American Activities and answered the kinds of questions Miller later refused. Subsequently, both Kazan and Miller presented their respective waterfront dramas: Kazan's, a film collaboration with Budd Schulberg called *On the Waterfront*, and Miller's, *A View from the Bridge*.

Quite a few critics have since noticed that the Kazan-Schulberg film offers as its hero a man who testifies before a congressional committee and names names, and who is heroic precisely because he does speak out and defy the neighborhood code of 'deaf and dumb,' while Miller's play is about an individual whose act of informing is roundly condemned not only by his community, but by his author as well. To imply, as some observers have, that Miller's drama is his personal reply to *On the Waterfront*, makes about as much sense to me as suggesting that *Peyton Place* was written as a rebuttal to *Our Town*. The divergent points of view

At the end of the drama, Eddie is still driven by a passion, but it no longer involves his niece and Rodolpho, whose wedding he is even willing to attend. Marco is the man he is after, Marco, who has cursed and shamed him in front of the community, Marco, who has publicly spat upon the name of Eddie Carbone. When Beatrice begs her husband to tell her what more he wants, he hurls at her the only answer he can.

'I want my name!' he cries. 'Marco's got my name!'

To Eddie, as to John Proctor, the name has a dual significance: it is the symbol of personal integrity and supreme selfhood, but it is also the symbol of a connection, a communion with one's fellow-men, without which the self becomes a vacuum. Eddie Carbone, the hollow man, wants to restore this significance and when Marco challenges him from the street, Eddie spews back his defiance and his final self-justification:

'Yeah, Marco! Eddie Carbone. Eddie Carbone. Eddie Carbone!'

Outside, he faces his antagonist and the rest of the neighborhood, and addresses them:

Maybe he comes to apologize to me. Heh, Marco? For what you said about me in front of the neighborhood? [*He is incensing himself and little bits of laughter even escape him as his eyes are murderous and he cracks his knuckles in his hands with a strange sort of relaxation*]

He knows that ain't right. To do like that? To a man? Which I put my roof over their head and my food in their mouth? Like in the Bible? Strangers I never seen in my whole life? To come out of the water and grab a girl for a passport? To go and take from your own family like from the stable—and

---

do suggest, however, that informing is not a phenomenon that can be analyzed abstractly. Neither drama attempts to do so, and to the extent that each sets the act in a particular context with specific motivations, it validates its premise.

Perhaps the more intriguing difference between the two works is inherent in their titles, which suggest two different lines of perspective. Kazan and Schulberg have focused on the waterfront from within; theirs is the more direct, engaged view. In using the narrator, Miller tries to examine his situation from a more disinterested vantage point.

This comparison offers no value judgments, but it does illuminate a particular strength of each drama. *On the Waterfront*'s power lies in its impassioned immediacy. The ultimate meaning of *A View from the Bridge* is centered in the detachment provided by its narrator's perspective.

never a word to me? And now accusations in the bargain? Wipin' the neighborhood with my name like a dirty rag! I want my name, Marco. Now gimme my name. . . .[12]

At first the statement appears to be a crude form of evasion. In his denunciation of Marco and Rodolpho, Eddie casts himself in the best possible light. Not only does he misinterpret Rodolpho's reasons for wanting to marry Catherine, but he flagrantly omits the two most important pieces of the drama: his own passion for the girl, and the betrayal that it precipitated. To assume, however, that Eddie is simply trying to bluff his way through a painful predicament is to miss the main point behind his words.

Only moments before, when Beatrice pleaded with him to give up Catherine, he cried out to her in shock and horror: 'That's what you think of me—that I would have such a thought?' Not only is Eddie unable to comprehend the motives which have triggered his act of informing, but even more importantly, these reasons have now paled beside the single dominant issue that obsesses him: the question of his honor.

Consequently, his statement before the neighborhood does not exhibit his chicanery, but his adamant loyalty to the communal code. The story Eddie tells is what he believes, what he *must* believe of himself if he is to retain his manhood.

From the moment he made the telephone call to the immigration authorities, he tried to annul his deed. His frantic attempt to save Marco and Rodolpho proved that the man who had betrayed them had been left behind in the phone booth; and by the time Eddie addresses the neighborhood that man is as foreign to him as the boy whose degradation he related to Catherine at the beginning of the play.

Eddie does not mention his victimization of Marco and Rodolpho because it is a sin so monstrous to him, so inherently alien to his concept of himself that he has blocked it out of his mind. He no longer knows nor wants to know why Marco is publicly blackening his name. He understands only that the name has been taken from him and that he must have it back, even at the price of a life—Marco's or his, or both. It is a doomed attempt because not even death can restore the severed bond, and although his demise in his wife's arms manifests a personal reconciliation,

[12] *Ibid.*, p.438.

it starkly illuminates his estragement from the outside world.*

Because in a moment of 'awesome passion' Eddie Carbone did what John Proctor stopped short of doing—yielded his name—his death is markedly different from Proctor's. It comes too late. It is not an affirmation, but a final and terrible act of desperation, a vain attempt to wipe a besmirched slate clean.

Eddie, however, is similar to the adamant New England farmer in one profound respect. Like Proctor, the longshoreman from Red Hook insists on his inviolable self-integrity. Miller defined this insistence years before he created either man, when in his essay 'Tragedy and the Common Man' he spoke of the hypothetical character

> who is ready to lay down his life if need be, to secure one thing—his sense of personal dignity . . . his 'rightful' position in society. Sometimes he is one who has been displaced from it, sometimes one who seeks to attain it for the first time, but the fateful wound from which the inevitable events spiral is *the wound of indignity*, and its dominant force is indignation. Tragedy, then, is the consequence of man's total compulsion to evaluate himself justly.[13]

Eddie Carbone, no less than John Proctor, is compelled to 'evaluate himself justly.' Although he lacks Proctor's higher consciousness, he shares with him—and with Joe Keller and Willie Loman—the intense need to claim what the playwright has termed 'his whole due as a personality,' and this is precisely what Alfieri is talking about in his final address to the audience:

> Most of the time now we settle for half and I like it better. But the truth is holy, and even as I know how wrong he was, and his death useless, I tremble, for I confess that something

---

* In the original version, Eddie dies in Catherine's arms rather than in Beatrice's. The alteration is hardly arbitrary. First, it points to a reconciliation between the husband and wife that is dramatically effective. Moreover, and more significantly, it reemphasizes the point that Miller is making throughout the final scenes: that Eddie's relationship with Catherine has become plainly secondary to his concern with his personal and public sense of respect, a concern in which his kinship to his wife and community would take precedence in his mind over his relationship to his niece.

[13] Miller, 'Tragedy and the Common Man,' The *New York Times*, February 27, 1949, Section 2, p.1. Italics my own.

perversely pure calls to me from his memory—not purely
good, but himself purely, for he allowed himself to be wholly
known and for that I think I will love him more than all my
sensible clients. And yet, it is better to settle for half, it must
be! And so I mourn him—I admit it—with a certain . . .
alarm.[14]

[14] Miller, 'A View from the Bridge,' *Collected Plays,* p.439. In the
original version, Alfieri's speech read as follows:

> Most of the time now we settle for half,
> And I like it better.
> And yet, when the tide is right
> And the green smell of the sea
> Floats in through my window,
> The waves of this bay
> Are the waves against Siracusa,
> And I see a face that suddenly seems carved;
> The eyes look like tunnels
> Leading back toward some ancestral beach
> Where all of us once lived.
> And I wonder at those times
> How much of all of us
> Really lives there yet,
> And when we will truly have moved on,
> On and away from that dark place,
> That world that has fallen to stones?
> This is the end of the story. Good night.

Again the revision is an immense advance over the original. The most
obvious improvement is in the writing. The strained lyricism, of which
'Siracusa' is the most glaring example, has been modified into a stronger,
more supple prose that is attuned to the demands of the story instead of
reclining in some verbal elysium above it.

But of much greater significance is the shift of thematic emphasis. In
his study *Arthur Miller* (New York: Grove, 1961, pp.103—104) Dennis
Welland recognized that while the original curtain speech set Eddie's story
in an historical perspective, the revision emphasized the moral perspective.

In the original, through Alfieri, Miller is stressing two things: the
primitivism still inherent in the human race, and the need for a civilized
society to move beyond the vendetta in settling its problems. Man, Miller
is reminding us, has not really changed all that much since Clytemnestra
helped Agamemnon scrub his back.

Its validity notwithstanding, the point is tangential to Eddie Carbone's
drama. His demonism, not his primitivism, is Eddie's defining characteristic.
He is not simply the embodiment of the atavistic potential in man (if he
were, the play would not require Alfieri, since Marco has already pointed
this out), but of his tragic possibility as well. There is something terrible
about the individual described by Alfieri in the original closing passage.
There is something both terrible *and sublime* about the man he ambivalently eulogizes in the revision. The difference is crucial.

Alfieri knows that society is dependent upon compromise and accommodation for its subsistence. He also knows that there are men like Carbone who cannot settle for half, who must make themselves 'wholly known,' and who—however perversely—are moved by an overwhelming desire for some vital kind of significance. Eddie shares this need with other Miller heroes who inevitably come into conflict with their social orders because in their insistence on claiming their 'whole due as a personality,' they fly in the teeth of any society's most basic demand of the individual: subordination.

The protagonist of *A View from the Bridge* is both frightening in his aberrancy and awesome in his total and irrevocable commitment to his concept of self, and it is this duality to which Alfieri refers when he confesses that 'something perversely pure' calls to him from Eddie's memory—'not purely good, but himself purely.' In Carbone, Miller has created the dark mirror image of John Proctor. Both men clash violently with their societies, but whereas the community in *The Crucible* is the transgressor against the individual's sanctity, in *A View from the Bridge* the protagonist is the violator of the communal codes, which are viewed as just. Consequently the rockbound adamancy which becomes Proctor's salvation can only propel Eddie Carbone to ruin.

A View from the Bridge manifests a deepeningly complex moral outlook on the part of its author. It illuminates his awareness that the total commitment to personal inviolability, which he previously admired almost unqualifiedly, can in extreme situations threaten the complementary allegiance Miller expects of his heroes: the responsibility to others in a world where private and public conscience should be synonymous. In his perverse ability to betray and destroy while remaining 'himself purely,' Eddie marks a departure from the protagonist of *The Crucible*. Concomitantly, by exhibiting the unique relationship between self-commitment and betrayal he vaguely previews Quentin's plight in *After the Fall*. However, Quentin can simultaneously relive and analyze the crucial events of his life. Eddie can only experience them; the comprehension and interpretation is left to Alfieri.

In the original version of the drama, the importance of the engaged narrator was pretentiously exaggerated. In the revision, Miller eliminated the pseudo-universality of his one-man chorus by allowing Alfieri to sound like an intelligent and sensitive immigrant lawyer instead of a floridly inept classical actor. But Alfieri is still a chorus, and his choral function is integral to the purpose of *A View from the Bridge* in a number of respects.

In his opening address to the audience, the multiplicity of his role is defined. He introduces himself as a lawyer:

> A lawyer means the law, and in Sicily, from where their fathers came, the law has not been a friendly idea since the Greeks were beaten. I am inclined to notice the ruins in things, perhaps because I was born in Italy. . . . I only came here when I was twenty-five. In those days, Al Capone, the greatest Carthaginian of all, was learning his trade on these pavements, and Frankie Yale himself was cut precisely in half by a machine gun on the corner of Union Street, two blocks away. Oh, there were many here who were justly shot by unjust men. Justice is very important here.[15]

Alfieri is not an attorney by coincidence. He represents two kinds of law: the state and federal statutes, and the moral and ethical codes within his particular society, tenets which sometimes run counter to the former. As an interpreter of the federal law that demands informing on illegal immigrants, Alfieri tacitly stands apart from the community, but as the mediator between his community's concept of justice and the external legal structure, he belongs. Thus by his profession he is involved in his specific society and yet detached enough to provide a perspective.

'This is Red Hook,' he continues, 'not Sicily.'

> This is the slum that faces the bay on the seaward side of the Brooklyn Bridge. This is the gullet of New York swallowing the tonnage of the world. And now we are quite civilized, quite American. Now we settle for half, and I like it better. I no longer keep a pistol in my filing cabinet. And my practice is entirely unromantic.[16]

The preceding comments set the play in both an historical and moral context. Red Hook, Brooklyn, United States of America: a civilization based of necessity upon 'settling for half,' and benefiting from its concessions.

[15] *Ibid.*, p.379.
[16] *Ibid.*, p.379.

He further sketches in the social setting, stressing the common-place quality of the civilized world with which he is now dealing:

> My wife has warned me, so have my friends; they tell me the people in this neighborhood lack elegance, glamor. After all, who have I dealt with in my life? Longshoremen and their wives, and fathers and grandfathers, compensation cases, evictions, family squabbles—the petty troubles of the poor—

He pauses for a moment as he thinks of the exception, the inevitable exception to the rule of the commonplace:

> and yet . . . every few years there is still a case, and as the parties tell me what the trouble is, the flat air in my office suddenly washes in with the green scent of the sea, the dust in this air is blown away and the thought comes that in some Caesar's year, in Calabria perhaps or on the cliff at Syracuse, another lawyer, quite differently dressed, heard the same complaint and sat there as powerless as I, and watched it run its bloody course.
> This one's name was Eddie Carbone, a longshoreman working the docks from Brooklyn Bridge to the breakwater where the open sea begins.[17]

Alfieri is emphasizing the bridge between present and past, not to fill Eddie's tale with the portent of Greek tragedy, but to illuminate the tragic inevitability of the human condition that permeates man's civilizing tendencies and poses a constant threat to them.

The final lines of Alfieri's opening monologue stress still another element in the story that is characteristic of most of Miller's dramas, the lawyer's feeling of helplessness in the face of Eddie's situation. Later in the play, after the longshoreman has come to request his help, he speaks of it again:

> There are times when you want to spread an alarm, but nothing has happened. I knew, I knew then and there—I could have finished the whole story that afternoon. It wasn't as if there was a mystery to unravel. I could see every step coming, step after step, like a dark figure walking down a hall toward a certain door. I knew where he was heading for, I knew

[17] *Ibid.*, p.379.

where he was going to end. And I sat here many afternoons asking myself why, being an intelligent man, I was so power-less to stop it.[18]

Alfieri manifests the helplessness of ordinary humanity in the path of impending catastrophe.

In Miller's plays, the bedeviled protagonists generally find them-selves beyond the aid of the everyday world. Ultimately unable to find either salvation or damnation within its legal and moral con-fines, they are forced to work their solitary ways through to their respective fates, adhering to laws and judgments often more harsh and inflexible than those established by any ordinary legislative or judicial body.

Alfieri's final and most important function is to provide the articulation and distancing that the play requires. By verbalizing and defining what is inexplicable for Eddie, the narrator constantly reminds the audience that there is more to Carbone's story than the overt spectacle of a confused man blindly driving himself to destruction. By affording the view implied in the drama's title, Alfieri enables us to make the connections between the specific individual and the general human condition he personifies.

Consequently, the problem is not whether the play needs the engaged narrator. Without him *A View from the Bridge* would be about as meaningful as *Our Town* without the Stage Manager and *The Glass Menagerie* without Tom Wingfield. The rub is that even though Alfieri is crucial to the drama and is employed quite adeptly, he cannot totally cope with the obstacle he was created to over-come. He narrows but does not close the gap between the nature of the tale and the intentions of the teller.

Inherent in the events and characters of the story is an intense emotionality. The play is not quite melodrama; it contains no battle between angels of light and angels of darkness. But it does have a strong operatic quality. It is bursting with all the ingredients of an Italianate court revenge drama, and its temperature level blazes considerably above 98.6°.

Aware of this, Miller initially tried to temper the excessive emotionality by stylizing the play's action and poetically high-lighting the role of his narrator. But the action became too remote, Alfieri too prominent and the drama uncomfortably resembled a

[18] *Ibid.*, p.410.

grisly ballet presided over by a pretentiously solemn dance master.

Although the revision is a marked improvement, Alfieri is still somewhat of an anachronism, and he fights a losing battle for audience attention against Eddie Carbone's powerful, lurid story.

The question is not whether Alfieri has the right to tell us that there is more to this tale than the events alone would indicate. He most certainly does, and there most certainly is. The trouble is that the action is so dominant that any attempts to stand beyond it and explain its broader implications is doomed to partial success, at best.

Miller knew that there was more to the story of Eddie Carbone than the skeletal framework of the tale suggested, and in the figure of Alfieri he tried to tell us so. Unfortunately his one-man Aeschylian chorus cannot wholly offset the glaringly Senecan quality of the drama he is interpreting. Consequently, the play never quite attains the balance for which its author strove.

Like Miller's, Alfieri's view may indeed be from the bridge, but the spectator's is eye level down below, and from this vantage point the sound and fury continually threaten to overwhelm the significance.

16

'Everything's always changing, isn't it?'

In the darkened theater the large screen shows Clark Gable and Marilyn Monroe driving by truck through a Nevada night. They have just been through a bitter argument and are now attempting a reconciliation. She snuggles against him and her face is radiant with love and hope.

'If . . . if we weren't afraid!' she exclaims. 'And there could be a child. And we could make it brave. One person in the world who would be brave from the beginning! I was scared to last night. But I'm not so much now. Are you?'[1]

In wordless reply he holds her tightly against him.

'How do you find your way back in the dark?' she asks, and he nods and indicates the star-filled sky before them.

'Just head for that big star straight on,' he answers in the familiar honey-gravel drawl. 'The highway's under it; take us right home.'

The camera pans from their faces, through the windshield, to the sky. The truck's headlights gradually disappear, and all that remains in the soundless night is the heaven full of stars, with one slightly but unmistakably larger than the rest.

An embarrassing cross between the fadeout of Owen Wister's *The Virginian* and the Nativity, the concluding scene of *The Misfits* misfires in two ways. To put it as kindly as possible, it is mawkish. But even more deplorably, it welds a conventional and clichéd happy ending (yes, they're still not *completely* out of the dark, but how can they miss it if they follow that star?) to a story that is one of the blackest and most despairing Arthur Miller has written.

The Misfits *is* about death, literally and figuratively, and in

---

[1] Arthur Miller, *The Misfits* (New York: Viking, 1961), p.132.

actuality there are very few stars to point the way out of the chaos and gloom that permeate the film. It is about death on many levels: the death of a world—the West as it once was—and the death of a myth—the dream of the West as it never quite was; the death of human relationships and the destruction of personal values. On its most elemental level it is about the death of some misfit horses, which symbolizes the figurative demise of some misfit people in a misfit world.

The movement of the film is circular, erratic, and bewildered, mirroring the attempts of its characters to grasp something fixed and durable, something which no longer exists because, as one of them observes, 'everything's always changing, isn't it?' The anguished search for permanence in a world of purposeless flux— this classical western fadeout notwithstanding—is the action of *The Misfits*.

The motion picture was combined from two Miller short stories, 'Please Don't Kill Anything,' and 'The Misfits.'

In the former, a man and a woman walking along a beach pause to watch some fishermen haul in their day's catch. Upset by the sight of dozens of unwanted fish dying helplessly on the sand, the young woman begs her companion to toss them back. Although he is embarrassed, particularly with the amused fishermen watching him, he follows her bidding. But after he has almost cleared the beach, the strange rescue operation is confused by a stray dog who retrieves a fish each time he throws it into the sea.

'There you are,' says the man with bemused irritation. 'This guy was trained to help man; man has to eat and something's got to die. . . .'

And when a minnow slips out of the mouth of the sea robin the girl has been trying to save, he tries to convince her of the predatory facts of life.

'See?' he adds. 'What about *that* little fish? You see? The victims make other victims.'

But his appeal to reason and logic falls on deaf ears.

'Well, hurry,' she urges, 'throw it back anyway.'

She then distracts the dog long enough for him to toss the two remaining fish into the water, and the couple depart, the man glad that he has satisfied her whim, and the girl pleased at the prospect that the rescued sea robins would live to 'see their children grown up!'

This charming and delicately humorous story points directly to the character of Roslyn in *The Misfits*. Its female protagonist shares with Roslyn a marked Schweitzerian reverence for life that avoids oversentimentality because it is admittedly contradictory and irrational. It flies in the face of her companion's rather didactic reasoning, and is refreshing in its innocence and spontaneity. When Roslyn pleads with her lover, Gay, not to kill the rabbits that are scavenging their new garden, and later to release the mustangs he has been hunting, she exhibits this same simplicity and tenderness. However, while the man in the short story 'Please Don't Kill Anything' is not being asked to give up something of himself in granting the girl her wish, Gay is. The stakes are higher in the film, and Roslyn's demands are more urgent, and more central to her relationship with the aging cowboy.

Another similarity between the girl and Roslyn is their tenacity. Beneath their naïveté and wonder, the two women exhibit a strong will and determination. Each gets her way, and Roslyn in particular shows a strength of character not immediately apparent behind her golden femininity, but crucial to her role in the lives of the misfits.

While 'Please Don't Kill Anything' provided the initial conception of Roslyn, the short story with the same name as the film introduced the three men in her life. During June of 1956, while he was in Reno obtaining a divorce from his first wife, Miller accepted the invitation of three cowboys to accompany them on a hunt for misfit horses (so called because they are too small to ride) in the surrounding mountains.

The writer was fascinated by the mechanized routine the cowboys followed. One man flew an old plane into the hills and flushed the horses out, while the other two lassoed and weighed them down with heavy tires attached to the ropes. Then they rounded up the animals to sell them for dog food. Although Miller was repelled by the fate of the horses, he was haunted by the lives of the men who trapped them, and using his companions as prototypes, he wrote a story about three of these last frontiersmen, Gay, Perce, and Guido, on a similar hunt.

These men track the mustangs because the experience seems to them the last exercise by which they can assert their maverick freedom and also make enough money to retain it.

At first, the observation that 'it's better'n wages,' strikes a chord of joyful independence, but as it is repeated throughout the story, it wears down. At the conclusion, with just five horses in tow, including a mare and her colt, the three cowboys manifest little of the rugged frontier spirit to which they so adamantly and pathetically cling. Because the horses are going to be sold by the pound, the men remind themselves to water them so the excess weight will fetch a better price. Then, vaguely embarrassed and frustrated, they return to civilization.

In his film script, Miller blended the two stories together. A woman named Roslyn, who was mentioned as Gay's mistress, was created into a major figure with many of the characteristics of the girl in 'Please Don't Kill Anything.' She is now a divorcée in Reno, who becomes involved with the three cowboys and accompanies them through a series of episodes that dramatize the aimlessness of their lives. Their erratic odyssey in and around Reno culminates in the exhausting mustang hunt described in the short story, and their relationships hit a crescendo as the men and the girl clash over the hunt's causes and consequences.

The tacit leader of the masculine trio is Gay Langland, whom Miller describes as a rather hedonistic, somewhat cynical man who 'cannot follow' but simultaneously 'has no desire to lead.'

> It is always a question of arranging for the next few days . . . beyond that there is only the state, and he knows people all over it. Homeless, he is always home inside his shoes and jeans and shirt, and interested. When he listens, he seems to feel that life is a pageant that is sometimes loud, sometimes soft, sometimes a headshaking absurdity, and sometimes dangerous. It is a pageant with no head and no tail. He listens, he is interested, and like a woodchuck he can go suddenly into the ground and come up later in another place. He needs no guile because he has never required himself to promise anything, so his betrayals are minor and do not cling.[2]

Gay's casual acceptance of the headless and tailless absurdity of life is his prominent characteristic at the beginning of the film. Although puzzled by a world bereft of any purpose, he has not allowed his bewilderment to stymie him.

'Just live,' is his motto, and when he is asked how, he replies:

[2] *Ibid.*, pp.13–14.

'Well . . . you start by going to sleep. Then you get up when you feel like it. Then you scratch yourself, fry some eggs, see what kind of day it is, throw a stone, ride a horse, visit, whistle. . . .'[3]

In the beginning of the story his spontaneous existence provides Gay with an illusory confidence and serenity which draw Roslyn to him, and which contrast starkly with the painful bewilderment of his young friend, Perce Howland.

Like Gay, Perce seems to exhibit a nonchalant and guileless outlook toward life; but where Gay has defined his existence for himself, Perce has not. His bronc-busting is a young man's self-conscious and freewheeling attempt to come to some kind of definition, even if it means breaking his neck in the process. And it is significant that while Roslyn is drawn to Gay's quiet assurance, she is simultaneously attracted to Perce's insecurity and his lavish and rather perilous efforts to overcome it.

Roslyn is also attracted to Guido, the third member of the trio, but theirs is the one relationship which turns sour. An ex-bomber pilot who is now a widower, Guido is steeped in remorse and self-pity.

'How do you get to know somebody?' he asks her. 'I can't make a landing. And I can't get up to God either. Help me.'

But his appeal for comfort emanates from a calculating guile that Gay and Perce noticeably lack. He is a taker, masochistically luxuriating in his self-imposed helplessness, not only eliciting but thriving on the sympathy of others. At first Roslyn extends him that sympathy, but when she perceives the monumental selfishness that lies beneath Guido's scratchings for affection, she can only show contempt.

'You were never sad for anybody in your life, Guido!' she concludes bitterly. 'You only know the sad words! You could blow up the whole world, and all you'd ever feel is sorry for yourself!'

Guido is not a cardboard villain, and in some respects, namely his affability and apparent heartiness, he is rather likable. But in his narcissistic concern with his personal anguish he uses other people. He is more than merely pitiful and selfish, he is also cruel, and as his relationships to the others develop it becomes apparent that this man who thrives on sympathy is willing to give none, either to people or to the horses he hunts with his airplane and gun.

[3] *Ibid.*, p.18

Unlike Gay, Perce, and Roslyn, Guido not only refuses to seek a meaning beyond despair, but actually discovers his stability in a cultivated hopelessness. He is the most lost of the misfits because he has made an absolute of loss, which he worships to the exclusion of all other values.

Loss.

The film traces it on various levels. The myth of the great frontier is moribund; the hope held by Biff Loman that the West is still the panacea for the urban malaise, still synonymous with freedom, independence, and the inherent worth of a man, is now presented as a romantic and hopelessly sentimental dream. In contrast to Biff's rhapsodic description of the power and promise of the wide open spaces—'all I want is out there, waiting for me'—is the sight which greets Roslyn and the men as they accompany Perce to the rodeo:

> A long, gradual curve of highway lies directly ahead, an arc of concrete raised above the valley bottom of white gypsum. At the distant end of the road is a row of wooden buildings and beyond them the mountains piled up like dumps of slag the color of soot. From this distance the desolation is almost supernatural, the mind struggling with the question of why men would ever have settled here.[4]

As *The Misfits* flashes across the screen its images of the bedrock reality beneath the legend—the sterile glitter of Reno, the alkali wastes of the surrounding and encompassing countryside, and the shabby little towns that sprawl like mournful tumbleweeds across it—Biff's ideal is relegated forever to the junk heap of tarnished illusions. And certifying the death of the myth: the shoddy spectacle of the last of the rugged individualists—the American cowboy—hunting mangy horses with airplane, rifle, and rubber tires, to sell them for dog food because 'it's better'n wages.'

But the destruction of the western myth is not the most important loss in *The Misfits*. Beyond the myth there is still the reality of society, family, and self. The family comes in for the playwright's most scathing indictment, with one character after another playing out the motifs of betrayal and loss that mark every familial relationship in the film.

⁴ *Ibid.*, p.56.

Roslyn has been betrayed in both her childhood and marriage by parents and a husband who abrogated their responsibilities toward her. Rather than being precise, the betrayals were characterized by their vagueness, and Roslyn summarizes them in her recollection that although her mother, father, and husband were physically present, they made no efforts to relate to her, 'they weren't . . . *there.*'

Gay's life is also tinged with betrayal, from the bitter memory of his wife's adultery to his impotent rage and sorrow at his children's embarrassed avoidance of him when he accidentally meets them on the street.

Perce's recollections are similarly marked. After his father died in a hunting accident, his mother betrayed her husband's memory and her son's love by quickly marrying a fortune hunter who promptly cheated Perce out of the ownership of his father's ranch. 'Sure enough, the wedding night he turns around and offers me wages. On my own father's place.' And with this confession, the comment that 'it's better'n wages' proves to have a special and bitter meaning for Perce Howland.

Guido differs from the other three in that he is not the betrayed but the betrayer. In his self-absorption he had never fully allowed his wife to share his existence, and he currently uses her death and the death of their stillborn child as a maudlin rationalization for avoiding this admission and sinking more deeply into the bog of self-pity that his life has become.

The stark symbol of the dissolution of loyalty and love that pervades the lives of all four characters is Guido's unfinished house in the desert outside of Reno. Mirroring the family within the society, it is a sepulcher set in an encompassing wasteland, a grim reminder of the past and a mocking challenge to the future.

Just as the skeletal house is the dominant image for the breakdown of the family, Reno is used by Miller as the representation of the society outside of, yet interrelated to, the family. It is gaudy, noisy, valueless, and numb, existing chiefly on the exploitation of human misery, and, like a garish buzzard, feeding off the decay of the family structure.

From the opening scene of the film, in which Guido's truck weaves through its crowded streets, Reno offers illustrations of chaos and ironic contradiction. A woman asks for directions and admits to Guido that 'it's awfully confusin' here.' In a supermarket, another woman with a bag of groceries in one hand pulls at a lever of a slot machine with the other. A young couple gaze tenderly at bridal gowns in a store window next to a door which reads 'Divorce Actions One Flight Up.' And as these images flash by the truck, a local disc jockey brags over the radio that for the third month in a row Reno has topped Las Vegas in the granting of divorces.

'No doubt about it, pardners,' he exults in a nasal twang, 'we are the Divorce Capital of the World.'

The confusion of Reno spills over and is intensified in the ensuing excursions of the three cowboys and the girl. They are continually in motion, riding from town to Guido's house in the desert, then bumping across the sandy wastes to the rodeo and watching Perce experience the convulsive plunging of horses and bulls, subsequently indulging in a night of forced revelry, and finally tapering off in the drunken return to that corpse of a house.

Only in the mustang hunt is the motion centralized, as the project evolves into an almost ritualistic confrontation between man and the stark world of nature from which he hopes to return, not only refreshed but in a sense purified. Miller is using the mystique of the hunt very much the way it has been employed in American literature from Cooper to Hemingway—as a testing and strengthening of character through conflict with a world tougher and more elemental than the complex and debilitating civilization that has become so inimical to any true self-awareness. The sense of unity and self-contained purpose that marks the kinship of Gay, Perce, and Guido as they set off on the hunt recalls similar allegiances and intentions in stories like *The Leatherstocking Tales, Moby Dick, The Bear,* and *The Old Man and the Sea.*

Miller, however, does not allow his heroes to revel in their newly gained equilibrium for long, for in *The Misfits* even this bold confrontation between the individual and the natural world is tainted. The hunt is the final, almost grotesque attempt to cling to the hope that innocence can still be claimed, that some kind of permanence yet exists, and that certain values still are valid.

The mustang hunt is an illusion. It is also a fraud.

Gay tries to rationalize it to Roslyn, and more importantly to himself, when he attempts to link his current actions to those of the past.

'When I started, they used a lot of them I caught. There was mustang blood pullin' all the plows in the West; they couldn't have settled here without somebody caught mustangs for them.'

But he knows this is no longer true.

'It . . . it just got changed around, see? I'm doin' the same thing I ever did. It's just that they . . . they changed it around,' he explains apologetically. 'There was no such thing as a can of dog food in those days. It . . . it was a good thing to do, honey, it was a man's work, and I know how to do it.'[5]

Gay is not to blame because things got changed around; he is still doing what he has always done, and for the same reasons:

'This is how I dance, Roslyn. And if they made somethin' else out of it, well . . . I can't run the world any more than you could. I hunt these horses to keep myself free. That's all.'[6]

But it is not all. When the roundup nets a grand total of seven mustangs, including a mare and her colt, the tawdriness of the proceedings is painfully apparent, and when Gay answers Perce's observation that it 'doesn't make much sense for six,' with the refrain that it is still 'better'n wages,' no further comment is necessary. The statement has evolved into a hollow parody of itself.

It is *not* better than wages, because it *is* wages. Although he has tried to divorce the hunt from its consequences, Gay finds that he cannot. As he gazes at the little band of mustangs and thinks of the fate to which he has condemned them for a few dollars, he is keenly aware of how pitifully 'it got changed around.' The hunt has not freed him from the warped and grasping world; instead it has become part of it. Exploitation, the keynote amid the tinsel of Reno, is also the keynote amid the alkali wastes of the last frontier. Deerslayer may not want to face the fact, but he works for Continental Meatpackers.

The three men do not hunt horses to keep themselves free; they do so to pretend they are free. The hunt is a sham and the deceivers are the deceived. This is the lacerating truth that an enraged Roslyn finally hurls in their faces.

'You liars! All of you! Liars!' she screams after watching them divide their prospective earnings. 'You. With your God's country. Freedom!'

[5] *Ibid.*, p.93.
[6] *Ibid.*, p.94.

Gay tries to cut her short. 'We've had it now, Roslyn,' he warns her.

'You sure did,' she counters, '—more than *you'll* ever know. But you didn't want it. Nobody does. I pity you all. You know everything except what it feels like to be alive, sweet dead men.'[7]

'*She's crazy!*'

Guido's infuriated scream is the only answer she receives, the shrill reply of a man who will not face any truth inimical to his vision. The other two men remain silent, but the searing truth of her words has scorched them. Perce is the first to act, and while Gay is helping Guido repair his plane the young man frees the horses. Gay quickly pursues them and manages to track down a mare and a stallion. Roping the female is no problem but recapturing the stallion erupts into a kicking and clawing battle between the wild horse and the lone man.

This time Gay discards what in his story, *The Bear,* William Faulkner called 'the lifeless mechanicals.' There is no airplane now to flush the horses out of the craggy canyons, no truck to overtake them, and no heavy tires to weigh them down. Just the man and the animal in a contest of strength and cunning; and suddenly, unexpectedly, the conflict takes on the purity and honesty of action and meaning for which Gay has longed.

The battle is rapid, brutal, and exhausting, and when it is over, Gay has won. And with victory, he cuts the stallion and mare loose. When Guido perplexedly asks him why he almost broke his neck trying to catch the horse in the first place, Gay replies: 'Just . . . done it. Don't like nobody makin' up my mind for me, that's all.'

Roslyn has provided the goad and incentive, but Gay has not freed the animals solely for her sake. The combat with the mustang has been a self-contained act—not an exploitation, but a test. And passing it, Gay is reconciled with the horse, with the girl, and most truly, with himself.

Just as Roslyn's condemnation had forced him to look honestly at the deception he was living, his triumph over the renegade stallion frees him to admit the truth beneath this deception:

God damn them all! They changed it. Changed it all around. They smeared it all over with blood, turned it into shit and

[7] *Ibid.,* p.118.

money just like everything else. You know that. I know that. It's just ropin' a dream now. Find some other way to know you're alive . . . if they got another way, any more.[8]

Like preceding Miller heroes, Gay must be pushed beyond what he had considered his limits. He has to experience 'the wound of indignity' before he can arrive at any new comprehension. Gay's knowledge, however, differs from his predecessors'. It is the realization that any kind of certainty is a delusion, and that even the self-integrity that he has momentarily recaptured in his battle with the mustang, can also be illusionary, and cruelly so.

'Oh, Gay, what is there?' Roslyn cries out in bewilderment and desperation. 'Do you know? What is there that stays?'

John Proctor would have replied: the Name. Gay can only answer, 'God knows. Everything I ever see was comin' or goin' away. Same as you. Maybe the only thing is . . . the knowin'.'[9]

The statement is almost a verbatim anticipation of Quentin's anguished comment at the conclusion of *After the Fall*, and if it represents a new awareness it is hardly a cause for rejoicing. What, after all, is the 'knowin'' but the recognition of the terrible impermanence and instability of things, of the individual's isolation and inability to relate meaningfully, and of the absurdity of even trying.

Nevertheless Gay and Roslyn do try. They make a tentative and hopeful effort to move beyond this knowledge and return from the abyss of despair into which Guido has plunged himself. But while the motivation for the attempt is credible, its execution is much too glib. Translated on the screen, the final sequence so resembles the clichéd, rose-tinted fadeout that was once the trademark of Hollywood at its slickest and stickiest that it completely blurs the genuinely poignant quality of their relationship and blunts the development of their story. As the film ends, Gay and Roslyn appear to recapture a kind of innocence, an effect precisely counter to what their experience demands. They should not be returning to Eden, but trying to live in a world after the Fall. And in that world one does not follow large, bright stars to Bethlehem, even on a second coming.

The conclusion is the most obvious but by no means the sole

[8] *Ibid.*, pp.129–130.
[9] *Ibid.*, p.131.

weakness of *The Misfits*. With only a few exceptions the dialogue is the worst Miller has ever written. Vague, self-conscious, often pretentious, it is so misshapenly pregnant with portent that one almost longs for a miscarriage.

Consider the following exercise in generality delivered by Roslyn to her friend Isabelle: 'I don't know anymore. Maybe you're not supposed to believe anything people say. Maybe it's not even fair to them.' To which Isabelle, not to be undone, replies: 'Well ... don't ask me, dear. This world and I have always been strangers —down deep, I mean.'

Somewhat later, Guido and Roslyn prance through one of their pseudophilosophical minuets. 'You really want to live, don't you?' he asks her. 'Doesn't everybody?' she parries. 'No,' he concludes disconsolately, 'I think most of us are just looking for a place to hide and watch it all go by.'

And the final scene's Big Question—' how do you find your way back in the dark?'—almost invites the melodic reply, 'When you walk through a storm, keep your head up high. . . .'

The dialogue is flabby and porous because the characters are for the most part poorly conceived. They are less individuals than they are variations on a theme, more like personifications of ideas than rounded human beings.

Their lack of depth is more obvious in the text than on the screen, because the film was fortunate enough to have four powerful and unique personalities to flesh out the major roles. No one could very well accuse Clark Gable or Marilyn Monroe of vagueness, and Montgomery Clift made something poignant and true out of the young bronc-buster. Perhaps the best acting in the movie was Eli Wallach's as Guido: spreading an ingratiating veneer over the underlying nastiness of the character, Wallach turned him into just the right kind of uneasy combination of sympathetic charm and whining selfishness.

However, without the vitality of these actors, the characters noticeably lack dimension.

The characterization of Roslyn best illustrates this weakness. She is the catalyst of the tale, the idealist who enters the world of the misfits and, although hurt and seeking some kind of meaningful direction herself, shows by her strength, courage, and belief how terribly crippled the others really are. To Gay's hedonistic 'just live' she poses the film's thematic counterpoint—'how can you just live?'—with its implication that life must have definition and meaning.

But who is Roslyn?

She has a vague past and an uncertain future; unfortunately, her present is also marked by obscurity.

She is not so much defined by solid characterization as by the semimagical effects she seems to have on all who cross her path, be they our three heroes or a group of saloon revelers who are hypnotized into adoration as they watch her set some kind of record for paddle ball (granted, the undulating motion of her derriere provides a corporeal rather than spiritual motive for their particular veneration, but the result is still unmistakably reverence).

Increasingly, she elicits verbal bouquets from the new men in her life.

'You're a real beautiful woman. It's . . . almost kind of an honor sittin' next to you. You just shine in my eyes,' gawks Gay in open-mouthed admiration.

'You got something,' confides Guido a little later on, 'that big connection. You're really hooked in; whatever happens to any-body, it happens to you. That's a blessing.'

'How come you got so much trust in your eyes?' Perce asks reverently. 'Do I?' she purrs.

'Like you were just born,' he affirms, obviously never having seen a newborn baby.

As critic Henry Popkin has caustically pointed out, this is 'characterization by compliment,'[10] and it presents us with a symbol rather than an individual. Roslyn shines, trusts, and con-nects; she has what one character terms 'the gift of life.' Mother, child, sister, or wife—just say hello to her and make a wish. Cleavage is lowered and hemline raised, but she is still the Good Fairy. In perhaps the finest acting of her tragically brief career, Marilyn Monroe did her best with Roslyn, but she was struggling to give substance to a shadow.

The Misfits does not lack valid themes. Indeed, it shows a definite and stimulating development in Miller's outlook and thought. But too much of the work is about theme, at the expense of character, and consequently the film is weakest when the actors have their mouths open and strongest when the camera is following

[10] Henry Popkin, 'Arthur Miller Out West,' *Commentary*, 31 (May, 1961), pp.433–436.

their peregrinations. The visual images of Reno, the wasteland outside, the rodeo sequences, and the final grim and gritty mustang hunt, culminating in Gay's duel with the wild stallion—these endow the film with dramatic power.

Whatever the reason, or more accurately, the amalgam of reasons, the best of *The Misfits* belongs to director John Huston, Eli Wallach, Clark Gable, Marilyn Monroe, and Montgomery Clift. Its weakest moments must be placed at the typewriter of the man who wrote the screenplay. Ironically, like the individuals whose story it dramatizes, the motion picture is most accurately defined and summed up by its title.

17

'We are very dangerous!'

One year after America's most celebrated marriage of 1956, *Look* presented a feature article in which the two participants voiced their opinions on their first twelve months together, and on their hopes and ambitions for the future. The interview glowed with sweetness and light.

'When Arthur's parents told me, "Darling at last you have a father and mother," this was the wonderful moment of my life—next to marrying their son,' rhapsodized Marilyn Monroe.[1]

Her husband amply returned the compliment. Professing to be a new man at forty-one, he commented that the past year had been 'the most learning year of my life. I've learned about living from her. . . . It's impossible to have a superficial relationship with her. She's too honest and earthy for anything phoney. She has an enormous sense of play, inventiveness—and unexpectedness—not only as a wife, but as an actress. She could never be dull.'[2]

If Marilyn was not dull, neither was the first year of Arthur Miller's marriage to her. It was enlivened by his lengthy battle with the House Committee on Un-American Activities, and more intimately and painfully it was blemished by the loss of their expected child in a miscarriage. But there were good times, too. The summer of 1957 was spent in Amagansett, a small village near the tip of Long Island, where they relaxed, fished, swam, and drove an old jeep across dusty roads and sandy beaches.

'We even get along in a car,' Marilyn exclaimed. 'He drives, but he doesn't have any sense of direction.'

[1] Jack Hamilton, 'Marilyn's New Life,' *Look*, 21 (October 1, 1957), p.110.

[2] *Ibid.*, p.114.

Looking to the future, Mrs Miller answered questions about her career, in the affirmative. With her husband's blessings she would continue working in films.

'I took her as a serious actress even before I met her,' the playwright added by way of bolstering her resolution. 'I think she's an adroit comedienne, but I also think she might be turned into the greatest tragic actress that can be imagined '[3]

But, she emphasized, her husband's work would take precedence; it would be 'the center of our lives.' And again underscoring her affirmation, Miller confided that he had been preparing a drama that he hoped would be ready for production in the next couple of months.

However, months spilled over into years and no new Arthur Miller play materialized. In *The Prince and the Showgirl, Bus Stop,* and *Some Like It Hot,* Marilyn Monroe began to prove herself the adroit comedienne her husband had visualized, but as her career boomed, his lay dormant. Miller explains that the slump in his writing began before his marriage to Marilyn, but it is clear that it continued throughout the marriage and the tensions and frictions of that relationship. It is difficult to judge whether the halt in his productivity led to his increasing involvement in his wife's career, or vice versa, but he became her unofficial manager during the filming of the *The Prince and the Showgirl,* watching over her and keeping her going during spells of depression and anxiety. This absorption became so deep that in ensuing films he did everything from helping select production stills to choosing her leading men.

When he attempted to return to his writing, he struggled up one blind alley after another. An effort to expand his short story, 'The Misfits,' into a novel was never realized, and a full-length play which had preoccupied him during the first year of the marriage was finally relegated to the waste basket.

As he subordinated his energies to his glamorous wife, the glow of their first months together began to fade. Another attempt to have a child ended in a miscarriage. Bitterness increased as personalities clashed and personal and professional frustrations churned to a boil. She began to distrust his involvement in her affairs. Their life grew more abrasive with each additional pressure, and remorselessly their marriage eroded.

[3] *Ibid.,* p.114.

After Marilyn's second miscarriage, Miller adapted 'The Misfits' into a screenplay and created the character of Roslyn for her. Like the actress, Roslyn was hurt by parental neglect and a broken marriage, and although dazzlingly beautiful, felt lost and confused. Unlike her prototype, Roslyn found her salvation. But the second Mrs Miller, who specialized in happy endings on celluloid, was destined to fall catastrophically short of one in her personal life.

In the early autumn of 1960 the Millers were on location in Nevada for the shooting of the film. The semi-ghost town of Dayton was the locale and served as an appropriate backdrop for the deteriorating final stages of the marriage. During the subsequent filming, the actress broke down and was sent by director John Huston to a hospital for a week's recuperation. She finished her scenes, but with the completion of the movie the termination of the marriage was made official. In November, after their return to New York, Arthur Miller and Marilyn Monroe announced their 'amicable estrangement.' The blandness of the term must have seemed particularly mocking to both of them. A few months later they were divorced.

' Other marriages have survived the goldfish bowl existence that was their lot,' the playwright commented tersely. 'But we've just resigned ourselves to the plain fact that ours didn't work, that's all.'

It was hardly all, as *After The Fall* would indicate, but it was as much as Miller wanted to discuss at the time.

On February 17, 1962, the dramatist married for the third time. His bride was Ingeborg Morath, a thirty-eight-year-old Austrian-born, free-lance photographer. A rather tall, attractive woman with high cheekbones, short brown hair, and deep blue eyes, she was the daughter of research chemists and was educated in Berlin, Budapest and Vienna. Formerly a journalist and critic in Vienna, she also held the position of Austrian bureau chief of the American-owned magazine, *Heute*. After living a while in Paris she married an English journalist and resided in London. By the time her marriage ended in divorce in 1954, she had taken up photography and become a highly skilled professional photographer. On assignment to take rehearsal pictures of the company of *The Misfits*, she met Arthur Miller. A year and a half after they were married, Ingeborg presented her husband with a daughter, whom they named Rebecca.

But between his marriage and the birth of his daughter, Marilyn Monroe reentered Miller's life one last time. On Sunday, August 5, 1962, newspapers, television, and radio headlined the story. The golden girl was dead. The most exciting and celebrated star of her generation, the woman in whom her ex-husband had once noticed 'a spontaneous joy,' had died alone in a sumptuous house that had turned into a drug- and alcohol-ridden cage. Almost two years before her death, the actress had commented on the girl she was portraying in *The Misfits*.

'Well she *knows* a lot more at the end,' Marilyn confided to an interviewer on the set. 'But I think she hasn't anything more of an idea where she is *going* than she had at the beginning.'

The observation could have served as her own epitaph.

Refusing to attend her funeral because it would be like a 'circus,' Miller replied to a reporter's typical request to summarize his life with her.

'How can I capsulize Marilyn?' he answered helplessly. 'The more you know about people the more complex they are to you. They're all writing about her and they can't because they don't know anything about her. They're writing a lot of rubbish. If she were simple, it would have been easy to help her.'[4]

Miller was writing about her, too, but not rubbish. In 1962, prior to her death, he had worked out the main portion of a new play. Although it encompassed semiautobiographical elements from his life with Marilyn Monroe, its antecedents stretched back a number of years to a drama on which he had been working prior to their marriage.

In the summer of 1959 he spoke of being immersed in a project he had begun a few years previously, about 'the present day, about people who lived through the events of the thirties and forties, and are now face to face with their lives in a world they never made. I am trying to define what a human being should be, how he can survive in today's society without having to appear to be a different person from what he basically is.'[5]

In October of 1962, Robert Whitehead, the creator and organizer of the fledgling Repertory Theater of Lincoln Center, announced that Miller had submitted his latest drama to the company as its

---

[4] Miller, quoted in *New York Post*, August 7, 1962.
[5] Miller, quoted in Kenneth Alsop, 'A Conversation with Arthur Miller', *Encounter*, 13 (July, 1959), p.59.

inaugural production. Even as this announcement was made, the playwright was laboriously trimming a mountain of preparatory and exploratory material into a workable script. By the spring of 1963, Elia Kazan, co-director of the Theater, took on the staging of the play. The long-standing coolness between him and Miller had thawed, and the two men began a series of conferences to work out the presentation of the new drama.

As construction began in Greenwich Village on the ANTA Washington Square Theater, which was to be the temporary home for the repertory company until a permanent lodging could be erected at Lincoln Center, Miller and Kazan shaped their ideas for staging the intricate and discursive play. Throughout the summer they met whenever and wherever they could: at the playwright's home in Connecticut, at the Chelsea Hotel in Manhattan, in restaurants, offices, and even in taxis. While the flat, prefabricated shed that would serve as the roof of the new theater rose in view of New York University drama students listening to lectures on *Death of a Salesman* and *The Crucible*, the writer and the director analyzed the characters of the new play, debated motivation, argued over thematic interpretation, and molded stage settings in modeling clay.

On October 24, 1963, the ANTA Theater was still not ready when the cast assembled for the first rehearsal, which would feature Miller's reading of the play. With the triple incentive of the emergence of a new repertory company, the reemergence of a major American dramatist, and the titillating rumors of a scandalously autobiographical peep show, the event was covered by both the television and newspaper media. In a setting that appeared to be a cross between the Sermon on the Mount and Sunday afternoon at Disneyland, the playwright, bombarded by lights and cameras, read the title and intoned the opening stage directions: '*After the Fall*—the action takes place in the mind, thought, and memory of Quentin.'

For a while the distinct possibility loomed that he would get no further, as the television crews requested him to repeat the performance for various camera angles. But finally the lights were dimmed, the cameras switched off, and the microphones packed away. As the reporters scurried off to meet the omnipresent deadlines, Miller and his cast got down to the business at hand. To give the actors the overall concept of the work, he read it through in its entirety in a recitation that began in the late afternoon and lasted into the night. When it was over, Jason Robards, who would portray Quentin, Barbara Loden, who would play Maggie, and the rest of the group knew that the complex and torturous drama would provide a stern test for the new company.

As the project moved into high gear in the autumn of 1963, Miller spent most of his time working with Kazan, production designer Jo Mielziner, and the performers. Even as the play took shape in rehearsals, he continued to mold it, revising and finally completing the second act. Although the ANTA Washington Square Theater was still under construction, the stage area was ready, and in December the company moved in for the final month of preparation, rehearsing by night as the workmen labored by day to finish the building. The race ended in a photo finish.

Miller's first play in almost nine years, *After the Fall* premiered on January 23, 1964 in the midst of a deluge of publicity that all but turned it into the circus that the playwright had tried to escape by avoiding Marilyn Monroe's funeral. Except that this time Miller was accused of staging the spectacle himself, coming neither to praise nor to bury Marilyn, but to exploit her. Just about everyone who wrote a column on the Eastern seaboard had something personal to say, and as a result the drama received a barrage of mixed notices that ranged from the warmest accolades to the bitterest denunciations. The playwright was hailed by a few for returning to the stage in full command of his talent, and castigated by others for indulging in a public display of literary masturbation. After about three weeks of reviews and word-of-mouth publicity, only one thing seemed to be clear: very few persons were bored with the play.

The defense of *After the Fall* was led by the *New York Times'* critic, Howard Taubman, who concluded a highly favorable review, in which he adamantly refused to become embroiled in the drama's autobiographical overtones, by urging his readers to 'rejoice that Arthur Miller is back with a play worthy of his mettle.'[6] Norman Nadel of the New York *World-Telegram & Sun* was equally impressed by the drama's 'fine structure' and 'searing power.'

'It will be a long time,' he wrote, 'before another playwright will

[6] Howard Taubman, The *New York Times*, January 24, 1964, p.18.

reveal more about the form and content of man's selfexamination.'[7]

Richard Watts, writing in the *New York Post,* was less exhilarated than his two colleagues. Although he admitted that the play was 'impressive' and had scenes that were 'powerful and striking,' he found himself generally disappointed with its 'waywardness' and 'self-indulgence.' He then struck the chord which, over the following weeks, would reach symphonic proportions, when he noted that the drama was permeated by 'an air of self-exculpation that grows a little uncomfortable.'[8]

Compared to the broadside leveled against the play by the majority of magazine critics, Mr Watts's review appeared to be a rhapsodic endorsement. Although Theophilus Lewis, writing in *America,* concluded a laudatory critique with the comment that *After the Fall* was 'an electrifying experience,' he stood virtually alone among his colleagues.

More characteristic of the mood of these men was John McCarten's opinion in the *New Yorker* that the play was 'desultory' and 'garrulous.' *Time* refused to treat it as anything but an autobiography and referred to its protagonist as 'Quentin-Miller,' a character who comes off 'badly.' According to *Time,* the drama's ultimate message was nothing more than the advice that 'when life becomes unbearable, find a new woman and start a new life.'[9] Writing in the *New York Herald Tribune*'s *Book Review,* Richard Gilman coldly pronounced the play a 'disastrous failure,' a pretended exorcism that was in reality an exercise in self-justification. Gilman then took out after its author for past failures, and concluded that the trouble with Miller was that he was 'made a god on the strength of one play,' *Death of a Salesman,* and has been trying ever since to live up to his artificial position of 'playwright of passion and ideas.'[10]

But the penultimate of pans was delivered by Robert Brustein from his turret at the *New Republic.* A week before Saint Valentine's Day, bow and arrow in hand, he took dead aim at the drama and twanged away.

[7] Norman Nadel, *The World-Telegram & Sun,* February 3, 1964, p.26.

[8] Richard Watts, Jr, *New York Post,* January 24, 1964, p.38.

[9] *Time,* 83 (January 31, 1964), p.54.

[10] Richard Gilman, *New York Herald Tribune Book Review,* May 8, 1964, p.7.

'*After the Fall,*' he thundered, 'is a three-and-one-half hour breach of taste, a confessional autobiography of embarrassing explicitness,' in which 'Mr Miller is dancing a spiritual striptease while the band plays mea culpa.' Although the playwright might have thought he was universalizing his experience into a parable of guilt and innocence, he only succeeded in creating 'a piece of tabloid gossip, an act of exhibitionism, which makes us all voyeurs.'

And even as titillation, added Mr Brustein, making sure the arrows were firmly embedded, the play was 'wretched . . . shapeless, tedious, overwritten, and confused,' composed of 'endless palaver,' with shallow characterization. While the drama pretended to be revelatory, the 'real discoveries were being concealed or had yet to be made,' and while Miller scourged himself for his inability to love, 'he still conducts an involuntary vendetta against the former objects of his love.'[11]

Thus, concluded the *New Republic*'s drama critic, not only was *After the Fall* a disaster because it was badly written and structured, but also because the playwright's intentions were either unconsciously muddled, or, if he did know what he was doing, downright treacherous.

If this was Brustein's Valentine message, one can only shudder at the contemplation of what he might have said on Halloween.

I have cited the preceding review at some length because to me it reveals how erroneously the play was approached by several ordinarily perceptive and discriminating critics. What is particularly disturbing about the critique (and a number of less ably written commentaries) is firstly its adamant refusal to consider the play as anything but strict autobiography, secondly—and as a corollary to the initial assumption—its conviction that the autobiography is dishonest, and thirdly, the stridently moralistic tone of its condemnation.

After the Fall contains autobiographical elements. Quentin approximates Miller, Maggie, the late Marilyn Monroe, and a number of other characters undoubtedly have their real life counterparts. But the same could be noted of *All My Sons, Death of a Salesman,* and *A Memory of Two Mondays.* Drama cannot be shunted off as invalid simply because it is autobiographical, no matter how

embarrassing the autobiography may be. Ibsen was frankly autobiographical in most of his plays, and many of his characters are
cruel portraits of individuals he knew both intimately and casually.
Chekhov's dramas are peopled with figures out of his personal
experiences. And Strindberg carried on voluntary and involuntary
vendettas against his wives in the majority of his naturalistic
works.

The issue should not be whether a play is autobiographical but
how it utilizes its autobiographical material. If the characters and
situations fit into the framework the dramatist has created for them
they are valid, irrespective of their relationship to 'real life.'

To the charge that *After the Fall* fails to shape its autobiographical material into a meaningful dramatic experience, I can
only ask: Does the play fail its viewer or do some viewers fail
the play by riveting their attention so strongly to the autobiographical overtones that they insist on its subjective incoherence
and shapelessness even in the face of contradictory evidence? Do
they fail, in other words, to trust the tale because they find it simple
and perhaps gratifying to distrust the teller?

'Mr Miller,' wrote critic Brustein, 'is dancing a spiritual striptease while the band plays mea culpa.'

Nice image, but for all its wittiness it manifests precisely the
above feeling. First, the play is assumed to be Miller's compulsive
public confessional, and then it is scored as dishonest whenever
it appears to stray from the straight and narrow autobiographical
guidelines the critic has staked out for it.

The shakiness of this position is evident. *After the Fall* was not
judged on its merits or demerits as a play, but on its adherence
to its author's life, and, even more garishly, to his innermost
motives in dramatizing the events of this life. Consequently a reviewer could feel justified in condemning the 'excessive self-consciousness' of the drama without bothering to ask himself why
Miller's excessive self-consciousness was any more reprehensible
than Strindberg's, Kafka's, Proust's, or O'Neill's.

The most intriguing element in much of the critical response
to *After the Fall* was the moral posturing. Not in recent memory
have I seen a play so strikingly galvanize a goodly number of its
reviewers into shrill defenders of public morality. Nor have I
read so many reviews that in their eagerness to censure a drama
for its breach of taste, proved infinitely more tasteless than their

target. Not only were many of the attacks blatantly unfair, but, even more unfortunately, by harping on *After the Fall*'s gossipy pertinence to its author's life, many critics and viewers wholly missed the genuine stature of the finest play Miller had written since *The Crucible.*

After the Fall dramatizes the story of Quentin, a lawyer who has been living 'merely in the service of [his] success.' Addressing an unidentified 'Listener,' Quentin relives and examines some of the important attachments in his life. He analyzes his relationships with his father, mother, and brother; he recalls his two marriages, the first to Louise, which floundered and broke on the shoals of disinterest and noncommunion and the second to Maggie, which began with high hopes and the quest for love, and ended in hatred, guilt, recrimination, and death; and he remembers an involvement with Felice, a young woman whose idolization of him makes him realize with concurrent pangs of selfishness and shame his power over another person's life.

He also reviews two important friendships: with Lou, a gentle, sensitive professor who committed suicide after being harassed by a congressional investigating committee, and with Mickey, a fellow attorney who did testify and knuckled under to the committee's demands that he inform. And throughout his contemplation of these harrowing relationships, Quentin attempts to discover what bond, if any, exists between himself and the concentration camp whose blasted stone tower remains a focal image in his mind throughout the play.

He probes these relationships because he has come to a moment of painful decision. Having fled from a series of major and minor upheavals, he has finally arrived at a point where he must find himself if he is to marry Holga, the new woman in his life, and make a fresh start with her.

To Quentin at the beginning of the play, existence has proved to be 'pointless litigation . . . before an empty bench. Which is, of course, another way of saying despair.' The rest of the drama is the tortured chronicle of how this man plummeted to such moral and spiritual depths. At the conclusion, after reviewing the wreckage of his life and the lives he has helped to smash, he arrives at the simple but profound realization that love and compassion are not enough, that life—as Holga has tried to tell him earlier—must be taken for the absurdity it is, and that we are—for all our denials—'very dangerous!' And then, wondering if 'the knowing is all,' he attempts to move beyond despair, fearfully but hopefully reaching out to the woman who waits for him.

Because the action takes place 'in the mind, thought, and memory of the protagonist,' the form of *After the Fall* is loose and free-flowing, encompassing psychological rather than chrono-logical time. The play does not unfold in a linear arc but in a series of recollections and associations as Quentin's thoughts glide back and forth in time and space. Everything the audience sees is viewed through the reflector of his memory, and consequently the viewer never gets an objective picture of any of the people in Quentin's life. They are ghosts, phantoms flaring fitfully in the recesses of 'a mind questing over its own surfaces and into its depths.'

This structure is deceptive because superficially it suggests arbitrariness and confusion. Quentin sometimes retreats from certain thoughts and memories; recollections crop up when they are not wanted; often a line of dialogue or a gesture may touch off a whole series of responses and associations; an entire incident may be fully formulated and dramatized in Quentin's mind, or a character may quickly and silently flit across the stage as he is sud-denly sprung loose from the gulf of memory. However, as the drama develops, its movement becomes increasingly centrifugal. With every recollection, Quentin is clarifying the blurred past, ad-justing the lens of his perception, and bringing his life slowly and torturously into sharper focus. The process is familiar. Like the thematic development of all of Miller's dramas, the movement of *After the Fall* is toward deepening awareness and significance.

After the Fall also resembles the majority of Miller's plays in another respect. It is structured as a trial. Quentin speaks to an amorphous Listener who might represent a number of things: he might possibly be a friend of Quentin's, or maybe his analyst, since a nervous breakdown is implied in the initial exposition. He might even be God. However, since the drama unravels within the mind of its protagonist, the Listener can be most reasonably and meaningfully interpreted as Quentin himself, and the conversation as an inner dialogue. The technique of the play is thus psycho-analytical, but as critic William Packard has astutely observed, the psychoanalysis is set 'within a metaphor of law.'[12] Quentin's initial remarks quickly and clearly establish the revelance of this metaphor:

> You know, more and more I think that for many years I looked at life like a case at law, a series of proofs. When you're young you prove how brave you are, or smart; then what a good lover; then, a good father; finally how wise, or powerful or what-the-hell-ever. But underlying it all, I see now, there was a presumption. That I was moving on an upward path toward some elevation, where—God knows what— I would be justified, or even condemned—a verdict anyway. I think now that my disaster really began when I looked up one day—and the bench was empty. No judge in sight. And all that remained was the endless argument with oneself—this pointless litigation of existence before an empty bench.[13]

The drama begins characteristically with a lawyer's opening statement before the bench, albeit an empty one.

Quentin has lost the glib optimism of the young lawyer who prepares a brief with an observable and provable resolution in sight. He can no longer view his existence as a series of proofs leading upward to some kind of surety. But even though he is wryly embarrassed at his smugly legalistic approach of former days he still observes his life through an attorney's eye. He analyzes himself, but in the process turns his examination into a trial in which he is not only both defendant and prosecutor, but judge and jury as well. Actually, investigation would be a better term than trial, since the procedure is not meant to culminate in either absolution or condemnation, but in comprehension.

Although in its dramatization of the processes of a man's mind *After the Fall* bears a structural resemblance to *Death of a Salesman*, the two plays are markedly dissimilar. While both Willy Loman and Quentin are involved in intense searches for comprehension of their lives, Willy's quest is marked by a grim irony: the intensity of his efforts is constantly undermined by the narrowness of his perception. Quentin is far more intelligent, subtle, and conscious than Willy, and as a result his perception is much greater.

---

[13] Miller, *After the Fall* (New York: Viking, 1964), p.3.
This quotation and subsequent ones, unless otherwise specified, are taken from the final revised stage version of the play.

Engaged in a search which by nature is agonizingly personal, Quentin goes about it with an objectivity totally lacking in Miller's anguished salesman. Because of this approach Quentin has been termed cold and detached, and his drama lacking in compassion and genuine feeling. Interestingly these were the same epithets that initially greeted *The Crucible,* and they underscore, I believe, an important problem in coming to terms with both the Salem play and *After the Fall.*

It has been, is, and perhaps always will be easier to grasp and accept a character who undergoes a clearly delineated emotional experience than one whose development is cerebral as well as emotional. The analytical man is generally shunted off as too cold, dispassionate, and withdrawn, and a play centering on him is vulnerable to the critical comment George Jean Nathan made when he found *The Crucible* 'too remote from the heart.'

We do not mind giving our hearts to a character on the stage; on the contrary, we are thankful for the opportunity. Thus, in *After the Fall* we readily embrace Maggie. She is wholly enveloped in her anguish, unwilling and pathetically unable to plumb the meaning of her suffering, and she is certainly not 'remote from the heart.' We feel for her even as we squint uneasily and distrustfully at Quentin. We are perturbed because he will not allow us to touch and comfort him, and we are distrustful because we are not convinced that a man who verbalizes his suffering so distinctly is actually as anguished as he claims to be.

In Pirandello's *Six Characters in Search of an Author,* the Father points unerringly to the plight of Quentin and other articulate but 'remote' protagonists in Miller's dramas when he replies to the Stage Manager's attempts to abort his 'philosophizing.'

> Believe me, I feel what I think; and I seem to be philosophizing only for those who do not think what they feel, because they blind themselves with their own sentiment. I know that for many people this self-blinding seems much more 'human'; but the contrary is really true. For man never reasons so much and becomes so introspective as when he suffers; since he is anxious to get at the cause of his sufferings, to learn who has produced them, and whether it is just or unjust that he should have to bear them. . . . The animals suffer without reasoning about their sufferings. But take the case of a man who suffers and begins to reason about it. Oh no! it

can't be allowed! Let him suffer like an animal, and then—
ah yes, he is 'human!'[14]

Quentin suffers *and* reasons, and if this process renders him
unemotional it is because the audience is measuring emotion with
an empathic footrule. *After the Fall* has a great depth of emotion,
but it extends beyond sentiment and is integrally linked to discovery and self-awareness. Quentin will never elicit the reaction that
Willy Loman does because he is too cognizant of his anguish to
give himself wholly to it, too perceptive to suffer unthinkingly. It
is just about impossible to have a good cry over him because he
asks for more than a purging of the tear ducts. He asks us not just
to feel, but to know *why* we feel. He demands more of us than love
or sympathy; he calls for comprehension. Quentin is aiming not
only at the heart, but at the mind.

Quentin is a man who has fallen from the illusion of grace, the
comfortable certainty of purpose. Leafing through the once tightly
and handsomely bound casebook of his life, he discovers page after
page of loss: the loss of faith, the loss of love, the loss of innocence, and, finally, the loss of identity.

'I've lost the sense of some absolute necessity,' he confesses to
his Listener.

> . . . It sounds foolish, but I feel . . . unblessed. And I keep
> looking back to when there seemed to be some duty in the
> sky. I had a dinner table and a wife—a child and the world
> so wonderfully threatened by injustices I was born to correct!
> It seems so fine! Remember—when there were good people
> and bad people? And how easy it was to tell! The worst
> son of a bitch, if he loved Jews and hated Hitler, he was a
> buddy. Like some kind of paradise compared to this.[15]

But if the world was some kind of paradise, it was an Eden
maintained through a rigorously self-imposed moral blindness.

'Until I begin to look at it,' Quentin confides shamefacedly. 'God,
when I think of what I believed, I want to hide!'

[14] From *Naked Masks: Five Plays* by Luigi Pirandello. Edited by Eric
Bentley. Copyright, 1922, 1952, by E. P. Dutton & Co., Inc. Renewal,
1950, in the names of Stefano, Fausto and Lietta Pirandello. Reprinted by
permission of the publishers, p.267.
[15] Miller, *After the Fall*, p.22.

He then remembers an incident from the past when the wife of his best friend Lou tantalized him by stripping out of a wet bathing suit in his presence. With 'a laugh of great pain,' he cries out to the Listener:

> I tell you I didn't believe she knew she was naked! It's Eden! . . . Well, because she was *married*! How could a woman who can tell when the Budapest String Quartet is playing off key; who refuses to wear silk stockings because the Japanese are invading Manchuria; whose husband, my friend, a saintly professor of law, is editing my first appeal to the Supreme Court on the grass outside that window—I could see the top of his head past her tit, for God's sake! Of course I saw, but it's what you allow yourself to admit! *To admit what you see endangers principles!*[16]

Although the sequence seems fairly inconsequential in the light of Quentin's larger problems, it beautifully illustrates the technique Miller employs throughout the play to delineate the process of his protagonist's thought. Characteristically, Quentin's mind continually interrelates specific situations with general concepts. In this instance the vivid and embarrassing recollection particularizes the abstract statement about his moral and intellectual innocence which preceded it, and then concludes on an appropriate generalization which exposes not only the naïveté of his former moral stance, but its hypocrisy as well.

'*To admit what you see endangers principles.*'

The movement of *After the Fall* is from the adamant and self-deceiving insistence on innocence, to the admission, not of its loss —but of its nonexistence. Quentin has fallen because he has gradually and increasingly made himself admit what he has seen, and he has seen failure and betrayal. He has witnessed the failure of love and trust between his parents, he has recognized it in his own marriages and in the lives of his friends, and finally he has observed it on a societal and corporate national level, symbolized by the sinister tower of the concentration camp. As in *The Misfits*, the betrayal of love is the keynote to almost every relationship in the play, and image after image of deceit shimmers and crystallizes as Quentin dredges these betrayals out of his past.

[16] *Ibid.*, p.23. Italics my own.

He recalls his mother's deception of him as a child when she lied about the rest of the family's outing at Atlantic City. With much greater pain he remembers her betrayal of his father, first in turning toward their children because of her shame over his intellectual inferiority, and then in her humiliation of him when his business collapses in the Depression. Her curse, 'You are an idiot!' flares like an agonizing ember in Quentin's consciousness, symbolizing for him the hurt, frustration, and ultimate betrayal of love. Afterward, the father and mother face each other like two strangers in a stance that will be repeated by other persons in Quentin's life.

He also recalls his father's tearful anguish at hearing of his wife's death, 'but still and all, a couple of months later he bothered to register and vote. . . . Well, I mean . . . it didn't kill him either, with all his tears.' Quentin is immediately ashamed of his interpretation of his father's resumption of everyday activities.

'I don't know what the hell I'm driving at,' he quickly interpolates.

But he does know. He is driving at betrayal, and if he has read too much into his father's actions it is because they are being viewed through the prism of a mind haunted by treachery, ranging from Lou's betrayal by his wife Elsie, who coerced him into falsifying a book to further his career, to Mickey's more heinous sellout of the tortured professor to an investigating committee, and covering also Quentin's personal betrayals by each of his wives.

But most clearly and chillingly, Quentin becomes aware of his own complicity in deception and betrayal: in his desertion of his father to go to college; in his tacit willingness to allow his brother to remain in the business to help finance his education; in his egocentric manipulation of Felice, the young divorcée whose blatant and embarrassing idolization of him he self-consciously encourages; in his indifferent treatment of Louise, who rightly accuses him of self-absorption although it is an accusation that could be made of her, as well as of almost every other character in the play; in his ambivalence toward Lou, which is manifested in the rush of relief he feels upon learning that his friend has committed suicide and thus removed the problem of defending him against the investigating committee's charges; and finally and most agonizingly, in his victimization of Maggie, initially in his motives for marrying her, and then most horribly exhibited in his abandonment of her to destruction when their marriage shatters.

And by that withdrawal the two most terrible betrayals of Quentin's life are insolubly welded. At the close of the first act, he relives his feelings at hearing of Lou's death beneath a subway train.

'When I saw him last week he said a dreadful thing. I tried not to hear it,' he tells Louise, and in reply to her request for an explanation, he exclaims: 'That I turned out to be the only friend he had.'

'Why is that dreadful?' she asks.

'It just was,' Quentin replies *evasively, almost slyly,* 'I don't know why.'

Then, stepping out of the past, he approaches the Listener, 'tears forming in his eyes,' and he clarifies the equivocal answer he gave his wife:

I didn't dare know why! But I dare now. It was dreadful because I was not his friend either, and he knew it. I'd have stuck it out to the end but I hated the danger in it for myself, and he saw through my faithfulness; and he was not telling me what a friend I was, he was praying I would be—'Please be my friend, Quentin,' is what he was saying to me, 'I am drowning, throw me a rope!' Because I wanted out, to be a good American again, kosher again—and proved it in the joy . . . the joy . . . the joy I felt now that my danger had spilled out on the subway track![17]

As Quentin speaks the tower blazes into life, Maggie's difficult breathing is heard, and he turns painfully away from the vision and the sound. However, his odyssey eventually brings him back, and at the conclusion of the final act, with Maggie gasping out her life, Quentin stands over her and again voices the ambivalent joy he felt at the news of Lou's death.

'And her precious seconds squirming in my hand alive as bugs; and I heard,' he confesses to the darkness around him. 'Those deep, unnatural breaths, like the footfalls of my coming peace— and knew . . . I wanted them.'

By what justification can he turn away from Lou and Maggie?

'In whose name do you ever turn your back—but in your own? In Quentin's name! Always in your own blood-covered name you turn your back!'

[17] *Ibid.,* pp.58–59.

The alternate title to the play was *The Survivor*. It was hardly an arbitrary choice. Almost every individual in the drama deceives and betrays others for his personal survival. They are not inherently cruel or sadistic—on the contrary, they are basically decent—but to survive (and each defines survival differently) they sacrifice each other, and then, to live with themselves after the betrayals, they attempt to accept the comforting illusion of innocence.

Separateness and innocence.

Sought by Quentin's mother in the betrayal of her husband, and in her adamant denial of it moments later.

'What *I* said?' she cries to the child who has overheard her attack on his father. 'Why what did I say? Well I was a little angry, that's all, but I never said *that*. I think he's a wonderful man! [*Laughs*] How could I say a thing like that? Quentin! I didn't say anything! Darling, I didn't say anything!'

Separateness and innocence.

Craved by Mickey as he explains to Quentin his intention to betray Lou to the investigating committee.

'I only know one thing, Quent, I want to live an open life, a straightforward life.'

This new desire is further elaborated when Mickey tells Lou why he is going to name names:

I despise the Party, and have for many years. Just like you. Yet there is something . . . that closes my throat when I think of telling names. What am I defending? It's a dream, now, a dream of solidarity. But the fact is, *I have no solidarity with the people I could name—excepting for you.* And not because we were Communists together, but because we were young together. Because we—when we talked it was like some brotherhood opposed to all the world's injustice. Therefore, in the name of that love, I ought to be true to myself now. And the truth, Lou, my truth, is that I think the Party *is* a conspiracy—let me finish. I think we *were* swindled; they took our lust for the right and used it for Russian purposes. And I don't think we can go on turning our backs on the truth simply because the reactionaries are saying it. What I propose—is that *we try to separate our love for one another from this political morass.*[18]

[18] *Ibid.*, p.35. Italics my own.

Separateness and innocence. The horror lies not only in what Mickey is about to do to his friend, but in his fervent attempt to convince himself of the decency and integrity of his motivation. Much of what he has said is undoubtedly true, but the truth of the situation he is describing, and his personal reasons for acting are separated by a deep chasm that can be spanned only by a footbridge of rationalizations.

The theme and conflict of *The Crucible* is being reenacted in this sequence, as a man attempts to separate private and public commitment so that he can take shelter in the subjective truths of his private world. Lou cuts to the core of their dilemma when he reminds Mickey that 'if everyone broke faith there would be no civilization.'

'There is only one truth here,' he exclaims angrily. 'You are terrified! They have bought your soul!'

Not only does the statement clearly recall Proctor's need to retain his name, but it also points directly to Leduc's scathing attack on Monceau in *Incident at Vichy* when he scornfully recognizes that the actor's heart 'is conquered territory.'

But Lou does not have the final word, for there *is* more than one truth. Bitterly stung by the relevance of his friend's words, Mickey flings back another. He reminds Lou of the book his wife made him falsify to protect his career.

'She has taken your soul!' he cries.

Their truths are far from equal, but the point is clearly and painfully made: who, for survival, does not betray—a person, a trust, a principle, oneself? Lou is more honest than Quentin's mother or Mickey; he does not attempt to cloak himself in innocence by denying his friend's accusation.

'You are a monster,' he exclaims, and bursts into tears.

Separateness and innocence are also sought by Louise, who reminds Quentin that he demands too much of people.

'You want a woman to provide an—atmosphere, in which there are never any issues, and you'll fly around in a constant bath of praise—Quentin, I am not a praise machine! I am not a blur and I am not your mother! I am a separate person!'

Like Mickey's explanation to Lou, Louise's self-defense is not invalid; but the objectivity of her criticism and her motivations for it are two distinct things.

Characteristically, Quentin's mind links the personal conflict

between himself and Louise to a broader one involving the plight
of his friend Lou.

'I got the same idea,' he says to her, 'when I realized that Lou
had gone from one of his former students to another and none
would take him—'

Equally characteristically, Louise interrupts her husband. 'What's
Lou got to do with it?' she snaps uncomprehendingly. Her truth,
like Mickey's, is self-contained, but Quentin's continually expands
outward and now he follows its implications. When Louise allows
that his defense of Lou is admirable, Quentin examines the motives
behind it:

> Yes, but I am doing what you call an admirable thing be-
> cause I can't bear to be a separate person. I think so. I really
> don't want to be known as a Red lawyer, and I really don't
> want the newspapers to eat me alive; and if it came down to
> it, Lou could defend himself. But when that decent, broken
> man who never wanted anything but the good of the world,
> sits across my desk—I don't know how to say that my interests
> are no longer the same as his, and that if he doesn't change
> I consign him to hell because we are separate persons.[19]

Louise still does not understand what her private problems with
Quentin have to do with his relationship to Lou, and in the ensuing dialogue with her husband the anguish of their marriage is
darkly illuminated:

LOUISE: You are completely confused! Lou's case has nothing—

QUENTIN: I am telling you my confusion! I think Mickey also
became a separate person—

LOUISE: You're incredible!

QUENTIN: I think of my mother, I think she almost became—

LOUISE: Are you identifying *me* with—

QUENTIN: Louise, I am asking you to explain this to me because
this is when I go blind! When you've finally become a separate
person, what the hell is there?

LOUISE: [*with a certain unsteady pride*] Maturity.

QUENTIN: I don't know what that means.

[19] *Ibid.*, p.41.

LOUISE: It means that you know another person exists, Quentin. . . .

QUENTIN: It's probably the symptom of a typical case of some kind, but I swear, Louise, if you would just once, of your own free will, as right as you are—if you would come to me and say that something, something important was your fault and that you were sorry, it would help. Louise?

[*In her pride she is silent, in her refusal to be brought down again*]

LOUISE: Good God! What an idiot![20]

Louise's bristling innocence is impenetrable. It is simultaneously her haven and her weapon against what she considers to be her husband's ridiculous and impossible demands upon her. She sees him withdrawing but still ironically demanding her continued absorption in him, and she adamantly refuses. Uncertain and fearful, she justifies her unwillingness to emerge from the cocoon of her separateness by labeling it maturity, and even though she is annoyed at being compared with his mother, she treats Quentin with a kind of maternal condescension. Deeply wounded by her husband, she cannot recognize the depth of his pain, and rather than make the attempt, which would entail responsibility and self-sacrifice, she simplifies their problems by ascribing his anguish to immaturity. It is easier to retreat into self-justification from the wreckage of a marriage than to examine its causes in depth.

But Louise's inability and reluctance to recognize all the ramifications of Quentin's dilemma does not invalidate her insight. On the contrary, she displays an acute comprehension of two facets of her husband's character that are crucial to his problems. She recognizes his continual need for assurance and praise, and she perceptively notes the curious relationship between his desire for connection and his marked inability to connect. When he unfairly berates her for refusing to help him make up his mind about defending Lou, she points unerringly to the heart of his confusion.

'You have to decide what you feel about a certain human being,' she reminds him. 'For once in your life. And then maybe you'll decide what you feel about other human beings. Clearly and decisively.'

It is hardly coincidental that Quentin's consideration of this problem, with respect to Holga, is a primary motivation that triggers the action of the play.

Louise has defined the contradiction in Quentin toward which his thought and the drama's development converges. As he admits to her, he 'cannot bear to be a separate person,' and yet he chooses separateness repeatedly when commitment threatens his equilibrium. Thus, although he sincerely affirms his allegiance to Lou, he asks her only moments later whether he should defend him.

Mickey cannot bear to be a separate person either. Just prior to informing Lou of his intention to testify before the investigating committee, he describes to Quentin how the colleagues in his law firm reacted to his admission that he had been a member of the Communist party.

'I wish you'd have seen their faces when I told them. Men I've worked with for thirteen years. Played tennis; intimate friends, you know? And as soon as I said "I had been"—stones.'[21]

Mickey will sell his soul not to be separate, and yet he is ready and willing to disengage himself from his best friend to retain his tenuous connection to this rock pile. The play is not only concerned with the price of connection, but with its very meaning.

In the original version, Mickey concluded his preceding comment to Quentin with the observation that 'I could feel their backs turning on me. It was horrible! As though—they would let me die.'

Significantly the concentration camp tower was illuminated and Maggie appeared in her bed and called out softly to Quentin, who turned away. Indeed 'they' would let Mickey die, just as he would abandon Lou to his destruction, and Quentin would feel the thrill of relief at the news of Lou's death and the anticipation of Maggie's.

Separateness and innocence.

A vital part of Quentin's self-knowledge is the growing realization that he is not as different from his mother, Louise, and Mickey as he would have initially liked to believe.

The second act of *After the Fall* is dominated by the relationship of Maggie and Quentin. In Act One, Miller has carefully introduced his protagonist and created a series of characters and se-

---

[21] *Ibid.*, p.33.

quences to illuminate the depth and complexity of his problems. In the concluding act, although these characters still move through the labyrinth of Quentin's mind, the issues raised in the preceding episodes are dramatically centralized in one situation—the most intimate and most anguished, the most hopeful and the most cruelly disillusioned relationship in Quentin's life: his marriage to Maggie. It is this relationship which brings him to his greatest despair, and, concomitantly, to his most profound awareness.

Superficially Maggie resembles the golden girl, Roslyn. She is beautiful, naïve, frank, and like the heroine of *The Misfits* she appears to have a zest for living. However, while Roslyn is essentially defined by these external characteristics, Maggie is not. As her characterization deepens, she emerges as a kind of rebuttal to Roslyn, still the glowing, radiant dream on the surface, but embodying a nightmare reality at the core.

Making the least claim on innocence, she is nevertheless the most innocent character in the play, and simultaneously the most poignant and terrible personification of the self-destructive quality of blind innocence. As soon as the superficial joy of life is penetrated, her uncertainty and fear spurt to the surface like a poisonous fountain. Haunted by the grim remembrances of things past, not the least of which is the memory of her mother's attempt to kill her, she desperately craves the certainty of love.

At first her faith and adulation are manna for Quentin's faltering ego. The adoration he received from Felice is now heightened and expanded by Maggie, who is initially as much a symbol for him as she is a human being. She is the relief he has been seeking amid the guilt-ridden debris of his broken marriage and the death of his friend; she is the vital human connection in a dislocated chain of ambivalent relationships; she is a life buoy of assurance in a whirlpool of doubt. And most gratifyingly, she is someone to be saved, a promiscuous but inherently innocent Magdalene over whom he can play God. Once, after Felice had come to him, he had stood against the wall of his hotel room, arms outspread between two light fixtures. In his marriage to Maggie the literal pose quickly deepens into a pervasively figurative one.

Initially he savors her infinite trust, but he soon realizes that infinite love implies an infinite capacity for self-sacrifice, and that infinite faith on the part of the recipient of love calls for infinite responsibility on the part of the donor. Out of their personal needs

Maggie and Quentin ask too much of each other, and because they cannot give enough, their marriage becomes everything from which they have tried to flee. The dream of heaven explodes into the reality of hell.

In a final, excruciating scene, they move reluctantly toward a reckoning.

'Tell me what happened!' she sobs; and crying, he faces her.

'Maggie, we . . . used one another,' he replies.

'Not me, not me!' she insists.

Her denial is not simply evasion; it is a rockbound belief in her own innocence, an innocence which Quentin finally attempts to burst in the hope of saving her life. As he tries to make her surrender the pills with which she is attempting suicide, he answers her:

Yes, you. And I. 'To live,' we cried, and 'Now,' we cried. And loved each other's innocence as though to love enough what was not there would cover up what was. But there is an angel, and night and day he brings back to us what we want to lose. So you must love him because he keeps truth in the world. You eat those pills to blind yourself, but if you could only say, 'I have been cruel,' this frightening room would open! If you could say, 'I have been kicked around, but I have been just as inexcusably vicious to others. . . . And I am full of hatred; I, Maggie, sweet lover of all life—I hate the world!

Hate women, hate men, hate all who will not grovel at my feet proclaiming my limitless love for ever and ever!

But no pill can make us innocent. Throw them in the sea, throw death in the sea and all your innocence. Do the hardest thing of all—see your own hatred, and live![22]

This is Quentin's insight and truth, what climbing to survival over the bodies of loved ones has taught him, and he tries desperately to communicate it to Maggie. But she refuses to acknowledge it. Death is a simpler end to torture than knowledge, particularly when the knowledge may only increase the torture.

Unable and unwilling to decipher his meaning and apply it to herself, Maggie counteracts Quentin's insight with a valid one of her own, namely that he, the dispenser of truth, cannot face it either.

'What about your hatred?' she spews. 'You know when I wanted

[22] *Ibid.*, pp.107–108.

to die. When I read what you wrote, kiddo. Two months after we were married kiddo.'

Now Quentin is evasive. 'Let's keep it true,' he exclaims. 'You told me you tried to die long before you met me.'

He is probably right, but like Mickey and Louise he is juggling observable facts to escape from a deeper truth, and both he and Maggie know it. Again, the man who cannot bear to be a separate person is dissociating himself from responsibility when his safety is jeopardized. But Maggie will not allow him to escape.

'So you're not even there, huh. I didn't even meet you. You coward. What about your hatred?'

As he turns away from her in shame, she reminds him of the note she found that he had written to himself, and she flings its contents into his face: 'The only one I will ever love is my daughter. If only I could find an honorable way to die.'

Trying to make Maggie face truth about herself, Quentin finds that she has reversed the situation and put him on the defensive. However, with a lifetime of deceptions swirling in his memory he refuses to take any exits to innocence. He admits that he betrayed their marriage by his inability to overcome the shame that he felt whenever he thought of her promiscuous past or saw her with men who might have had her. And noticing the distrust in his eyes, she had finally accused him of being cold and remote, thus echoing the judgment his first wife had hurled at him.

'That I could have brought two women so different to the same accusation—it closed a circle for me,' he confesses. 'And I wanted to face the worst thing I could imagine—that I could not love. And I wrote it down, like a letter from hell.'

The angel has brought him back to what he wanted to lose, and with the proof that his marriage to Maggie was not a progression but a shameful variation of the basic problems of his first marriage, a circle closes. Now Quentin has confronted a bitter truth, and from the depths of his shame, amid the rubble of his principles, he quietly tries to reach his wife one last time.

'Maggie,' he pleads, 'we were born of many errors; a human being has to forgive himself! Neither of us is innocent. What more do you want?'

'Love me,' she replies.

What Maggie still wants is what she has always wanted: infinite love, a blessing, salvation. Moments earlier she referred to Lazarus, whom she believes to be a woman, and whose story Quentin had previously related to her. God had resurrected Lazarus out of the power of infinite love; but Quentin knows at last that when a man dares reach for that, 'he is reaching only for the power.' This is what he has done with Maggie, concealing his hubris in the downy illusion of limitless love. But now, with only the truth left between them, his words explode that illusion.

'It isn't my love you want anymore,' he cries half in truth and half in rationalization, 'it's my destruction!' And then with a chilling pang of self-recognition, as he tries to wrench the sleeping pills from her hand: 'You're not going to kill me, Maggie.'

Quentin refuses to take the responsibility for her life, which in her final anguish and hatred she hurls at him, but in the act of refusal he cannot but help acknowledge that he is choosing his survival at the expense of hers. Unspoken, Mickey's words echo mockingly in the black void around them:

'They would let me die.'

And another circle is closed as Quentin again sees the specter of betrayal freeze into fact. Only one final recognition remains, and in the ensuing struggle with Maggie, he achieves it.

As they wrestle for the pills he grabs her wrist, trying to pry her hands open. Then, suddenly and clearly, he lunges for her throat. But as his grip closes on her, the image of his mother flashes into his mind and he again recalls the early childhood betrayal when he was left behind on a family vacation. He springs back from Maggie and stands transfixed as his mother backs into his open and grasping hands, which tighten around her neck.

Miller is by no means suggesting that all of Quentin's problems can be traced back to a traumatic afternoon of his youth, or even to ambivalent feelings toward his parents. Earlier in the play, Quentin dismissed this nickel psychologizing with his caustically rhetorical question, 'Shall we lay it all to mothers?' What the playwright does consider in this sequence is the possibility that the adult male is capable of doing what the angry and confused child had pondered years earlier, that—as Quentin notes only minutes later—'the wish to kill is never killed' no matter how much one may attempt to delude himself with sophisticated rationalizations. As his mother gasps for breath, he releases her, horror-struck, and a question that is not a question but the final, irrevocable knowledge, forms on his lips.

'Murder?'

The third circle slams shut for Quentin.

'Now we both know.' Maggie rasps as her knowledge and his coalesce, for his attack has also conjured up her first betrayal—her mother's attempt on her life. As she sees that the Savior is also the Destroyer, her illusion of salvation is shattered, only her victimized innocence remains, and her death becomes inevitable. And for Quentin, not just the realization that he would let her die, but the recognition that he would kill her, points to the deep and terrifying chasm at the end of his search.

'How is that possible—' he cries, 'I loved that girl!'

But he already knows how it is possible.

'Love, is love enough?' he replies to himself. 'What love, what wave of pity will ever reach this knowledge—I know how to kill. . . . I know.'

Quentin turns toward the blasted stone tower of the concentration camp, which had flared into grisly prominence at every instance of betrayal in the play, and is now blazing fiercely and implacably as the most awesome manifestation of the failure of love and the fact of betrayal. In the first act, after recalling his feelings at Lou's death, he had also looked to the tower and tried to define its relevance for him.

> This is not some crazy aberration of human nature to me. I can easily see the perfectly normal contractors and their cigars, the carpenters, plumbers, sitting at their ease over lunch pails; I can see them laying the pipes to run the blood out of this mansion; good fathers, devoted sons, grateful that someone else will die, not they, and how can one understand that, if one is innocent? If somewhere in one's soul there is no accomplice—of that joy, that joy, that joy when a burden dies . . . and leaves you safe? [*Maggie's difficult breathing is heard*][23]

The knowledge inherent in these words is a precursor of the awareness Quentin attains at the end of the play, but at this point it is still tentative and groping, concluding on a question. However, after his recollection of Maggie's destruction, the question marks finally give way to exclamation points as he perceives the

[23] *Ibid.*, p.59.

nature and meaning of his mind's anguished journey.

'Or is it possible,' he muses as he moves toward the tower and considers the deceit and cruelty of which he is capable, 'that this is not bizarre . . . to anyone?'

And I am not alone, and no man lives who would not rather be the sole survivor of this place than all its finest victims! What is the cure? Who can be innocent again on this mountain of skulls? I tell you what I know! My brothers died here— [*He looks from the tower down at the fallen Maggie*]—but my brothers built this place; our hearts have cut these stones! And what's the cure? . . . No, not love! I loved them all, all! And gave them willingly to failure and to death that I might live, as they gave me and gave each other, with a word, a look, a trick, a truth, a lie—and all in love![24]

After the Fall carries the bleak despair of *The Misfits* as far as Miller can take it. To the breakdown of belief in family and society, which the screenplay of the last frontier depicts, the play-wright has added the dissolution of faith in the individual. Quentin experiences the total destruction of every absolute in which he ever sought certainty, including the ideal of self-integrity which heretofore remained the life preserver in the troubled waters be-setting so many of Miller's former heroes.

'Is the knowing all?' asks Quentin as he echoes Gay Langland's bewilderment in *The Misfits*.

Following the development of Miller's earlier dramas, the move-ment of *After the Fall* is toward increasing awareness and moral focus. But unlike the other plays, *After the Fall* does not drama-tize the resolution and commitment gained from increased com-prehension, but rather the skepticism and dismay, for the realiza-tion at which Quentin arrives is the recognition that self-knowledge—faced honestly and unflinchingly—tears to pathetic tatters all hopes, illusions, and ideals, and shows human existence for what it is: an absurdity, personified by the figure who haunts Holga's recurrent and troubled thoughts.

'The same dream returned each night,' she confides to Quentin as she tells him of her life in Germany during the war. 'I had a child, and even in the dream I saw it was my life, and it was an

[24] *Ibid.*, p.113.

idiot, and I ran away. But it always crept onto my lap again, clutched at my clothes.'

This dream, recalled by Quentin early in the play, points to the abyss toward which he stumbles. However, the image of absurdity which so quickly and clearly elicits despair, also signals the possibility of a tentative movement beyond it.

'Until I thought,' Holga continues, 'if I could kiss it, whatever in it was my own, perhaps I could sleep. And I bent to its broken face, and it was horrible . . . but I kissed it.'[25]

'That woman hopes!' Quentin cries out in amazement when Holga comes to him at the conclusion. He wonders how anyone can still hope in the face of the knowledge that they now share. But her interpretation of the dream comes back to him— 'I think one must finally take one's life in one's arms, Quentin,'—and he faces the Listener, struck by a new thought:

> Or is that exactly why she hopes, because she knows? What burning cities taught her and the death of love taught me: that we are very dangerous!
>
> [*Staring, seeing his vision*]
>
> And that, that's why I wake each morning like a boy—even now, even now! I swear to you, I could love the world again![26]

With this statement Quentin returns to the unreasonable hope which he verbalized at the beginning of the play:

> A couple of weeks ago I suddenly became aware of a strange fact. With all this darkness, the truth is that every morning when I awake, I'm full of hope! With everything I know—I open my eyes, I'm like a boy! For an instant there's some unformed promise in the air. I jump out of bed, I shave, I can't wait to finish breakfast—and then, it seeps into my room, my life, and its pointlessness. And I thought—if I could corner that hope, find what it consists of and either kill it for a lie, or really make it mine. . . .[27]

Miller has begun the play with its tentative resolution, but in

[25] *Ibid.*, p.22.
[26] *Ibid.*, p113.
[27] *Ibid.*, pp.113–114.

the beginning it is an abstract statement, an unexplored and un-explained feeling which haunts Quentin and demands what he has demanded from his existence—the blessing of certainty. At the conclusion, although his words superficially parallel his opening comments, they evolve out of a recognition that he must live in the knowledge that makes a mockery of certainty and blessedness.

> Is the knowing all? To know, and even happily, that we meet unblessed; not in some garden of wax fruit and painted trees, that lie of Eden, but after, after the Fall, after many, many deaths. Is the knowing all? And the wish to kill is never killed, but with some gift of courage one may look into its face when it appears, and with a stroke of love—as to an idiot in the house—forgive it! again and again . . . forever?[28]

After the Fall juxtaposes a man's agonizing confrontation of the heart of darkness in himself and in humanity with the tenuous and illogical hope that springs, not from the evasion of know-ledge, but from its acceptance. Like the protagonist of Dante's *Inferno*, Quentin has found himself in the 'middle of the journey of [his] life, in a dark wood where the straight way was lost,' and in the subsequent search for the way out, has come to understand his complicity in that darkness, a complicity centered in the phenomenon of separateness. His separateness, however, cannot wholly eradicate the fact that he still lives in a world of other men, in which choice and responsibility are implied.

To Quentin's anguished recognition that 'I gave them willingly to failure and to death that I might live, as they gave me and gave each other,' Miller opposes Lou's belief that 'if everyone broke faith, there would be no civilization.'

Each is a truth. At the end of *After the Fall* Quentin attempts to restore some of that faith, not glibly and certainly not con-fidently.

'No, it's not certainty,' he remarks. 'I don't feel that. But it does seem feasible . . . not to be afraid. Perhaps it's all one has.'

He knows that he can no longer live in the spurious illusions of innocence and must accept the complete possibility of the hell of which he is capable. But: he must live. With innocence gone, the vacuum is easily filled with despair, 'and, of course, despair can be a way of life; but you have to believe in it, pick it up, take it to

[28] *Ibid.*, p.114.

heart. . . .' Quentin cannot. He can no more make an absolute of despair than he can of innocence. Consequently, and paradoxically, his potential damnation is simultaneously his hope.

The image of Lazarus, which symbolized Maggie's pathetic need for blessedness and Quentin's ultimate unwillingness and inability to provide it, now develops a fuller dimension. It manifests the possibility of a slow and painful resurrection for Quentin, an uncertain movement out of the black limbo of self-pity and despair toward a new attempt at connection, free from guarantees, comforting ideals, and 'the sense of some absolute necessity.'

Quentin may lack John Proctor's ultimate strength and steadfastness, but he is still able to move beyond Guido's whining self-immolation.

> He turns upstage. He hesitates; all his people face him. He walks toward Louise, pausing; but she turns her face away. He goes on and pauses beside Mother, who stands in uncomprehending sorrow; he gestures as though he touched her, and she looks up at him and dares a smile, and he smiles back. He pauses at his dejected Father and Dan, and with a slight gesture magically makes them stand. Felice is about to raise her hand in blessing—he shakes her hand, aborting her enslavement. He passes Mickey and Lou and turns back to Maggie; she rises from the floor, webbed in with her demons, trying to awake. And with his life following him he climbs toward Holga, who raises her arm as though seeing him, and speaks with great love. . . .[29]

As she greets him, a whispering rises from all his ghosts, and for a moment the void is filled with the hiss of memory. But although these pathetic Furies will remain in his mind, 'endlessly alive,' Quentin straightens himself against their sound and resolutely walks toward Holga, holding out his hand. The drama closes quietly and appropriately on his final word.

'Hello.'

[29] *Ibid.*, p.114.

18

They stand there, forever

incomprehensible to one another

About the time that he was writing *A View from the Bridge*, Arthur Miller heard a story from a friend that caught his imagination and held it over the years with a tenacity that amazed and perplexed him.

The story dealt with an acquaintance of Miller's friend who was picked up one day on a street in Vichy, France, in 1942, taken to a police station, and without any clarification, ordered to await further developments. Although he was Jewish the man was puzzled by his detention because it was not in keeping with the political situation in Vichy, was was relatively stable. The Petain regime had rather successfully warded off the more brutal aspects of the Nazi occupation, including the enforcement of racial laws, and with easily purchased forged papers even a Jewish refugee could live essentially unmolested in the so-called Unoccupied Zone extending over the southern half of the country.

After waiting uneasily on a bench, he was directed to a line of persons, each of whom had been summoned in the same manner as he. Every few minutes a door at the front of the queue would open, a Vichy policeman would coldly beckon, and a man would enter the inner office. Some soon reappeared and fled silently and nervously into the tenuous freedom outside, but the majority were not seen again. The rumor that the Gestapo were conducting a program to weed out Jews by evidence of circumcision soon edged chillingly down the line.

Hearing this, the man grew certain that his destruction was near, and as the door opened and closed and the line became shorter, he felt as if he were on a conveyor belt that was slowly but irrevocably propelling him to oblivion. Finally only one other person stood between him and the entrance, and moments later the last human buffer was removed when this individual was ordered into the office. The Jew stood alone, waiting for the senseless but inevitable axe to fall.

The door opened and the previous suspect emerged, ostensibly a free man. The policeman had not yet reentered, but the Jew stood frozen, awaiting his fate. Then, suddenly, the stranger walked up to him, thrust his pass into his hand, and whispered for him to escape. He did. He had never before seen the man who saved his life, and he never saw him again.

From the moment he heard it and on into the ensuing years, the story became a part of Miller's consciousness. Its meaning shifted continually, sometimes becoming sharp and lucid, other times remaining tantalizingly blurred; but the individual who traded his life for another man's stalked the playwright's imagination, sometimes even drawn out of his private thoughts by public events.

> That faceless, unknown man would pop up in my mind when I read about the people in Queens refusing to call the police while a woman was being stabbed to death outside their windows. He would form himself in the air when I listened to delinquent boys whose many different distortions of character seemed to spring from a common want of human solidarity. Friends troubled by having to do things they disapproved of brought him to mind, people for whom the very concept of choosing their actions was a long forgotten thing. Wherever I felt the seemingly implacable tide of human drift and the withering of will, in myself and in others, this faceless person came to mind. And he appears most clearly and imperatively amid the jumble of emotions surrounding the Negro in this country, and the whole unsettled moral problem of the destruction of the Jews in Europe.[1]

However, the possibility that a drama could evolve out of this character and situation did not occur to the playwright until he completed *After the Fall* and suddenly realized that the meaning inherent in the twenty-three-year-old tale had been woven into the fabric of his latest play.

'Before that,' he recalled, 'it had been simply a fact, a feature of

[1] Arthur Miller, 'Our Guilt for the World's Evil,' *The New York Times Magazine* (January 3, 1965), p.10.

existence which sometimes brought exhilaration with it, sometimes a vacant wonder, and sometimes even resentment.'[2]

Now the fact took on significance, and like *Death of a Salesman*, which formed itself instantaneously out of images that had lain dormant in his imagination for a number of years, *Incident at Vichy* 'burst open complete in almost all its details.' The result was a drama written at blinding speed, completed in a little over a month, and exploring, as did *After the Fall*, man's relationship to justice and injustice, guilt and responsibility, separateness and commitment, in a world irretrievably east of Eden.

Incident at Vichy was Miller's second and final offering to the Lincoln Center Repertory Theater, from which he withdrew, along with producer Robert Whitehead and director Elia Kazan, after two stormy seasons of dissension that permeated the fledgling enterprise. *Incident at Vichy* opened on the third of December, 1964, and subsequently alternated in repertory with *After the Fall*. It was staged by Harold Clurman and featured Joseph Wiseman as Leduc, the Jewish psychiatrist; David Wayne as Prince Von Berg, his Catholic benefactor; and Hal Holbrook as a reluctant German officer; and with David J. Stewart (Monceau); Michael Strong (Lebeau); Stanley Beck (Marchand); and Will Lee (the old Jew) as four prominent suspects.

The play garnered glaringly mixed notices that ran the gamut from the *New York Times'* Howard Taubman's ecstatic paean that Miller's new drama 'returns the theatre to greatness,' to the *New York Daily News'* Douglas Watts's dismissal of it as 'contrived claptrap.' And even Watts's judgment paled alongside the pronouncement of Robert Brustein, who pitchforked the play with obvious relish. Mr Brustein felt that *Incident at Vichy* had sharply bypassed greatness and plunged instead into a sargasso sea of World War II Hollywood hokum.

Generally, however, the reviewers steered clear of both blessings and brickbats. To a number of critics who viewed *After the Fall* as Miller's catastrophe, *Incident at Vichy* seemed to be a step in the direction of creative recuperation. On the other hand, a few critics who greatly admired *After the Fall* were disappointed with the new effort, which they interpreted as a dramatically inferior postscript to the preceding play.

Actually it is quite difficult, and perhaps not really fair, to com-

[2] *Ibid.*, p.10.

pare *Incident at Vichy* with *After the Fall*, since the two plays are
radically different in form, characterization, and action. Unquestionably, *Incident at Vichy* lacks the fascination of *After the Fall*.
Its setting and dramatic time quite literal, its characters stripped of
any existence beyond the situation which unwillingly relates them,
and its action compressed and linear, the drama does not approach
the virtuosity and intricacy of the previous play. Instead it aims
a blunt and unavoidable blow directly at its audience.

Presented without an intermission, *Incident at Vichy* dramatizes approximately ninety minutes in the lives of a few men in
a detention room in Vichy in the autumn of 1942. As they sit
on a long bench in front of an inner office, waiting for a mysterious
interrogation, they can hear a concertina playing 'Lilli Marlene'
from a cafe across the street. Listening to this tantalizing reminder
of the outside world, they grow increasingly anxious, but they
remain silent, afraid to substantiate their apprehension by vocal-
izing it.

Finally a young painter, Lebeau, is no longer able to keep quiet
about his premonitions, and he begins to ask questions which dip
and flap like sinister little black bats in the stale air of the dingy
room. He wonders if they could be in a police station, if the others
were picked up as arbitrarily as he, and if perhaps there might be
some 'racial implication' to the roundup. Despite their uneasiness
at his queries, the other men gradually and grudgingly begin to
talk.

Marchand, a businessman who seems confident, brusquely assures
them that they are undergoing nothing more than a routine document check, and an electrician named Bayard, an actor, Monceau,
a waiter from the cafe, and a fifteen-year-old boy try to bask
in the warmth of his apparent sureness. Only a gypsy seated at the
far end of the bench is tacitly but clearly excluded from their
tenuous fellowship.

Nevertheless Lebeau's fears are not allayed, and he continues
his annoying interrogation. Afraid to spell out the word which
hangs like a suspended axe over their heads, he euphemistically
sidles up to the truth when he questions Bayard.

'Does he know,' he asks, referring to the German major who
is one of their captors, 'that you're a . . . Peruvian?'

The electrician's reply ironically heightens the consideration it
is intended to obliterate.

'Don't discuss that here, for Gods sake!' he snaps. 'What's the matter with you?'

Discussion, however, is quickly rendered unnecessary when three new men are hauled into the room. Two, an Austrian nobleman and a psychiatrist, are only casually inspected by the group, but the third rivets their attention. An aged, bearded man in a long threadbare coat, and carrying a large sackcloth bundle, he silently and immediately crystallizes their fears and makes a mockery of Lebeau's euphemism and Bayard's attempt to censor it.

The apprehensions and hopes of the men then rapidly fluctuate. The presence of the old Jew terrifies the others, but their discovery that the nobleman, Prince Von Berg, is a Catholic, stokes the embers of their wavering hope. However, the optimistic theory, advanced by Monceau and seconded by Marchand, that the gypsy is being detained because he is probably suspected of stealing a large pot he carries with him, is countered by Bayard's reminder that gypsies have the same rating as Jews in the Nazi Racial Laws. Next, Lebeau's attempt to soften the implication of a roundup of Jews, by suggesting that it may only be part of a forced labor program, is grimly canceled by the electrician's recollection of a freight train, crammed with people and bound for Poland, which only the day before had pulled into the railroad yard in which he worked.

'Concentration camp?' asks Leduc, the psychiatrist, as he catches Bayard's meaning.

'Why?' replies Monceau. 'A lot of people have been volunteering for work in Germany.'

Bayard extinguishes this possibility immediately.

'The cars are locked on the outside,' he says quietly. 'And they stink. You can smell the stench a hundred yards away. Babies are crying inside. You can hear them. And women. They don't lock volunteers in that way. I never heard of it.'[3]

But although their fears grow stronger, their hope is suddenly fanned. Marchand, the first to be summoned into the inner office, is released, much to the wonderment of the others. Daring to hope again that they are only being subjected to a passport check, they start to put their papers in order. However, their tentative optimism is quickly aborted: the waiter's employer, who has been in the

[3] Miller, *Incident at Vichy* (New York: Viking, 1965), p.16.

office to serve coffee, has overheard the conversations within. He informs his employe of the actual reason for their detainment: Jews are being collected for shipment to concentration camps, and in the inner office a 'racial anthropologist,' with the reluctant aid of the German major (a line soldier recuperating from battle wounds), is checking each suspect for circumcision.

Their last glimmer of hope snuffed out, each man then tries as best he can to prepare himself for his ordeal.

Bayard has already begun his attempt. A Communist, he bolsters his courage with an objective vision of the historical process, which he equates with progress and enlightenment.

'It is faith in the future; and the future is Socialist. And that is what *I* take in there with *me*,' he exclaims.

And when Leduc replies, 'You means it's important not to feel alone . . .?' Bayard amplifies his credo: 'None of us is alone. We're members of history. Some of us don't know it, but you'd better learn it for your own preservation.'[4]

Although Bayard's belief is noble and comforting, to Leduc it is curious because it transforms the individual into a symbol.

'Yes. Why not?' counters Bayard. 'Symbols, yes. . . . What am I to them personally? Do they know me? You react personally to this, they'll turn you into an idiot. You can't make sense of this on a personal basis.'[5]

However, for Leduc, as for Quentin and Proctor and the majority of Miller heroes back to Lawrence Newman of *Focus*, there is no basis save a personal one: 'But the difficulty is—what can one be if not oneself?'

Admitting that Bayard's belief in the subordination of the individual to the collective WE might be 'the best way to hold on to oneself' in a time of crisis, Leduc is nonetheless unready and unwilling to apply this tenet to himself.

'It's only that ordinarily one tries to experience life, to be in spirit where one's body is,' he concludes. 'For some of us it's difficult to shift gears and go into reverse.'[6]

If Leduc has delineated the weakness of Bayard's vision, the electrician's rejoinder illuminates the agonizing paradox of the psychiatrist's will to believe.

[4] *Ibid.*, p.31.

[5] *Ibid.*, p.31.

[6] *Ibid.*, p.32.

'You think a man can be himself in this society?' he replies. 'When millions go hungry and a few live like kings, and whole races are slaves to the stock market—how can you be yourself in such a world? I put in ten hours a day for a few francs, I see people who never bend their backs and they own the planet. . . . How can my spirit be where my body is? I'd have to be an ape.'

Consequently, his spirit is 'in the future. In the day when the working class is master of the world.'[7] Adamantly clutching his 'fact' that 'class interest makes history, not individuals,' Bayard takes refuge from the arrows of outrageous fortune behind the shield of historical process.

However, his defense is suddenly challenged by Von Berg.

'But the facts . . .' the gentle nobleman reminds him, 'Dear sir, what if the facts are dreadful? And will always be dreadful?'

'So is childbirth,' replies Bayard, 'so is . . .'

But Von Berg does not wait for him to complete his analogy.

'But a child comes of it,' he exclaims. 'What if nothing comes of the facts but endless disaster?'

And then in sorrow and respect for the man whose reluctant opponent he has become, the Austrian prince administers the *coup de grace* to Bayard's faith in the common people.

'Ninety-nine per cent of the Nazis are ordinary working people,' he sadly reminds his companion. Only a very few individuals cannot be propagandized.

'You mean this whole world is going to hang on that thread?' Bayard replies incredulously. 'If I thought that, I wouldn't have the strength to walk through that door, I wouldn't know how to put one foot in front of the other.'[8]

Bayard's belief emanates from what Quentin terms 'that duty in the sky . . . the sense of some absolute necessity . . . that lie of Eden.' The electrician may be able to die for a cause, but he needs a guarantee, a certification of validity, without which, like the soldier Watson of *Situation Normal*, he cannot 'go through hell completely on his own steam, alone.'

Although Bayard clings to his own faith in the collective potential of mankind, and walks courageously into the interrogation room to

[7] *Ibid.*, p.32.
[8] *Ibid.*, p.34.

put his conviction to the test, the psychiatrist and the nobleman have already demonstrated its inadequacy.

With Bayard gone and their fate apparently sealed, Leduc proposes that the remaining able-bodied men overpower the guard at the outer door and make a run for freedom. But his desperate plan is blocked by the actor Monceau, who refuses to aid him because he cannot accept the monstrous intentions of his captors. His bland passivity rests on a dual faith: his abstract belief in reason and logic, and his specific reliance on his own personality, which he equates with his creativity as an artist.

To the waiter's revelation that Jews are being sent to concentration camp furnaces in Poland, Monceau replies that 'that is the most fantastic idiocy I ever heard in my life,' and justifies his exclamation by the observation that the wholesale slaughter of a people is absurd.

'What good are dead Jews to them? They want free labor. It's senseless. You can say whatever you like, but the Germans are not illogical.'[9]

Neither is Monceau, and his logic leads him to yet another deceptive conclusion.

'I played in Germany,' he affirms. 'That audience could not burn up actors in a furnace.'

And turning to Von Berg, he demands confirmation of his statement. However, neither the prince nor Leduc can grant it. Both men realize that Monceau's logical approach to his plight is leading him away from its reality. Both are aware of the truth of Leduc's comment that 'you cannot wager your life on a purely rational analysis of this situation.'

As he feels his faith in logic eroding before their scrutiny, the actor falls back on his reliance on his personal skills. He replies to Leduc's amazement at his confidence by telling the psychiatrist that he simply refuses to play a part that is not applicable to him.

'Everyone is playing the victim these days; hopeless, hysterical, they always assume the worst,' he whistles in the ominous gloom. 'You accuse us of acting the part the Germans created for us; I think you're the one who's doing that by acting so desperate.'[10]

But Leduc stalks him. 'In other words,' he answers, 'you will create yourself.'

[9] *Ibid.*, p.37.

[10] *Ibid.*, p.48

'Every actor creates himself,' Monceau replies haughtily.

'But when they tell you to open your fly.'

Monceau is mutely furious at the doctor's sardonic challenge, which has swiftly and deftly sliced through the rationalization in which he had wrapped himself. However, this does not shake the actor out of his willed passivity. Still refusing to help the psychiatrist make a break for the street, he again reverts to reason.

'The fact is there are laws and every government enforces its laws; and I want it understood that I have nothing to do with any of this talk,' Monceau declares.

> I go on the assumption that if I obey the law with dignity I will live in peace. I may not like the law, but evidently the majority does, or they would overthrow it. And I'm speaking now of the French majority, who outnumber the Germans in this town fifty to one. And if by some miracle you did knock out that guard you would find yourself in a city where not one person in a thousand would help you. And it's got nothing to do with being Jewish or not Jewish. It is what the world is, so why don't you stop insulting others with romantic challenges![11]

Monceau's argument is the antithesis of Bayard's. Unlike the idealistic worker, the actor is quite realistic about people and their motivations, and finds no comfort in contemplating the humanitarian potential of the collective majority. He swings like an erratic aerialist between the self-esteem embodied in a desperate belief in his personality, and the self-deprecation inherent in his conviction that the individual's subordination to corporate authority will assure him—if not freedom—at least survival. Like Mickey of *After the Fall*, Monceau seeks accommodation as the crucial prerequisite for preservation.

'In short,' Leduc replies scathingly, 'because the world is indifferent you will wait calmly and with great dignity—to open your fly.'

Monceau's final words to the psychiatrist further delineate the man behind the actor's mask and the personal truth behind the general outlook.

'I'll tell you what I think,' he declares in anger and in fright.

[11] *Ibid.*, p.52.

'I think it's people like you who have brought this on us. People who gives Jews a reputation for subversion, and this Talmudic analysis, and this everlasting, niggling discontent.'[12]

'Your heart is conquered territory, mister,' snaps Leduc. The debate is over.

When Leduc attempts to escape without Monceau's help, he is stopped by the German officer who informs him that flight would be impossible: sentries are posted on both sides of the street. As the two men eye each other warily, the major drunkenly confesses his revulsion with his task.

'Can you believe that?' he asks, grasping for an affirmative answer from the man he grudgingly respects.

'I'd believe it if you shot yourself,' Leduc replies flatly. 'And better yet, if you took a few of them with you.'

With a 'manic amusement, yet deeply questioning,' the major urges the psychiatrists on, asking him what would be gained if he let Leduc go free.

'I will love you as long as I live,' Leduc answers. 'Will anyone do that now?'

The reply is so bizarre and anachronistic that it staggers the officer for a moment. An appeal to something so alien to the situation and climate, it seems to glow a moment like some incongruous candle at the bottom of a deep, murky abyss.

Then the German blows it out. Wiping the thought from his mind, as if it were a Judas kiss, he cries out to Leduc in fury and pain: 'There are no persons anymore, don't you see that? There will never be persons again. What do I care if you love me? Are you out of your mind? What am I, a dog that I must be loved?'[13]

The gospel of love has become as invalid as all the preceding beliefs in mankind, community, and individual personality.

Intrigued and angered by Leduc's assertion that he deserves to live more than his captor because he is incapable of acting like him and is thus 'better for the world,' the officer backs the doctor into a moral corner by asking him if he would refuse a pass to safety if the others were denied theirs. Leduc tries to evade an answer, but the major forces it out of him.

'Would you refuse?' he repeats sharply.

'No.'

[12] See note 11 above.

[13] *Ibid.*, p.54.

'And walk out of that door with a light heart?'

'I don't know.'

But Leduc does know and the German drives the knowledge home.

'I am trying to understand why you are better for the world than me,' he exclaims, sarcastically. '. . . Would you go out of that door with a light heart, run to your woman, drink a toast to your skin? . . . Why are you better than anybody else?'

'I have no duty to make a gift of myself to your sadism,' the doctor replies haltingly, enmeshing himself in his own argument. The major quickly draws the net tight.

'But I do?' he interjects, 'to others' sadism? Of myself? I have that duty and you do not? To make a gift of myself?'

'I have nothing to say.'[14]

The man who demonstrated the ineptitude of Bayard's and Monceau's faiths now finds his own beliefs choked off by his enemy. The individual integrity, which Leduc contrasted to Bayard's adherence to the Marxian dialectic and to Monceau's dependence on logic and his obedience to the majority will, suddenly reels under the baleful truth that the major forces him to admit and share: that self-preservation subordinates even honor and dignity. And although Leduc has nothing to say, Quentin's words seem to echo in the dark void.

'And no man lives who would not rather be the sole survivor of this place than all its finest victims!'

This is Leduc's ultimate knowledge and it renders him more isolated and disillusioned than anyone else in the play.

The tempo of the drama accelerates as the suspects are hurried along. Galvanized by the metallic 'Next!' of the captain of police, Lebeau, Monceau, and the young boy are taken individually into the inner office, until only Leduc, Von Berg, and the old Jew remain. Confronted with the wordless old man whose doom is sealed, and with the Gentile who will momentarily be free, Leduc allows his bitterness and helplessness to spill over into acrid despair.

'This is why one gets so furious,' he confides to the prince, 'because all this suffering is so pointless—it can never be a lesson, it can never have a meaning. And that is why it will be repeated again and again forever.'

'Because it cannot be shared? Von Berg asks.

[14] *Ibid.*, pp.56–57.

'Yes. Because it cannot be shared. It is total, absolute, waste.'[15]

Then the aged Jew is taken, and as his bundle is wrested away from him it bursts apart in a storm of feathers. While they gently settle in the darkening room, like a dying and wistful embodiment of softness and gentility, Von Berg, with obvious difficulty in facing the man he will survive, asks Leduc if he can at least depart with his friendship. The psychiatrist replies that he bears the aristocrat no particular malice:

> Prince, in my profession one gets the habit of looking at oneself quite impersonally. It is not you I am angry with. In one part of my mind it is not even this Nazi. I am only angry that I should have been born before the day when man has accepted his own nature; that he is *not* reasonable, that he is full of murder, that his ideals are only the little tax he pays for the right to hate and kill with a clear conscience. I am only angry that, knowing this, I still deluded myself. That there was not time to truly make part of myself what I know, and to teach others truth.[16]

In his retort, Von Berg reaches for an antidote to counteract the lethal nihilism of Leduc's proposition.

'There are ideals, Doctor, of another kind,' he exclaims. 'There are people who would find it easier to die than stain one finger with this murder. They exist. I swear it to you. People for whom everything is *not* permitted, foolish people and ineffectual, but they do exist and will not dishonor their tradition.'[17]

And he concludes with his initial request: 'I ask for your friendship.'

The disillusioned man and the idealist confront each other in the drama's crucial balance of beliefs, each challenging the other with his truth, and for a moment the equilibrium is maintained. Then, as the coarse laughter of the men humiliating the old Jew in the inner office breaks around them, Leduc drops another weight onto his scale.

'I owe you the truth, Prince,' he says quietly. 'You won't believe it now, but I wish you would think about it and what it means. I

[15] *Ibid.*, pp.61–62.

[16] *Ibid.*, p.65.

[17] *Ibid.*, pp.65–66.

have never analyzed a Gentile who did not have, somewhere hidden in his mind, a dislike if not hatred for the Jews.'

And in reply to Von Berg's alarmed denial, the psychiatrist continues:

> Until you know it is true of you you will destroy whatever truth can come of this atrocity. Part of knowing who we are is knowing we are not someone else. And Jew is only the name we give to that stranger, that agony we cannot feel, that death we look at like a cold abstraction. Each man has his Jew; it is the other. And the Jews have their Jews. And now, above all, you must see that you have yours—the man whose death leaves you relieved that you are not him, despite your decency. And that is why there is nothing—until you face your own complicity with this . . . your own humanity.[18]

'I tell you what I know!' cries Quentin to the Listener as he looks toward the image of the blasted stone tower of the concentration camp. 'My brothers died here—but my brothers built this place; our hearts have cut these stones!'

In a reasoned and carefully elucidated critique in the *New York Review of Books*, Philip Rahv commended the play's 'unquestionable dramatic tension,' but took its author to task for absorbing 'quite a few of the mystifications with which some of our intellectuals have been at once perplexing and diverting themselves.'

Citing Leduc's preceding speech as a case in point, the critic viewed it as a particularly feeble analysis of anti-Semitism, and reminded his readers that simpler and more pungent reasons than otherness draw Gentiles into disliking Jews. As an example, he suggested the 'tempting contradiction' in the Gentile image of the Jew. 'On the one hand they seem to be "pushy" and all too prosperous while on the other hand they seem so very helpless. It is this particular combination which invites the blows.'[19]

As long as Mr Rahv is not implying that the blows are invited solely by this 'particular combination,' there is no reason to dispute his assertion. However, the premise does not really invalidate Leduc's statement.

---

[18] *Ibid.*, p.66.

[19] Philip Rahv, 'Arthur Miller and the Fallacy of Profundity,' *The New York Review of Books*, 3 (January 14, 1964), p.3.

Rahv began his criticism of the passage by stating that he was not impressed by 'Miller's notion of anti-Semitism as his psychoanalyst voices it.' But Leduc's comment does not embody Miller's theory of anti-Semitism. The dramatist is not attributing the phenomenon to a single principle of human behavior; he is suggesting instead that *one* of the factors prevalent in anti-Semitism is inherent in human nature.

Mr Rahv casually swings around to this observation in his final comments about Leduc's speech, but he is still skeptical: 'And if Miller merely means to say that everyone wants to find someone he can look down upon or who might serve him as a scapegoat, that is the sheerest cliché.'[20]

The condescending tone of this statement is puzzling. As Leduc's words crackle like whiplashes in the narrow space between himself and Von Berg, they are no more a mere cliché than the number six million. They are not just abstractions; behind them, giving them terrible weight, are the sickening peals of laughter from the inner office, and the clacking wheels of crammed freight cars hurtling along steel rails to their barbed-wire destinations.

Moreover, the validity of Leduc's words are not just borne out by the Nazi barbarity, but by almost everything that has been happening among the internees of the detention station: by Marchand's refusal to look at the prisoners as he scurries past them after his release; by Lebeau's undefinable sense of guilt when he wishes he were Von Berg, innocent and separate; by Monceau's feelings of shame and resentment toward other Jews whose demeanor and actions, he thinks, have somehow obliquely put him in his present predicament; by the group's exclusion of the gypsy from their uneasy brotherhood; by the major's observation that everyone is at the muzzle end of someone else's revolver; by Leduc's bitter realization that he may be no better for the world than the captor he has vilified; and finally by the cultured innocence which Von Berg has used as a shield between himself and some of the facts of his life.

In the beginning of the play the Austrian prince has attempted to understand the Nazi phenomenon and his relationship to it by viewing it as something abominably uncultivated, an 'outburst of vulgarity' wholly alien to his sensibilities. But when he is reminded that Nazism is hardly restricted to the lower classes he can only

[20] *Ibid.*, p.3.

admit that he does not 'know what to say.' For the bulk of the ensuing hour his voice is muffled as he listens with growing mortification to the exchanges among the other men, and as he hears hopes, ideals, and rationalizations exploding like balloons in a shooting gallery, he tries desperately to cling to some belief that will leave him a shred of integrity.

'I deny that!' he cries angrily at Leduc's charge that he too, for all his decency, is not above the inhumanity he truly abhors. 'I deny that absolutely. I have never in my life said a word against your people. Is that your implication? That I have something to do with this monstrousness! I have put a pistol to my head! To my head!'[21]

But the protestation that Von Berg once contemplated suicide rather than yield to Nazism fails to impress the psychiatrist. Shifting from the abstract to the particular, he reminds the prince of his cousin Baron Kessler, a Nazi who persecuted Jewish doctors at a medical school which Leduc had attended, and forces him to admit that he was aware of what was happening.

Stunned and 'inward seeing,' Von Berg stammers his reply: 'Yes. I heard it. I . . . had forgotten it. You see, he was. . . .'

Leduc picks up the unfinished statement:

> . . . . Your cousin. I understand. And in any case, it is only a small part of Baron Kessler to you. I do understand it. But it is all of Baron Kessler to me. When you said his name, it was with love; and I am sure he must be a man of some kindness, with whom you can see eye to eye in many things. But when I hear that name I see a knife. You see now why I say there is nothing, and will be nothing, when even you cannot really put yourself in my place? Even you! And that is why your thoughts of suicide do not move me. It's not your guilt I want, it's your responsibility—that might have helped. Yes, if you had understood that Baron Kessler was in part, in some part, in some small and frightful part—doing your will. You might have done something then, with your standing, and your name and your decency, aside from shooting yourself![22]

Staring in full horror at the image of himself in the dark mirror Leduc holds up, Von Berg's final assurance crumbles.

'What can ever save us?' he shudders, covering his face with his

[21] Miller, *Incident at Vichy*, p.66.

[22] *Ibid.*, pp.67–68.

hands. And as he is taken into the office, the doctor sits motionless in the empty room, waiting fearfully and resignedly for inevitable destruction.

His sudden deliverance stuns him. Von Berg returns and hands Leduc his own pass; and after hesitating and protesting that the prince does not owe him any sacrifice, Leduc takes the piece of paper and escapes.

Because he is the most vocal and analytical individual in the play, and because his questions and comments seem essentially to be the author's, Leduc has been viewed by several critics as Miller's mouthpiece. This judgment, however, slights one crucial consideration: it does not differentiate between the doctor's role as the playwright's surrogate and as the object of his highly objective scrutiny.

Throughout the drama, Leduc speaks of making a break for freedom by overpowering the lone guard at the door, but he continually fails to act, ostensibly because he cannot muster enough support from his fellow inmates. Even when he finally convinces one other man, he hesitates because he then decides that three are needed. The major's revelation that sentries are posted at the street corners outside does not underscore the wisdom of Leduc's hesitancy, only in the light of subsequent events—the luck, and although the doctor constantly protests the inactivity of the others, he also does nothing until he is literally propelled by Von Berg. Verbally committed to a perilous but imperative action, he never takes it, and his inability to do so defines him as accurately as all his probing analysis and eloquent rhetoric.

Like Chris Keller of *All My Sons*, Leduc manifests a wide gulf between word and deed, between the voice and the man. He concludes his jeremiad to Von Berg by making a characteristically Millerish demand for the count's commitment. The exhortation, however, is drastically qualified by the unevadable fact that the morally indignant demander of responsibility has himself given very little, and furthermore, knows it.

A French officer who fought against the German invasion of his nation in 1940, Leduc has spent the past two years hiding with his wife and two children in the country, willingly detached from his homeland and his fellow Frenchmen. He cannot even employ Joe Keller's excuse of family love to rationalize his lack of responsibility, because his marriage is a failure and he is living with his wife only because the dangerous times have made a formal separation difficult. In the light of this absence of both public and private commitment, the reason for his capture is mordantly ironic: he had come to town to attempt to find some codeine for his wife's toothache, 'for a goddamned toothache! So what, she doesn't sleep for a couple of weeks! It was perfectly clear I shouldn't be taking the chance.'

The man who demands another person's responsibility has so abrogated his own in every area of his life that when he is convinced he is going to die he asks the apparent survivor to explicitly describe to his wife the fate that awaits him.

'The furnaces, tell her that,' he instructs Von Berg, before realizing with guilt and shame that in his deepest despair he can still wish to inflict vengeance and pain on someone else.

Leduc is hardly a villain, but neither is he a shining hero or a one-dimensional polemic bugler for the playwright. He is an intelligent, perceptive, deeply troubled human being, brought in his predicament to an awareness of the weaknesses and cruelties in himself at a time when he had hoped to find some decency, perhaps even nobility. Throughout the play he has sought proof that the nature of man is not as base as the spiraling evidence of his analysis seems to suggest, but his confrontations with Monceau, the German major, and finally the best of them—Von Berg—only confirm his blackest suspicions about himself and about humanity in general. And as he hurls his awareness and despair at the Austrian prince, prefacing his last diatribe with the agonized recognition of 'what scum we are,' the man who does not want guilt is steeped in it, and Leduc's heart, profoundly more than Monceau's, is conquered territory.

Because critics insistent on viewing Leduc solely as Miller's mouthpiece interpreted the doctor's final assessment of human nature as the play's ultimate truth, the ending of *Incident at Vichy* was cited by many as a blatant deus ex machina, not only arbitrarily but contradictorily undermining the play's thematic development. It was chided in several reviews for being melodramatic gimmickry at best (one favorable reviewer earnestly but backhandedly complimented it for giving the drama a badly needed 'jolt'), and at worst, moral dishonesty and thematic doubledealing, wherein the playwright tried to have his cake while eating it by condemning mankind in one thundering exhalation and then glibly exonerating it.

To argue that the play's resolution is valid because it parallels the outcome of true story upon which it is based is of course useless and fallacious. The final scene is sound not because it approximates history but because it is integrally related to the purpose and characterization of the drama. Von Berg's decision does not constitute any arbitrarily manufactured deliverance from the blackness of Miller's vision, nor any unconscious blurring of it. It is the inevitable climax to which the action of the play has been building..

As in *The Misfits* and *After the Fall*, one movement of *Incident at Vichy* is toward despair, toward the loss of hopes, illusions, and rationalizations, toward the inadequacy of reason and logic as well as faith, toward the erosion of any value that might possibly endow the word humanity with some positive meaning. Credos and tenets topple like ninepins before the withering scrutiny of Leduc and the major until at the end, with the pointed exception of the old Jew, the moral fate of all the characters is crushingly wedged between the psychiatrist's observation of 'what scum we are' and Von Berg's anguished search for 'what can save us.'

But like the Reverend Hale's conclusion in *The Crucible* that 'before the laws of God we are as swine,' Leduc's cry is a self-contained accusation. It is not Miller's final judgment of the human race, but the doctor's savage indictment of himself. Unquestionably the playwright recognizes the truth in it, but unlike Leduc, for whom it has become the *whole* truth, for Miller it has not, as Von Berg's final question and the act emanating from it demonstrate.

'What can save us?'

For all its disillusionment the line is a query, not a conclusion. It is not a final negation but an attempt to find a meaning, and this effort provides the corollary action of the play.

'What can save us?'

Not Bayard's belief in the innate decency of the common people, nor Monceau's faith in the subjective personality; neither the major's pervasive cynicism nor Von Berg's controlled innocence. Not the lie of Eden, but also not the blanket acceptance of despair inherent in Leduc's final searing nihilism. Perhaps only, and most tenuously, hope lies in the individual's acceptance of responsibility in the full knowledge of his separateness and his destructive potential, before that responsibility has been utterly dissolved into the uselessness of guilt. Von Berg's final decision is precisely his acceptance, for once in his life, of that responsibility *before the fact,* an acceptance as integral to the meaning and development of his drama as the debilitating despair out of which it is wrenched.

Nonetheless, the objection has been advanced that the prince's action is a vain sacrifice, made less out of responsibility than out of an unwarranted guilt imposed upon him by the playwright.

The glaring weakness in this objection is the assumption that Miller is parceling out equal shares of responsibility for the horrors of Nazism to the entire human race. This is simply and clearly not so. Not one of the ten men waiting in the detention station can be even remotely compared with the racial 'anthropologist' who efficiently and sadistically controls their destinies. The dramatist is hardly suggesting that the victim is as responsible for his plight as the victimizer; and he no more claims that Von Berg is as culpable in the persecution of Jews as Baron Kessler than he equates the workmen who helped to construct the concentration camps with the creatures who conceived them.

Miller is grappling with *complicity,* not *equality,* in evil, and to interpret the former in terms of the latter is to distort the meaning of his play. He is not claiming that we are all equally guilty of injustice in the world, but rather that very few of us, for all our avowed decency, are wholly innocent.

In *Incident at Vichy,* Miller is much less concerned with defining the Nazi mentality than with dramatizing the reasoning of its uncomprehending accomplices. In fact, to the extent that he does attempt to analyze Nazism he becomes woefully confused. Philip Rahv was undeniably right when he suggested that the playwright was unnecessarily mystifying the Nazi mind by allowing Von Berg to define the Germans' actions as a compensation for their essential vacuity.

'They do these things not because they are German but because they are nothing,' the prince exclaims. 'It is the hallmark of the age—the less you exist the more important it is to make a clear impression.'[23]

As Rahv noted, it may be a hallmark of the age, but the explanation, its 'modish existentialist ring' notwithstanding, is pretty flabby. The Nazi phenomenon was not a compensatory mechanism

[23] *Ibid.,* p.38.

for some kind of metaphysical vacuum, but 'a willed contempt functionally serving as the rationalization, politically and culturally, of their urge to exterminate other peoples in order to make *Lebensraum* for themselves.'[24] They acted not because they were nothing, but because they were definitely something, and knew it.

However, Miller's rather hazy thinking with respect to Nazism does not invalidate the main purpose of his play. *Incident at Vichy* dramatizes not the villainy of the Nazis—which is scarcely worth reiterating—but the involvement of human beings with justice and injustice, self-preservation and commitment to others, which make for some of the conditions responsible for Nazism's growth and, by strong implication, for its possible resurrection.

Implicit in the play is the proposition that the events it dramatizes were not an isolated historical accident, an unexplainable earthquake engulfing millions of persons, but something recognizable, not only in political, social, and economic terms, but also in terms of human nature.

In *Incident at Vichy,* Miller is applying to a particular moment in history a consideration of a facet of human nature that he dramatized in a more personal context in *After the Fall*: the individual's potential for evil, coupled with his adamant refusal to acknowledge it in himself. At the end of the play Von Berg does not discover that he is or ever could be a Nazi. He discovers, in the awareness of his relief at escaping victimization, his relationship to—*not equality with*—the victimizers. It is a relationship based not simply on his desire for life, but on the grim fact that this desire makes him close his eyes to the injustice around him. And in refusing to face his particular kinship to this evil, no matter how gossamer the connection, he aids and abets it.

Incident at Vichy presents no solution to the problem of man's complicity with evil. It recognizes that the acknowledgment of this complicity elicits guilt which rushes into the vacuum left by the shattered illusion of innocence. And perceiving this, the play suggests that the way out of the resultant dilemma does not lie in the generalization of guilt, which is ultimately self-frustrating and self-defeating, as the plight of Leduc illustrates. Steeped in mortification, he generalizes his shame into a universal condition—'what scum we are'—and takes refuge from responsibility by losing himself in an abstraction.

Balancing Von Berg against Leduc, the drama implies that if guilt can be particularized and clarified, it can perhaps be transformed from masochistic despair into responsibility. This is what the prince does, and so doing sets a similar alternative before the man he saves. Symbolized by the wedding ring that has been given to Von Berg by the boy to return to his mother, and which the nobleman gives to Leduc along with his pass, guilt and responsibility are transmitted from one man to the other—the guilt of being the survivor, and the responsibility of transforming that guilt into something stronger and more positive than self-pity.

To his consternation, Leduc has received the proof for which he has been asking; his image of man has encountered its first exception. How he will act upon this evidence is a question the play rightly does not attempt to answer any more than Von Berg does. It is proper and sufficient that Leduc's drama begins as the prince's ends.

To debate the utility of Von Berg's final decision in terms of wisdom or waste is useless. Strictly speaking it is neither. A choice is made which is far too personal and impassioned to represent a circumscribed and articulate philosophy of life. The nobleman finds himself in the wrong place at the wrong time to be academic, and the choice he makes is the initial and crucial step a man takes on discovering himself in a world whose values have proved deceptive and destructive. A protest of the individual soul against inhumanity, it is the decision of a man who cannot survive at what he considers—wisely or foolishly—to be the price of his integrity. As he has said earlier, there are people for whom everything is *not* permitted. To his great surprise, he discovers he is one of them.

His brother's keeper? Probably. His own? Unquestionably.

If *Incident at Vichy* hurls a polemic at its audience, it does so with dramatic skill and power. The stark, drab setting is perfectly suited to the play's purpose. A kind of purgatory between the outer world where ordinary people are going about their daily business, and the hellish inner office in which that existence is being horribly undermined, the dimly lit room manifests the isolation and despair of each individual in it. And against the gray drabness of this forbidding no-man's-land, the thrust of the drama builds ominously and relentlessly through a carefully controlled interplay of action and dialogue.

Tension is initiated in the characters' quickening realization of the nature of their plight, and maintained and heightened by each succeeding exit made against the baleful light of the inner office. Paralleling the play's action, a skillfully balanced series of conversations develop and propel its argument to a final crescendo as each line of dialogue hurls the drama forward, simultaneously crystallizing the horror of the situation and narrowing the alternatives to it.

The dialogue serves yet another purpose. It not only reveals the growing awareness of most of the characters, but their helplessness as well.

'They rely on our own logic to immobilize us,' Leduc says of the Nazi operation, and the structural pattern of the play chillingly validates his remark.

In the midst of the verbal deluge only one man, Bayard, makes any valid gesture of escape, when he breaks the handles off the gypsy's pot for use as a wedge on the door of the freight car that will ship him to a concentration camp. The rest, including Leduc, take refuge in words. While the victims talk, the victimizers act, plucking one rider after another from the verbal carousel, and as the numbers dwindle the dialogue characteristically is intensified.

However, although Miller's use of dialogue helps to maintain the dramatic tension of *Incident at Vichy,* it also delineates the greatest weakness in the play. In carefully building toward the elucidation of his central issue, the dramatist tends to sacrifice characterization for thematic clarity, particularly with respect to secondary figures like Monceau, Bayard, and Lebeau. Although they occasionally flare into individuality, for the most part they are personified attitudes, and the rather obvious attempts to humanize them by endowing each with bits and pieces of personal history do not wholly compensate for the thematic functions that tend to weigh them down.

The subordination of their humanity to their didacticism is most apparent when they do not speak. Silent, they often ceases to exist, sitting instead in their appointed places like obedient marionettes waiting for the next tug of their verbal strings. Consequently, when the dialogue abates even momentarily the gulf between the play's polemic intent and its organic life becomes marked.

Walter Kerr's suggestion that 'it is better to make a man than to make a point,' which did not really apply to *The Crucible,* finds

its target more readily in *Incident at Vichy*. And of greater significance, to the extent that the man is subordinated to the point,
the point is also weakened. Doors slam, commands are barked,
shots are fired, persons are pushed, and numbers relentlessly
dwindle, but to the degree that invalidated arguments rather than
human beings enter the inner office, the power of the drama's
debate, though still considerable, never attains its full potential.

There are two exceptions to this debilitation by silence. The
old Jew does not speak a word, but as he sways wearily on the
wooden bench, his mouth working, perhaps in silent prayer or in
memory, and his eyes staring into a universe of private hopes
and dreads, he develops a terrible and tragic humanity that
needs no dialogue to define it. Similarily, Von Berg's ultimate
self-awareness and the deed it engenders are unheralded by any
bursts of rhetoric. The prince's sacrifice is accompanied only by
the command to the doctor to leave, and the reiteration of the
address to which Leduc must deliver the ring. His humanity also
need no further verbal definition.

At the conclusion, the Austrian prince and the German officer
face each other wordlessly.

> The moment lengthens, and lengthens yet. A look of anguish
> and fury is stiffening in the major's face; he is closing his fists.
> They stand there, forever incomprehensible to one another,
> looking into each other's eyes.[25]

And as four new suspects are dragged into the room, each in his
bewilderment and fear does not realize that standing before him
are two men separated by their destinies, two human alternatives
suspended in a critical and terrible polarity.

[25] Miller, *Incident at Vichy*, p.70.

19

'I just didn't want him to

end up on the grass'

Arthur Miller had often run the gauntlet that is sometimes called play rehearsals. But if he thought that after twenty-four years along the same blistering paths he was becoming inured to the fiery trials of his chosen profession, the pre-Broadway tribulations of *The Price* quickly convinced him he was not.

For over four months in 1967, Miller and director Ulu Grosbard, who had staged the powerful off-Broadway revival of *A View from the Bridge* in 1965, searched for an actor to portray the fifty-year-old policeman who is the key figure in *The Price*. They finally chose Jack Warden, and subsequently rounded out their four-character cast with Kate Reid, David Burns, and the quintessential and perennial Miller actor, Arthur Kennedy.

However, just before the tryouts in Philadelphia, Warden became seriously ill and literally had to be replaced overnight by Pat Hingle. The Philadelphia opening was postponed and round-the-clock rehearsals were scheduled to allow the newcomer time to acclimate himself. But although Hingle soon hit his stride and the performances rapidly gained a fine, honed edge, the play limped into New York two weeks behind schedule, and still beset with problems.

Miller and Grosbard could not agree on certain interpretations of character and theme, and finally the playwright took over the direction for the last week of Broadway previews. Then, as he tried to mold the production to his specifications, another crack appeared in the dike. Prior to opening night, David Burns was stricken with an intestinal ailment, and his understudy, Harold Gary, had to be pressed into service.

'This never happened to me before and, my God, I hope it never happens again,' Miller exclaimed with a stunned look on his face. 'I haven't slept; I feel I've been down here all my life. It's like *No Exit*—you can never get out!'[1]

It wasn't quite like *No Exit*. He got out. And so did *The Price*. Its premiere at the Morosco Theater on February 7, 1968 was greeted by more cordial reviews than any Miller drama since *Death of a Salesman*. Although many of the reviewers had reservations about its structure and resolution, the majority agreed with the *New York Times'* Clive Barnes, who viewed it as 'one of the most engrossing and entertaining plays that Miller has ever written.' A one-year run in New York, followed by a highly successful London opening, subsequently proved that quite a few theatergoers concurred with Mr Barnes's appraisal.

The Price is an intriguing play. In form and structure it hearkens back to *All My Sons*; in its themes it is similar to *After the Fall*. Consequently, while it seems somewhat dated (one reviewer wrote it off as 'vintage 1930s') it also appears to herald new directions in Miller's thought (another critic saw it exhibiting not one but 'two new faces' of its author).

Structurally the drama is less vintage 1930s than a solidly constructed, well-made play in the tradition of Ibsen in which the present conflict spirals out of an involved set of past relationships. The dialogue is basically expository and revelatory, probing the past and examining a house built on lies, while simultaneously leading to a series of discoveries that shatter the illusions that have enveloped and almost suffocated the house.

As the two brothers who form the play's dramatic nucleus square off against each other in a long, exhausting, and corrosive verbal fencing match, Miller returns to his perpetual gladiatorial arena, the family, in a renewed exploration of the relationship between actions and consequences, guilt and responsibility, and self-preservation and commitment to others. Throughout the harrowing, recrimination-filled afternoon, the echoes of previous family confrontations and conflicts reverberate across the footlights as brother lacerates brother in a desperate attempt to justify his life.

The Price dramatizes the ambivalent relationship of Victor and Walter Franz. The former is a fifty-year-old policeman facing the prospect of retirement with uncertainty and fear. Once a promising student, he had aborted his college education and subsequent career by choosing to remain with and support his bankrupt father during the Depression. Walter, on the other hand, had allowed nothing to deter him from his goals and had left home to pursue his studies in medicine. Doling out only token financial aid to his father and brother, Walter looked out for himself and quickly became a success in his profession. Estranged for many years, the two brothers now meet again when Victor summons Walter to help him dispose of the household belonging of their late father and mother.

As the men confront each other in the cluttered attic of their parents' home, one in his blue policeman's uniform and the other in his tan vicuna coat, their latent antagonism quickly flares into overt hostility, and some initial comments about the prices of furniture explode into a blistering quarrel over the less tangible but more pervasive prices each has paid for the life he has fashioned. With Victor's loyal but weary wife Esther, and an elderly Jewish furniture dealer named Gregory Solomon looking on like embarrassed and helpless referees, the two brothers begin to slash at each other through the accumulated layers of protective armor each has developed over the years.

Illusions and rationalizations are punctured by the verbal rapiers the two men wield against each other until at the end of the duel each has been laid bare to the bone of reality and forced to see some of the truths he has attempted to conceal. And each then departs, having gained some new awareness but still essentially powerless to alter the role he has played for more than half his life.

'Time you know is a terrible thing,' muses Solomon early in the play and points casually to the painful dilemma facing all four of the characters. In his own way each is attempting to find some sureties and enduring values in the face of the ceaseless and irrevocable movement of time which makes a mockery out of all attempts at permanence, blurring the once clear lines of demarcation between importance and triviality, and continually recalling choices made and sacrifices lived, without bestowing either the guarantee of rightness or the consolation of compassion.

The attic in which the play's action occurs brilliantly illuminates the ravages of time. Choked with a lifetime's accumulations—highlighted by the father's overstuffed armchair and the mother's gilded harp, the room is a mausoleum of memories, a grim, bittersweet, almost incomprehensible reminder of a past that no longer seems as meaningful or even true as it once was.

As the attic begins to resurrect his previous life, Victor grows increasingly uneasy. Faced with the prospect of retirement, he is afraid of the emptiness that lies ahead and amazed at the bleakness stretching out behind him.

'I'll be frank with you, kid,' he confides shakily to his wife, 'I look at my life and the whole thing is incomprehensible to me. I know all the reasons and all the reasons and all the reasons, and it ends up—nothing.'[2]

Victor has been dominated by his past, particularly by his father's catastrophe. Like Willy Loman, the elder Franz had worshiped the gods of material success and had viewed his bankruptcy as a fall from grace. But unlike the idealistic salesman, Franz took refuge from an alien, mocking world by fashioning a fortress out of despair and self-pity. And embracing defeat, he had allowed his son to become the keeper of his cold, flickering flame. Now, with his life permanently molded by his commitment to his father, Victor cannot shake off the nagging and frightening suspicion that the past twenty-eight years may not only have been a waste, but a lie.

'I'm not even sure any more what I was trying to accomplish,' he admits wearily. 'I look back now, and all I can see is a long, brainless walk in the street.'[3]

His doubt and confusion are shared by his wife. Frustrated by the shoddiness of their life, she feels particularly isolated since her son left for college. Intelligent and compassionate, she loves her husband but is bewildered at his indecisiveness, embarrassed by his uniform (which perpetually signals his income), and discouraged by the treadmill of their lives.

'It's that everything was always temporary with us,' she explains. 'It's like we never were anything, we were always about to be.'[4]

Her frustration is clearly exhibited in her dualistic attitude toward her brother-in-law. On the one hand she resents the aloof individual whose success has been a corollary of his abandonment

[2] Miller, *The Price* (New York: Viking, 1968), p.23

[3] *Ibid.,* p.48.

[4] *Ibid.,* p.18.

of his father and brother, and she proudly contrasts Victor's
fidelity to his father with Walter's calculated neglect. On the other
hand she is herself enmeshed in the success idea that Victor has
long abandoned, and even though she resents Walter's attitude
toward her husband, she respects and even begrudgingly admires
her brother-in-law's apparent purpose, confidence, and affluence.

Consequently when Walter proffers his help by offering his
brother his share of the sale, Esther quickly urges Victor to take
it, accepting Walter's kindness at face value. And in her demand
she berates her husband for his hesitancy.

'You throw this away,' she threatens, 'you've got to explain it
to me. You can't go on blaming him or the system or God knows
what else! You're free and you can't make a move, Victor, and
that's what's driving me crazy!'[5]

Contrasted with Victor's inertia is Walter's drive. However, although Walter has been a winner in the rat race, he has paid
dearly for the victory, and after a divorce and a nervous breakdown he realizes how meaningless the laurels can be. Having
peered into the abyss and survived, he now has a deeper comprehension of the motivations that spurred him.

> You start out wanting to be the best and there's no question
> that you do need a certain fanaticism. Until you've eliminated
> everything extraneous—including people. And of course the
> time comes when you realize that you haven't merely been
> specializing in something—something has been specializing in
> you. You become a kind of instrument . . . that cuts money
> out of people, or fame out of the world. And it finally makes
> you stupid. Power can do that. You get to think that because
> you frighten people they love you. Even that you love them—
> And the whole thing comes down to fear. . . . But there's one
> virtue in going nuts—provided you survive, of course. You
> get to see the terror—not the screaming kind, but the slow,
> daily fear you call ambition, and cautiousness, and piling up
> the money.[6]

And analyzing this terror, Walter relates it to his abandonment
of his father. He views his flight as an escape generated by the
annihilating fear that his father's failure and degradation could

---

[5] *Ibid.*, p.78.

[6] *Ibid.*, pp.82–83.

also be his legacy. He even suggests that Victor's choice to remain with the elder Franz was a manifestation of that same fear.

> Vic, we were both running from the same thing. I thought I wanted to be tops, but what it was was untouchable. I ended in a swamp of success and bankbooks, you on civil service. The difference is that you haven't hurt other people to defend yourself. And I've learned to respect that, Vic; you simply tried to make yourself useful.[7]

Thus for Walter, both sons had fled from their father's fate, one by challenging and hollowly triumphing over the system that had crushed the old man, and the other by turning his escape inward, trying to appease that selfsame system by offering himself as a sacrifice. These are Walter's opening truths, and he propounds them to his brother in a spirit of reconciliation.

His share of the profits from the sale of the furniture accompanies Walter's initial offer of friendship; the second offer involves a liaison position for Victor in the new wing of the hospital Walter currently supervises. But although Victor is dazzled by his brother's generosity, he is also uneasy with the simplicity of Walter's solutions. He knows that he hasn't the credentials for the position, and the more he considers the proposal, the more he detects the slightly sour smell of a bribe.

'I'm not sure I know what you want, Walter,' he says warily, and as Walter perceives the iciness in Victor's tone he realizes that his brother's friendship will not come easily. The glib hope of solidarity is dissolved and the two men face each other across the cluttered space, with their mother's harp and their father's chair standing like mute witnesses demanding their due. The room presses in on them, refusing to be cleared by heartening words and generous offers. Piled up like used furniture are months and years that will not be readily sold. Each has its price, and it is expensive.

Releasing a lifetime of pent-up resentment against his brother, Victor draws first blood when he reminds Walter that for all his rationalizations he cannot evade the fact that he ran out on his father and then tried to soothe his conscience by contributing five dollars a month for the old man's support. Walter parries his

[7] *Ibid.*, p.84.

brother's thrust by insisting that Victor's choice to remain with their father was foolish since the elder Franz was perfectly able to work and care for himself. And as Victor tries to sidestep this uncomfortable truth, Walter drives it home.

'He exploited you!' he exclaims.

Now Victor is defensive. Protesting that he was not his father's victim, he insists that his actions were determined solely by the situation.

'I made no choice,' he cries. 'The icebox was empty and the man was sitting there with his mouth open.'

With this reply the brothers temporarily check each other. Each has attempted to justify his actions and neither has been able to pierce the other's carefully constructed defense. Then, as they cautiously take each other's measure, Esther breaks the stalemate by citing Walter's refusal to lend his brother five hundred dollars to complete his education as the crux of Victor's resentment.

Admitting his shame, Walter reveals that he had subsequently telephoned Victor to make the loan, but was dissuaded from doing so by their father. Hearing from the old man of Victor's firm commitment to him, Walter then decided to withdraw his offer:

> I was never able to feel your kind of faith in him. . . . His selfishness—which was perfectly normal—was always obvious to me, but you never seemed to notice it. To the point where I used to blame myself for a lack of feeling. You understand? So when he said that you wanted to help him, I felt somehow that it'd be wrong for me to try to break it up between you. It seemed like interfering.[8]

Despite its validity, Walter's explanation is still an obvious rationalization, and Victor cuts through it with one deft rapier stroke when he sarcastically asks his brother how the loan would really have interfered.

'I'd have gone on supporting him; it would have let me finish school, that's all,' he exclaims.

Then he backs Walter to the wall.

'You didn't give me the money because you didn't want to,' he concludes bluntly. 'That's what it comes to doesn't it? Not that you had any obligation, but if you want to help somebody you do

[8] *Ibid.*, p.96.

it, if you don't you don't . . . we do what we want to do, don't we?'[9]

And demolishing Walter's justification, Victor angrily dismisses his brother's efforts at reconciliation.

You can't walk in with one splash and wash out twenty-eight years. There's a price people pay. I've paid it, it's all gone, I haven't got it any more. Just like you paid, didn't you? You've got no wife, you've lost your family, you're rattling around all over the place? Can you go home and start all over again from scratch? This is where we are; now, right here, now.[10]

Right here, and now, Victor seems to have the upper hand. He has shattered Walter's attempts to buy off the past, and his strength and honesty appear to illuminate the weakness and evasiveness of the surgeon's position. When Walter feebly returns to the proposition that their father was able to take care of himself, Victor cuts him down.

'Perfectly fit!' he cries. 'What about the inside of his head? The man was ashamed to go into the street. . . . I could have left him with your five dollars a month? I'm sorry, you can't brainwash me. . . . You had a responsibility here and you walked out on it.'[11]

Victor's words stun Walter, but he fights back. He had hoped for a reconciliation without reopening old wounds, but staggered by Victor's irate accusations, he counters with a truth of his own. He admits that the real reason he refused his father and brother financial aid was because the old man had a four thousand dollar nest egg from which he supported himself throughout the period of Victor's care. When Victor dazedly questions his father's motives Walter tries to explain that even though Victor was looking after him the old man never wholly believed that he would remain.

Stung by the revelation of his father's betrayal of his trust, and by the terrible implication that his sacrifice has been worthless, Victor still tries to pin the blame on Walter. He accuses his brother of complying with the elder Franz's treachery in a conspiracy of silence.

[9] *Ibid.*, p.97.
[10] *Ibid.*, p.98.
[11] *Ibid.*, p.101.

'You knew he had that kind of money, and came here many times, you sat here, the two of you, watching me walking around in this suit?' he cries bitterly.

However Walter is now on the offensive and he will not allow Victor to play the unqualified martyr any longer. Caustically reminding him that he could have financed his education easily by selling his mother's harp, he insists Victor suspected the truth about their father all along, but refused to face it, preferring instead to play the noble, self-sacrificing son.

'It's a fantasy, Victor. Your father was penniless and your brother a son of a bitch, and you play no part at all.'

And as Walter's truth slides home through the crumbling tissue of Victor's defense, Esther drives it still deeper.

'It was all an act!' she cries of her father-in-law's duplicity, 'he was a calculating liar! And in your heart you knew it! No wonder you're paralyzed—you haven't believed a word you've said all these years. We've been lying away our existence all these years; down the sewer, day after day . . . to protect a miserable cheap manipulator. No wonder it all seemed like a dream to me—it *was*; a god-damned nightmare.'[12]

His illusions in rubble around him, almost shuddering in pain and despair, Victor groggily tries to delve beneath the facts with which his brother and wife have confronted him.

'This isn't true, either,' he finally exclaims.

'We are dying, that's what's true!' Esther replies bitterly.

And in the teeth of this single, irrevocable certainty, hemmed in by the mocking shadows of the past, no longer able to draw sustenance from the martyr's myth, Victor defensively begins to probe Walter's truth. Although he is still attempting to justify his life, he is nevertheless determined to fully comprehend it. He admits that he had questioned his father about the money, only to be greeted with laughter.

Struck by that incongruous and chilling response, which has haunted him through the years, Victor had walked out of the house and into a nearby park.

The grass was covered with men. Like a battlefield; a big open-air flophouse. And not bums—some of them still had shined shoes and good hats, busted businessmen, lawyers,

[12] *Ibid.*, p.106.

skilled mechanics. Which I'd seen a hundred times. But suddenly—you know?— I *saw* it. There was no mercy. Any-
where. One day you're the head of the house, at the head
of the table, and suddenly you're shit. Overnight. And I
tried to figure out that laugh. How could he be holding out
on me when he loved me?[13]

He cries out his answer, the only answer that makes any
sense to him:

'He loved me, Esther! He just didn't want to end up on the
grass! It's not that you don't love somebody, it's that you've got
to survive. We know what that feels like, don't we?'[14]

She knows. And Walter knows.

Survival and betrayal. To survive, who would not betray? If the
elder Franz betrayed one son, was he not betrayed by the other,
and by his wife as well?

[Walter] kicked him in the face; my mother—the night he told
us he was bankrupt. . . . It was right on this couch. She was
all dressed up—for some affair, I think. Her hair was piled up,
and long earrings? And he had his tuxedo on . . . and made
us all sit down; and he told us it was all gone. And she
vomited. All over his arms. His hands. Just kept on vomiting,
like thirty-five years coming up. And he sat there. Stinking
like a sewer. And a look came onto his face. I'd never seen a
man look like that. He was sitting there, letting it dry on his
hands.[15]

Their lives reek with betrayals: a wife's betrayal of her husband, a father's betrayal of his son, another son's betrayal of his
father and brother, and the betrayal in Walter's and Victor's
families as well. As the mordant specters glower in the musty air
of the attic, Quentin's concluding words in *After the Fall* seem
to echo in sardonic affirmation:

I loved them all, all! And gave them willing to failure and
to death that I might live, as they gave me and gave each other,
with a word, a look, a trick, a truth, a lie—and all in love!

[13] *Ibid.*, p.107.
[14] See note 13 above.
[15] *Ibid.*, p.108.

Although Victor's admission is new, the awareness behind it is not. He always knew, and knowing, he acted. Against the facts of deception and betrayal, something had to be upheld.

'We do what we have to do,' he says simply. 'He couldn't believe in anybody anymore, and it was unbearable to me!'

So he made his commitment.

'Not that I excuse it; it was idiotic, nobody has to tell me that. But you're brought up to believe in one another, you're filled full of that crap—you can't help trying to keep it going, that's all. I thought if I stuck with him, if he could see that somebody was still . . . I can't explain it; I wanted to . . . stop it from falling apart.'[16]

In contrast to Walter's flight toward detachment, Victor has posited the countermovement toward involvement, an involvement born of a love that he tried to relocate in his family as a debt to an old man who had once believed in it.

Victor's words are comforting. They soothe, heal, and reestablish belief. In fact they could easily resolve the play. But *The Price* offers no easy resolutions, and with Walter's rejoinder it is quickly apparent that the agonizing search for final answers is not yet over.

'It won't work, Vic,' he says quietly. 'You see it yourself, don't you? It's not that at all.'

And with Victor and Esther staring mutely at him, he explodes his brother's stirring valedictory.

> Is it really something that fell apart? Were we really brought up to believe in one another? We were brought up to succeed, weren't we? Why else would he respect me so and not you? What fell apart? Was there ever any love here? When he needed her, she vomited. And when you needed him, he laughed. What was unbearable is not that it all fell apart, it was that there was never anything here.[17]

Not in anger, but in profound sadness, Walter has elucidated the underlying truth of the Franz family. The last illusions and rationalizations begin to evaporate as the three of them now gaze fearfully into the abyss of despair out of which they created their lives.

[16] *Ibid.*, p.108.
[17] *Ibid.*, p.109.

'But who . . . who can ever face that, Walter?' Esther asks sorrowfully.

'You have to!' he replies, and then turns to his brother.

'What you saw behind the library was not that there was no mercy in the world, kid,' he says resignedly. 'It's that there was no love in this house. There was no loyalty. There was nothing here but a straight financial arrangement. That's what was unbearable. And you proceeded to wipe out what you saw.'[18]

As his truth sinks in, Walter elaborates on it:

We invent ourselves, Vic, to wipe out what we know. You invent a life of self-sacrifice, a life of duty; but what never existed here cannot be upheld. You were not upholding something, you were denying what you knew they were. And denying yourself. And that's all that is standing between us now—an illusion, Vic. That I kicked them in the face and you must uphold them against me. But I only saw then what you see now—there was nothing here to betray.[19]

'To admit what you see endangers principles.'

Quentin's realization in *After the Fall* is equally applicable to Victor. He had always seen the pictures Walter now holds up before him, but he had attempted to blot them out. Unable to admit that little love or faith save his own existed in his family, he created the masochistically comforting illusion of love and trust betrayed, and for the rest of his life clung to it. Thus he has lived a lie, blaming an amorphous system for his father's downfall, and a specific brother for the old man's betrayal, and viewing himself as the martyred victim of his nobility.

'I am not your enemy,' Walter concludes. 'It is all an illusion and if you could walk through it, we could meet. . . .'

Walter's sincerity is unmistakable, but despite his renewed offer of friendship, something remains annoyingly out of focus. Victor is not the only one who still has an illusion to walk through.

'He doesn't follow me any more with that vomit on his hands,' Walter exclaims, refering to the memory of his father. 'I don't look high and low for some betrayal any more; my days belong to *me* now.'

[18] *Ibid.*, p.109.
[19] *Ibid.*, p.110.

Not quite. He is not as free from his father as he would like to believe. First of all, even though he boasts of finally living a 'real' life, no longer molded into the 'financial arrangement' which dominated the Franz home, almost all of Walter's actions in the play reverberate with the steady ring of a cash register as they contradict his assertion.

Secondly, and more importantly, if Walter is no longer pursued by the demanding apparition of his father, why has he come to his brother at this time, and what does he want from him? Friendship, he explains, free of delusions, based firmly upon the comprehension of truth.

But is this all?

Victor does not think so. Although he can see the validity of Walter's argument, he is also able to perceive the motivation behind it, and to his brother's demand that he face the facts of life, Victor retorts: 'But what do you face?' And overriding Walter's protests, he counters with his insight and his accusation:

> You came for the old handshake, didn't you! The okay! And you end up with the respect, the career, the money, and best of all, the thing that nobody else can tell you so you can believe it—that you're one hell of a guy and never harmed anybody in your life! Well, you won't get it, not till I get mine![20]

Still defensive, still seeking personal justification, Victor has nevertheless touched his brother's raw nerve. He has bared the wound of festering guilt beneath Walter's carefully applied bandage of logic and reason. Like Eugene O'Neill's compulsive salesman, Hickey, Walter exhibits in his attempts to destroy Victor's illusions, his own uncertainty and fear, his own nagging comprehension that for all his efforts at liberation he has not shaken himself loose from the ghosts that still pursue him. Having abandoned his father when the old man's plight became a threat to his career, Walter tried to justify his action by demonstrating that his flight was not a betrayal of love or faith because neither ever existed in the Franz home, and if 'what never existed cannot be upheld,' neither can it be destroyed.

However, he cannot dispel the awareness that his abandonment

[20] *Ibid.*, pp.111–112.

of his family was motivated mainly by self-preservation. The realization that his bleak description of his parents' home is essentially correct does not assuage the guilt emanating from his complicity in his father's betrayal.

Walter has gained his separation but he has paid his prices. Like the attic around him his life is littered with the debris of a broken marriage, a nervous breakdown, overwhelming loneliness, and omnipresent guilt. What he wants from Victor is not only reconciliation, the restoration of ties he had severed twenty-eight years ago, but a blessing, the guarantee and surety his brother's love and forgiveness will supply. He has accepted much of the responsibility for his life, something Victor has heretofore been unwilling to do, but he wants a reward for his efforts: he wants both his freedom and his innocence. He wants absolution.

With the contradiction of his life painfully exposed, Walter now strikes back at the brother who apparently refuses to resolve it.

'And you?' he rages. 'You never had any hatred for me? Never a wish to see me destroyed? To destroy me . . . with this saintly self-sacrifice, this mockery of sacrifice? What will you give me, Victor?'

Although Walter's condemnation perfectly defines much of his brother's distorted self-justification, it also illustrates how trapped Walter still is in his own maze. Accusing Victor of trying to play the tragic hero in a farce of self-deception, Walter ironically casts himself in a similar role. In reply to Walter's question, Victor speaks with a new sense of awareness.

'I don't have it to give you,' he says quietly and comprehendingly. 'Not any more. And you don't have it to give. And there's nothing to give—I see that now. I just didn't want him to end up on the grass. And he didn't. That's all it was, and *I don't need anything more*.'[21]

Walter still does, but it is not Victor's to give. Neither of them can provide the panacea for the other's life. This is Victor's final knowledge, but for Walter it is still not comprehensible.

'He is sacrificing his life to vengeance,' he exclaims to Esther. Then, turning to Victor: 'To prove with your failure what a treacherous son of a bitch I am!—to hang yourself in my doorway!'

[21] *Ibid.*, p.112. Italics my own.

His frustration and anger now embracing both his brother and his sister-in-law, Walter continues:

> You quit; both of you. You lay down and quit and that's the long and the short of all your ideology. It is all envy. . . . And to this moment you haven't the guts to face it! But your failure does not give you moral authority! Not with me! I *worked* for what I made and there are people walking around today who'd have been dead if I hadn't.
>
> [*pointing at his father's chair*]
> He was smarter than all of us—he saw what you wanted and he gave it to you! . . . You will never, never again make me ashamed![22]

Walter's parting salvo acts as both a sword and a shield. It hacks out truths about Victor, but it also provides a buffer between Walter and his own truths. Like Willy Loman accusing Biff of vengeance and spite when the young man tries to make him face his life, Walter uses his insight into his brother as a shield for himself. He still maintains a bristling and adamant defense.

His garish claim that his abandonment of his family led, via his profession, to the saving of many lives, is pathetically irrelevant to the present situation. And his final assertion that Victor will never again make him feel ashamed is equally misguided because he, not Victor, will continually provide the sword thrust of shame. The guilt he accuses his brother of making him feel is really his own, and no amount of truth about Victor will change or alleviate it.

As he strides out, Walter grabs Solomon and laughs angrily into the old man's face.

'Go ahead you old mutt—rob them blind,' he snarls, 'they love it!'

The exclamation shows that although Walter has bared the facts of Victor's life, he still has not wholly understood it. For Walter, his brother's relationship to the furniture dealer is similar to his attachment to his father: it appears to be another manifestation of Victor's masochistic desire for victimization and martyrdom. Rather than make a handsome profit on the sale of the furniture through Walter's manipulations, Victor stands by his agreement with Solomon. To the surgeon this is further proof of

[22] *Ibid.*, pp.112–113.

his brother's self-sacrificial attitude, and he throws it in Victor's face as he storms out.

What Walter cannot and will not see is that Victor's reaffirmation of the pact with the old man is not simply an illustration of self-immolation, but a gesture of faith, a preservation of a bond between the two men. Characteristically, Walter cannot grasp this any more than he can Victor's previous commitment to his father.

Although Victor's actions toward Solomon reorchestrate this commitment in a minor key, the ancient furniture dealer is by no means a reincarnation of the elder Franz. In fact, in just about every respect he is the antithesis of Victor's father.

In a play about survival and the prices it elicits, Gregory Solomon, the wandering Jew, is not only the crowning personification of man's will to survive, but of his unadulterated zest for living. Marvelously human and humorous, he is a combination of gentleman, sage, and aged imp. Exhibiting the wisdom of Solomon, the canniness of David Harum, and the indestructibility of Superman, he has spent almost a century traveling the earth, indulging in everything from a stint in the British Navy to an acrobatic act in vaudeville, outliving wives and children, and amassing and losing several fortunes. In marked contrast to the elder Franz, who crumpled under his first blow and embraced failure, Solomon has rebounded from at least four depressions dating all the way back to 1898. Almost ninety, he burns with a strong flame that consumes the fear of undertaking a new project in a blaze of anticipation and challenge.

Unlike the brothers he meets, he has lived so deeply because he has been able to face life without illusions. Living in an admittedly absurd world where 'it's impossible to know what is important,' he is convinced that one's existence is ultimately dependent upon the individual point of view, and his is rooted in a wry sense of humor and an unflinching belief in his dignity as a human being. His complicated and often hilarious bargaining process with Victor is not superfluous comic relief; it is a manifestation of the 'mental world' Solomon has fashioned for himself, the tradition to which he clings, the conviction that things have to be done in certain ways if they are to have any meaning and joy. For Solomon, as for his forebearers, life must be ritualized to make sense, and he goes about doing so with solemnity, gusto, and a few perfectly placed—and quite mischievous—winks.

Although he provides a great deal of rich humor, he is much more than simply a comic foil to the other characters. A multidimensional figure in his own right, he is also integral to the relationships and meaning of the play.

When Esther confesses to him that she still longs for the miraculous moment when 'some crazy kind of forgiveness will come and lift up everyone,' Solomon counters her hope for absolution with a poignant truth.

'I had a daughter, should rest in peace,' he replies softly, 'she took her own life. That's nearly fifty years. And every night I lay down to sleep, she's sitting there. I see her clear like I see you. But if it was a miracle and she came to life, what would I say to her?'[23]

Like Victor and Walter and Esther, he too has paid his prices for survival. The suicide of his young daughter haunts him with its implications of the failure of love and communication. But he has refused to weave his sorrow into a mourning shroud of guilt and self-recrimination. Nor has he attempted to avert reality by rationalizations or illusions. He too has invented himself, but according to the facts; not to wipe out what he knows, but to build upon it.

'Let me give you a piece of advice,' Solomon proposes to Victor early in the play. 'It's not that you can't believe nothing, that's not so hard—it's that you got to believe it. *That's* hard. And if you can't do that, my friend—you're a dead man!'[24]

The juxtaposition of belief and disbelief which marks so many of Miller's works is central to *The Price*. Solomon's comment is pertinent to both Walter and Victor, but the embodment of his advice is the old furniture dealer himself. According to Walter's logic, Solomon has little reason for existence, much less for undertaking the mammoth job of disposing of the Franz household. However Solomon is not about to treat his life logically. Admitting the implausibility of the task for a man his age, he nevertheless accepts it with a child's delight. And in the acceptance is his victory.

At the conclusion, after Walter has walked out of the room and out of his brother's life, Solomon and Victor close the sale. The transaction is much more than a straight financial arrangement.

[23] *Ibid.*, p.114.
[24] *Ibid.*, p.37.

For Solomon it signals a renewed hope, another lease of a life that he refuses to consign to a dusty attic. For Victor it is an act of trust that is and always was wholly consistent with his character.

Like his venerable companion, Victor could not live without belief, but unlike Solomon he needed external guarantees to validate his faith. Committing himself to his father, he then could not face the possibility that on the evidence of the facts his commitment was an absurdity—an act of faith where no faith had previously existed, a gesture of love where love had been a lie, a proof of solidarity where solidarity had been based upon a solvent bank account. When Walter saw these truths about his family he used his perception as a justification for flight. But Victor could not walk away. So he created something to believe in which would validate his staying. He fashioned the comforting myth that he was *restoring* certain values that had previously existed, when in reality he was *pledging* them in the face of their absence.

With the myth finally exploded by his brother, Victor achieves a new awareness, and is able to touch the core of his life. He receives Solomon's payment for the furniture, thus concluding the arrangement they had made before Walter's arrival. But now Victor's eyes are open. He is acting without illusions, free of the dream of martyrdom. And behind these actions is the comprehension that for all the subliminal motivations and invented rationalizations, he committed himself to his father, not *for* the old man's love, but *out of* his love for the old man.

'I just didn't want him to end up on the grass.'

Victor could no more walk away from his father, although there was no logical reason for remaining with him, than he can renege on his agreement with Solomon, even though sound monetary logic would dictate otherwise.

Victor has paid the prices for his illogicality. But Walter has paid for his logic as well. Victor's final truth is that the prices have all been met. For all his perception, Walter still cannot wholly accept this irrevocable fact.

Structurally, *The Price* is a tightly wound, electrically charged time bomb that begins to crackle the moment the curtain rises and detonates in a series of perfectly gauged explosions.

However, its precision is also its weakness. The play is too neat, too transparently artifact. Conversations dovetail into each other with computerized perfection; the question-response, accusation-defense dialogue between the two brothers is more the consequence of carefully calculated writing than of a realistic interplay of agonized souls; and the almost total recall of the two men is a heavy burden on an audience's credibility. And when the precision falters, the mechanical quality of *The Price*'s structure is even more obvious. For example, the sudden exhaustion which banishes the furniture dealer to another room while Walter and Victor indulge in their lacerating debate is a blatant maneuver on the part of the playwright. For all the genuine dramatic flame that is struck, the viewer is too often aware that the dramatist is manipulating an effective but flashy lighter.

Light and heat also mark the play's dialogue. At its best it illuminates and penetrates with searing force. At its worst its co-agulates into abstractions. When a character wonders 'what's it all about,' and another compares life to a masquerade, we are not singed by the blaze of truth, but merely oppressed by the tepid and musty ashes of rhetoric.

The conclusion of *The Price* was seen by many reviewers as yet another weakness. The apparent lack of a firm resolution was viewed as an unfortunate kind of flaccidity at best and a rather craven evasiveness at worst. As one critic summarized it, the effect was 'rather as though we'd followed a good detective story for 19 chapters only to discover that someone had torn out the 20th and last.'

With this view I firmly disagree. Granted, a missing final chapter in an Agatha Christie mystery would be unpardonable. But *The Price* is not a detective story, and it does not move toward any glib solutions. For all the revelations afforded them in their exhausting confrontation, Victor and Walter are powerless to change. Their lives have been molded by almost three decades of experience, and no conversation, however revelatory, can break or even per-ceptibly bend these molds.

The play moves toward comprehension, but comprehension is not synonymous with change. After Walter's departure, Victor and Esther turn toward each other, preparing to continue their life as best they can. Their action no more manifests defeat than it does victory. It is an acceptance with its implications of both: the defeat of bright dreams, and the victory over the deceptive illusions of innocence. They are neither condemned nor redeemed, only a little wiser, and concomitantly somewhat sadder. This is the resolution of *The Price*, the only resolution the drama can honestly arrive at.

Although it is a flawed play, *The Price* is still a powerful and provocative one. Despite the contrivance of its situation and the ponderousness of portions of its dialogue, its outstanding strength lies in its humanity, in its deeply sympathetic yet unsentimental depiction of genuine human beings caught in the ordinary but painful attempt to explain and justify their reasons for existence. It is a play of the heart and for the heart, and although it advocates very few truths, it unmistakably and hauntingly has caught many.

20

'Only connect'

In 1951 Arthur Miller wrote a short story entitled 'Monte Sant' Angelo.' It tells of two young Americans, Appello and Bernstein, who, on vacation in Italy, are looking for members, living and dead, of Appello's family. Unmoved by his friend's sentimental journey, Bernstein tags along reluctantly as Appello locates relatives and traces his lineage from town to town. The more Appello warms to his task and becomes familiar in his new surroundings, the more isolated and resentful Bernstein feels. Then one day while they are lunching at a small restaurant near a church whose vaults they have been searching for tombs of the Appello family, a curious incident befalls them.

As they eat, Bernstein finds himself drawn to a robust, middle-aged Italian peasant with whom they have exchanged casual greetings. The longer he watches the stranger, the surer he becomes that there is some kind of affinity between them. Finally the Italian completes his meal and prepares to leave. Scrutinizing the manner in which he places a freshly baked loaf of bread into his bundle and carefully ties it, Bernstein suddenly smiles his recognition. For the first time in days his eyes gleam animatedly, and he turns to Appello.

'He's Jewish, Vinny,' he exclaims.

When his friend asks him how he knows, Bernstein replies: 'The way he works that bundle. It's exactly the way my father used to tie a bundle. And my grandfather. The whole history is packing bundles and getting away. Nobody else can be as tender and delicate with bundles. That's a Jewish man tying a bundle.'[1]

---

[1] Arthur Miller, 'Monte Sant' Angelo,' *I Don't Need You Anymore* (New York: Viking, 1967), p.65.

When they question him, the peasant expresses bewilderment as to what a Jew even is.

'Are they Catholics?' he asks hopelessly.

Nevertheless, his name—which is a derivative of Moses—and his insistence on returning home before sunset on Friday because it is a custom in his family, convince the two Americans that although he does not know it, he is of Jewish stock.

After the man departs, Bernstein is strangely excited, and he urges Appello to continue his search for the tombs. Later in the day the friends find them and, standing before the evidence of his companion's heritage and continuity, Bernstein feels an overpowering joy.

'I feel like . . . at home in this place,' he affirms.

He did not move, seeking the root of an ecstasy he had not dreamed was part of his nature; he saw the amiable man trudging down the mountains, across the plains, on routes marked out for him by generations of men, a nameless traveler carrying home a warm bread on Friday night—and kneeling in church on Sunday. There was an irony in it he could not name. And yet pride was running through him. Of what he should be proud he had no clear idea; perhaps it was only that beneath the brainless crush of history a Jew had secretly survived, shorn of his consciousness, but forever caught by that final impudence of a Saturday Sabbath in a Catholic country; so that his very unawareness was proof, a proof as mute as stones, that a past lived. A past for me, Bernstein thought, astounded by its importance for him, when in fact he had never had a religion or even, he realized now, a history.[2]

In no other work is Miller's intrinsic Jewishness more clearly delineated than in 'Monte Sant' Angelo.' In the character of the surviving Jew who has lost all but a vestigial instinct of his heritage, Miller quietly but firmly expounds his faith in his cultural and moral tradition. And in Bernstein, the disconnected Jew who regains his sense of belonging, the writer delineates not only the Jewishness at the core of the story, but the outlook emanating from it that is integral to the body of his work.

Like 'Monte Sant' Angelo,' all of Miller's writing is invisibly prefaced by the words E. M. Forster inscribed in his novel, *Howards End.*

[2] *Ibid.,* p.69.

'Only Connect'

It is precisely this lack of connection, followed by the realization of its importance, and the ultimate commitment to its achievement, which forms the underlying thematic pattern of Miller's plays. For the playwright, vital human connection is the most difficult task an individual can set for himself, and yet no achievement is more indispensable if he is ever to assume what the dramatist has termed 'his rightful place in the world.'

However, 'rightful place' is rarely restricted to a niche in society. Miller is definitely a social dramatist, but in the broadest and deepest sense of the term. Although it is profoundly shaped by the experience of the Depression, Miller's drama is seldom a polemic in behalf of the common man against an economic superstructure. Rather, it cuts beneath particular systems to exhibit a concern with human destiny that may embrace but is certainly not defined by either politics or economics.

For Miller, drama asks 'how . . . we [are] to live . . . and that question is in . . . its best and most humane sense, not merely a private query.'[3] Against the inverted romanticism and circumscribed egocentricity of much of the modern theater, Miller propounds a drama that for all of its concern with the inner life, which is substantial, addresses itself to 'the world beyond the skin.' This is not a call for thesis drama, but a search for a balance between the social and the psychological, the outer and inner concerns of man.

'I am not calling for ideology,' the playwright wrote a few years ago. 'I am simply asking for a theater in which an adult who wants to live can find plays that will heighten his awareness of what living in our time involves.'[4]

> Society is inside of man and man is inside of society, and you cannot even create a truthfully drawn psychologically entity on the stage until you understand his social relations and their power to make him what he is and prevent him from being what he is not. The fish is in the water, and the water is in the fish.[5]

[3] Miller, 'On Social Plays,' *A View from the Bridge*, p.7.

[4] Miller, 'The State of the Theater,' *Harper's Magazine*, 221 (November, 1960). p.66.

[5] Miller, 'The Shadow of the Gods,' *Harper's Magazine*, 217 (August, 1958), p.39.

This intense commitment to moving beyond the closed ego is linked to an equally firm belief in man's ability to exercise responsibility. Miller does not deny the absurdity and existential loneliness of the human condition. *The Misfits, After the Fall, Incident at Vichy,* and *The Price* are cogent and painful testaments to its anguish. What he does challenge is the implication that the power of choice is negated by this anguish. For Miller, the exercise of will is always prevalent to some extent, and with it the concomitant possibility of tragic affirmation.

In an interesting and pertinent essay, William I. Oliver made the following comment about modern absurdist writers:

> Generally, absurdist writers . . . fail to give us a picture of man living beyond his confrontation with the abyss of ignorance and impotence. . . . Most of the absurdist writers limit their plays to dramatic definitions of absurdity or to depicting the plight of the immediate or naïve man who entertains illusions of power and definition without knowing that he is absurd. Having written one or two such plays, an author should at least begin to prepare himself to write about *the engaged man who has sought to live actively in the knowledge of his own absurdity.* Failing to develop in this direction casts the playwright in the unsavory role of a gloating harpy that delights in the misery of others—for notice that the absurdist playwright is already engaged in the game of value by the very fact of his playwriting. This strain of sentimentality and sadism is evident in the absurdists' fondness for images of man's impotent degradation.[6]

Although Miller's plays increasingly dramatize the absurdist element in human experience, he is never content with simply defining absurdity or chronicling its manifestations. Miller can recognize despair, but he cannot embrace it into a cult. For him the drama must move further and reach higher; it must explore the possibilities of the 'engaged man who has sought to live actively in the knowledge of his own absurdity.'

In 1944, the idealistic young writer concluded his disillusioning

[6] William I. Oliver, 'Between Absurdity and the Playwright,' *Modern Drama: Essays in Criticism,* eds. Travis Bogard and William I. Oliver (New York: Oxford University Press, 1965), p.13. Italics my own.

experiences in the army training camps with an adamant refusal to accept absurdity as an absolute. Referring in *Situation Normal* to the projected film for which he was compiling material, he flatly stated that it would have shown the meaning of the war.

'It must show something sane coming out of this horror,' he wrote. 'It must have a theme. . . . Something sane must come out of the story . . . something besides horror must be proved or only horror will remain.'[7]

Two decades later, in *Incident at Vichy*, Miller created a character who replied to this determination.

'This is why one gets so furious,' Leduc explains to Von Berg. 'Because all this suffering is so pointless—it can never be a lesson, it can never have a meaning. And that is why it will be repeated again and again forever. . . . It is total, absolute, waste.'[8]

But Leduc's paralyzing pessimism is countered by Von Berg's action. Like Proctor's movement toward those whose names he cannot sully, Quentin's tentative steps toward Holga, and Victor Franz's commitment to Gregory Solomon, the prince's gesture toward Leduc is a reaffirmation of a young writer's belief in and quest for meaning. Over the years the search has been stripped of much of its original naïveté and wonder; but although it has been tempered in doubt and despair, it has never been wholly submerged in nihilism.

'It's not that you can't believe nothing, that's not so hard—it's that you still got to believe it. *That's* hard. And if you can't do that, my friend—you're a dead man!'

Solomon's exhortation to Victor in *The Price* clearly exhibits Miller's insistence on meaning and the role of the individual in attaining it. In all his works, despite crushing obstacles, something is achieved, the possibility of responsibility and action is restored. Dignity is reaffirmed.

And because this possibility permeates his work, Arthur Miller is one of the most rebellious writers in the modern drama. His continuing exploration of the ramifications of determinism and free will, guilt and responsibility, drift and action, represents his revolt against a theater singing dirges of woe. Miller rebels against the fashionable complacency and chic lamentation that dominate so

---

[7] Miller, *Situation Normal*, p.175.

[8] Miller. *Incident at Vichy*, pp.61–62.

much of the contemporary stage, on, off, or below Broadway. His consideration of responsibility and free will is a challenge to the paralyzing morbidity of a drama which views man as trapped in a cosmic straitjacket, thrashing about in his pettiness and helplessness. His characters are not defined in terms of hysteria, but of history; they are not only affected by their world, they are able to affect it as well.

Miller does not invite his audience to luxuriate in a velvety cloak of universal despair and self-pity, nor does he subject us to sadomasochistic barrages under the shrill slogans of joy, freedom, and liberation. In a theater of angry young men, frustrated old men, and precocious adolescents of indeterminate age, Miller goes his own way, committed to a drama of communication, based on the reasonable assumption that the stage may still be the place for an aesthetic and civilizing act.

Because of his sense of purpose, Miller has been a target for adverse criticism. Reminding his audience, in his plays and in a virtual avalanche of essays about his work, of his intentions, he has made himself a prime mark for the slings and arrows of a number of critics. He has been chided for his strident moralizing and berated for his penchant for transforming the apparent into the appalling.

And often with good reason. The didacticism and polemicism inherent in his view of the theater and his role in it, occasionally turns his plays into tracts in which character and situation are plunged into a quagmire of verbiage.

However, the gulf between pamphleteering and playwriting is, most of the time, bridged by works that are stunning dramatic achievements. No Miller play is vapid, and his best ones strike an audience with triphammer force. Viewers shaken by *Death of a Salesman, The Crucible, A View from the Bridge, After the Fall, Incident at Vichy,* and *The Price* are jolted by the immediate emotional impact of something real, something vibrantly alive exploding at them with a burst of meaning and a ring of truth.

The impact is hardly accidental. Miller's plays are products of a meticulous craftsman with an unerring sense of the theater and the ability to create meaningful people in striking situations.

In an age of theatrical experimentation so feverish that it borders on malaria, Miller's drama has been considered by some reviewers as hopelessly passé in form and structure.

This kind of criticism is simply inaccurate. Although his work displays a continuity that makes a Miller play easily recognizable, his dramas are by no means carbon copies of each other, and if he shows no great penchant for indulging in structural hijinks, he nonetheless has experimented vitally and interestingly in all of his efforts.

The formalized, carefully hewed pattern of *All My Sons*, the semiexpressionistic form of *Death of a Salesman*, the austere structure and heightened dialogue of *The Crucible*, the blend of boisterous realism and elegiac lyricism of *A Memory of Two Mondays*, the breakneck pacing and engaged narrator of *A View from the Bridge*, the liquid mobility and complex interaction of *After the Fall*, the stark literalness of *Incident at Vichy*, and the compact, cumulative, expository power of *The Price* all attest to the playwright's desire and ability to make the form of his drama convey its meaning as graphically and forcefully as possible.

But the content is primary.

'There are two questions I ask myself over and over when I'm working,' Miller recently remarked. 'What do I mean? What am I trying to say?'

With each new play, as these questions are molded into dramatic life, the meaning and purpose of his craft continue to clarify themselves.

The production of a new play, I have often thought, is like another chance in life, a chance to emerge cleansed of one's imperfections. Here, as when one was very young, it seems possible again to attain even greatness, or happiness, or some otherwise unattainable joy.[9]

In his recollection of how Lee J. Cobb took on the character of Willy Loman during the rehearsals of *Death of a Salesman*, Miller eloquently described this somber and 'otherwise unattainable joy.'

For the first ten days of rehearsals Cobb merely sat on the stage 'like a great lump, a sick seal, a mourning walrus,' while the rest of the cast acclimated themselves to the play. As the days flew by, a gradual wave of uncertainty began to mount. Director Elia Kazan and the playwright anxiously watched their star, pretending not to be worried, but secretly wondering if their choice was to

[9] Miller, 'The American Theater,' *Holiday*, 17 (January, 1955), p.102.

prove disastrous. Then, one afternoon, in the musty rehearsal hall, Cobb simply rose from his chair, shuffled over to Mildred Dunnock, and began his opening lines.

'I'm tired to the death,' he sighed from deep within himself. 'I couldn't make it. I just couldn't make it, Linda.'

'And the theater vanished,' Miller exclaimed.

The stage vanished. The chill of an age-old recognition shuddered my spine; a voice was sounding in the dimly lit air up front, a created spirit, an incarnation, a Godlike creation was taking place; a new human being was being formed before all our eyes, born for the first time on this earth, made real by an act of will, by an artist's summoning up all his memories and his intelligence; a birth was taking place . . . a man was here transcending the limits of his body and his own history. . . . I knew then that something astounding was being made here. . . . There was a new fact of life, there was an alteration of history for all of us that afternoon.

There is a certain immortality involved in theater, not created by monuments and books, but through the knowledge the actor keeps to his dying day that on a certain afternoon in an empty and dusty theater, he cast a shadow of a being that was not himself but the distillation of all he had ever observed; all the unsingable heartsong the ordinary man may feel but never utter, he gave voice to. And by that he somehow joins the ages.[10]

Most significant in his recollection is Miller's stress on the combination of individual will and creative spirit. The playright's exultation at Cobb's 'transcending the limits of his body and his own history' to infuse with life the character Miller had already created on paper, is integrally linked to the joy the writer felt when he knew that once and forever he had captured the humanity of his character by his own act of will and the 'summoning up of all his memories and . . . intelligence.'

Nor is the feeling very different from the exultation of a John Proctor or a Count Von Berg, who in totally different spheres of human experience transcend the limits of their bodies and histories to declare themselves as men. It is ultimately the admiration and wonder of an individual at his renewed realizátion, in the full

[10] *Ibid.*, p.103.

awareness of emptiness and despair, that the possibility of affirmation is never wholly extinguished, that against the iron barriers of necessity and determinism, the paradox of will still exists, and that in both the particular and the general, 'we are,' in the playwright's words, 'made, and yet are more than what made us.'

Attention must be paid.

This is the demand behind every one of Miller's dramas. It is an exhortation that can and does occasionally become strident. But beneath its stridency, it illuminates the intense desire of one man to carry on a continuing and meaningful dialogue with other men, not as a writer ahead of his time or above his time, but profoundly of his time.

More often than not, the dialogue has been dramatically validated. Hopefully, it will continue to be.

SELECTED BIBLIOGRAPHY

Works by Arthur Miller

PLAYS (chronologically)

Honors at Dawn (unpublished), 1936. Typescript in the Hopwood Room, University of Michigan.

No Villain (unpublished), 1937. Typescript in the Hopwood Room, University of Michigan.

They Too Arise (unpublished revision of *No Villain*), 1938. Typescript in the Theater Collection, New York Public Library, Lincoln Center.

The Grass Still Grows (unpublished revision of *They Too Arise*), 1939. Typescript in the Academic Center Library, University of Texas.

Listen My Children (written with Norman Rosten, unpublished), 1939. Typescript in the Library of Congress.

The Half-Bridge (unpublished), 1943. Typescript in the Academic Center Library, University of Texas.

'That They May Win', (one-act). In Margaret Mayorga, ed. *The Best One-Act Plays of 1944*. New York: Dodd, Mead, 1945. Pp.45–60.

'The Man Who Had All the Luck'. In Edwin Seaver, ed., *Cross-Section: A Collection of New American Writing*. New York: Fischer, 1944. Pp.486–552.

All My Sons. New York: Reynal & Hitchcock, 1947.

Death of a Salesman. New York: Viking, 1949. London: Cresset Press, 1949.

An Enemy of the People (adaptation). New York: Viking, 1951.

The Crucible. New York: Viking, 1953. London: Cresset Press, 1956.

A View from the Bridge. All My Sons. Harmondsworth: Penguin, 1961.

A View from the Bridge (two one-act plays: 'A View from the Bridge' and 'A Memory of Two Mondays'). New York: Viking, 1955.

A View from the Bridge. London: Cresset Press, 1957.

A View from the Bridge (revised two-act play). New York: Viking, 1960.

After the Fall. New York: Viking, 1964. London: Secker & Warburg, 1965.

———. (Revised Final Stage Version). New York: Viking, 1964.

Incident at Vichy. New York: Viking, 1965. London: Secker & Warburg, 1966.

The Price. New York: Viking, 1968. London: Secker & Warburg, 1968.

RADIO SCRIPTS (chronologically)

'The Pussycat and the Expert Plumber Who Became a Man'. In William Kozlenko, ed., *One-Hundred Non-royalty Radio Plays*. New York: Greenberg, 1941. Pp.20–30.

'William Ireland's Confession'. In Kozlenko, *One-Hundred Non-royalty Radio Plays*. Pp.512–521.

'The Four Freedoms' (unpublished), 1942. Typescript in the Library of Congress.

'Grandpa and the Statue'. In Erik Barnouw, ed., *Radio Drama in Action*. New York: Farrar & Rinehart, 1945. Pp.267–281.

'The Story of Gus'. In Joseph Liss, ed., *Radio's Best Plays*. New York: Greenberg, 1947. Pp.303–320.

REPORTAGE

Situation Normal. New York: Reynal & Hitchcock, 1944.

PROSE FICTION (chronologically)

Focus. New York: Reynal & Hitchcock, 1945. London: Gollancz, 1949.

'It Takes a Thief'. *Collier's*, 119 (Feb. 8, 1947), 23, 75–76.

'Monte Saint Angelo'. *Harper's* 202 (March, 1951), 39–47.

The Hook (unpublished screenplay), 1951. Typescript in the Academic Center Library, University of Texas.

'The Misfits'. *Esquire*, 48 (Oct., 1957), 158–166.

'Bridge to a Savage World'. *Esquire*, 50 (Oct., 1958), 185–190.

'I Don't Need You Any More'. *Esquire*, 52 (Dec., 1959), 270–309.

'Please Don't Kill Anything'. *Noble Savage*, 1 (March, 1960), 126–131.

'The Prophecy'. *Esquire*, 56 (Dec., 1961), 140–141, 268–287.

The Misfits (cinematic novella). New York: Viking, 1961. London: Secker & Warburg, 1961.

'Glimpse at a Jockey'. *Noble Savage*, 5 (Oct., 1962), 138–240.

I Don't Need You Any More (collected short stories). New York: Viking, 1967. London: Secker & Warburg, 1967.

ESSAYS AND INTERVIEWS (chronologically)

'Subsidized Theater'. *The New York Times* (June 22, 1947), Sec. 2, p.1.

'Tragedy and the Common Man'. *The New York Times* (Feb. 27, 1949), Sec. 2, pp.1, 3.

'Arthur Miller on "The Nature of Tragedy"'. *The New York Herald Tribune* (March 27, 1949), Sec. 5, pp.1, 2.

'The "Salesman" Has a Birthday'. *The New York Times* (Feb. 5, 1950), Sec. 2, pp.1, 3.

Preface to the adaptation of Henrik Ibsen's *An Enemy of the People*. New York: Viking, 1951. Pp.7–12.

'Many Writers: Few Plays'. *The New York Times* (Aug. 10, 1952), Sec. 2, p.1.

'Journey to "The Crucible"'. *The New York Times* (Feb. 8, 1953), Sec. 2, p.3.

'Arthur Miller Discusses *The Crucible*'. Interview by John and Alice Griffen, *Theater Arts*, 37 (Oct., 1953), 33–34.

'University of Michigan'. *Holiday* 14 (Dec. 1953), 68–71, 128–132, 136–137, 140–143.

'A Modest Proposal for Pacification of the Public Temper'. *Nation* 179 (July 3, 1954), 5–8.

'The American Theater'. *Holiday*, 17 (Jan., 1955), 90–98, 101–102, 104.

'A Boy Grew in Brooklyn'. *Holiday* 17 (March, 1955), 54–55, 117, 119–120, 122–124.

'Picking a Cast'. *The New York Times* (Aug. 21, 1955), Sec. 2, p.1.

'On Social Plays'. Preface to original edition of *A View from the Bridge.* New York: Viking, 1955. Pp.1–18. Reprinted under title of 'A View of One-Actors', *The New York Times* (Sept. 25, 1955), Sec. 2, pp.1, 3.

'The Family in Modern Drama'. *Atlantic Monthly*, 197 (April, 1956), 35–41.

'Concerning the Boom'. *International Theatre Annual*, 1, ed., Harold Hobson. London: John Calder, 1956. Pp.85–88.

'The Playwright and the Atomic World'. *Colorado Quarterly*, 5, 1956), 117–137.

'The Writer in America'. *Mainstream*, 10 (July, 1957), 43–46.

Introduction to *Arthur Miller's Collected Plays*. New York: Viking, 1957. Pp.3–55.

'Brewed in "The Crucible"'. *The New York Times* (March 9, 1958), Sec. 2, p.3.

'The Shadows of the Gods'. *Harper's*, 217 (Aug., 1958), 35–43.

'My Wife Marilyn'. *Life*, 50 (Dec. 22, 1958), 146–147.

'Morality and Modern Drama'. Transcript of radio interview by Phillip Gelb, *Educational Theatre Journal*, 10 (1958), 190–202.

'A Conversation with Arthur Miller'. Interview by Kenneth Alsop, *Encounter* 13 (July, 1959), 58–60.

'The State of the Theatre: A Conversation with Arthur Miller'. Interview by Henry Brandon, *London Sunday Times* (March 20, 1960). Reprinted in *Harper's*, 221 (Nov., 1960), 63–69. Also reprinted in Henry Brandon, *As We Are*. New York: Doubleday, 1961.

'The Bored and the Violent'. *Harper's*, 225 (Nov., 1962), 50–56.

'A New Era in American Theatre?' *Drama Survey*, 3 (1963), 70–71.

'Lincoln Repertory Theater—Challenge and Hope'. *The New York Times* (Jan. 19, 1964), Sec, 2, pp.1, 3.

'Arthur Miller's Quest for Truth'. Interview by William Goyen, *The New York Herald Tribune* (Jan. 19, 1964), Magazine, p.35.

'With Respect for Her Agony—But with Love'. *Life* 56 (Feb. 7, 1964), 66.

'Question: "Am I My Brother's Keeper?"'. Interview by Barbara Gelb, *The New York Times* (Nov. 29, 1964), Sec. 2, pp.1, 3.

'Our Guilt for the World's Evil'. *The New York Times* (Jan. 3, 1965), Sec. 6, pp.10–11, 48.

'"After the Fall": An Author's View'. *New Haven Register* (April 25, 1965), Features, p.9.

'What Makes Plays Endure?' *The New York Times* (Aug. 15, 1965), Sec. 2, pp.1, 3.

'It Could Happen Here—And Did'. *The New York Times* (April 30, 1967), Sec. D, p.17.

'Arthur Miller Ponders "The Price"'. Interview by Joan Barthel, *The New York Times* (Jan. 28, 1968), Sec. 2, pp.1, 5.

Works about Arthur Miller

Adler, Henry. 'To Hell with Society'. *Tulane Drama Review*, 4 (May, 1960), 53–76.

Barksdale, Richard K. 'Social Background in the Plays of Miller and Williams'. *College Language Association Journal*, 6 (March, 1963), 161–169.

Bentley, Eric. *In Search of Theater*. New York: Knopf, 1953. London: Dobson, 1954.

———. *What is Theatre?* Boston: Beacon, 1956. London: Dobson, 1957.

Bettina, Sister M. 'Willy Loman's Brother Ben: Tragic Insight in *Death of a Salesman*'. *Modern Drama*, 4 (Feb., 1962), 409–412.

Bierman, Judah; Hart, James; and Johnson, Stanley, eds. *The Dramatic Experience*. Englewood Cliffs, N.J.: Prentice-Hall, 1958. Folkestone: Bailey and Swinfen, 1958.

Brien, Alan. 'There Was a Jolly Miller'. *The Spectator*, 6789 (Aug. 8, 1958), 191–192.

Broussard, Louis. *American Drama: Contemporary Allegory from Eugene O'Neill to Tennessee Williams*. Norman, Oklahoma: University of Oklahoma Press, 1962.

Brustein, Robert. 'Arthur Miller's Mea Culpa'. *New Republic*, 150 (Feb. 8, 1964), 26–30.

———. 'Why American Plays Are Not Literature'. *Harper's*, 219 (Oct., 1959), 167–172.

Caputi, Anthony. 'The Shallows of Modern Serious Drama'. *Modern Drama*, 4 (Sept., 1961), 111–116.

Clark, Eleanor. 'Death of a Salesman'. *Partisan Review*, 16 (June, 1949), 631–635.

Clurman, Harold. 'Director's Notes: *Incident at Vichy*'. *Tulane Drama Review*, 9 (Summer, 1965), 77–90.

———. *Lies Like Truth*. New York: Grove, 1958. London: Macmillan, 1958.

Dillingham, William B. 'Arthur Miller and the Loss of Conscience'. *Emory University Quarterly*, 16 (Spring, 1960), 40–50.

Downer, Alan S. 'Mr Williams and Mr Miller'. *Furioso*, 4 (Summer, 1949), 66–70.

———. *Recent American Drama* (pamphlet). Minneapolis: University of Minnesota Press, 1961.

Driver, Tom Faw. 'Strength and Weakness in Arthur Miller'. *Tulane Drama Review*, 4 (May, 1960), 45–52.

Dusenbury, Winifred L. *The Theme of Loneliness in Modern American Drama.* Gainesville, Florida: University of Florida Press, 1960.

Eissenstat, Martha Turnquist. 'Arthur Miller: A Bibliography'. *Modern Drama*, 5 (May, 1962), 93–106.

Findlater, Richard. 'No Time for Tragedy?' *Twentieth Century*, 161 (Jan., 1957), 56–66.

Flaxman, Seymour L. 'The Debt of Williams and Miller to Ibsen and Strindberg'. *Comparative Literature Studies* (Special Advance Issue), (1963), 51–59.

Fruchter, Norm. 'On the Frontier'. *Encore,* 9 (Jan., 1962), 17–27.

Fuller, A. Howard. 'A Salesman Is Everybody'. *Fortune*, 39 (May, 1949), 79–80.

Ganz, Arthur. 'The Silence of Arthur Miller'. *Drama Survey*, 3 (1963), 224–237.

———. 'Arthur Miller: After the Silence'. *Drama Survey*, 3 (1964), 520–530.

Gassner, John. *Form and Idea in Modern Theatre.* New York: Dryden, 1956. *Directions in Modern Theatre and Drama* (revised edition). London: Holt, Rinehart and Winston, 1965.

———. *Theatre at the Crossroads.* New York and London: Holt, Rinehart and Winston, 1960.

———. *The Theatre in Our Times.* New York: Crown, 1954.

Goode, James. *The Story of 'The Misfits'.* Indianapolis: Bobbs-Merrill, 1963.

Hanscom, Leslie. ' "After the Fall": Arthur Miller's Return'. *Newsweek,* 63 (Feb. 3, 1964), 49–52.

Hogan, Robert. *Arthur Miller* (pamphlet). Minneapolis: University of Minnesota Press, 1964.

Huftel, Sheila. *Arthur Miller: The Burning Glass.* New York: Citadel, 1965. London: W. H. Allen, 1965.

Hurrell, John D., ed. *Two Modern American Tragedies: Reviews and Criticism of 'Death of a Salesman' and 'A Streetcar Named Desire'* New York: Scribner's, 1961.

Hynes, Joseph A. 'Arthur Miller and the Impasse of Naturalism'. *South Atlantic Quarterly*, 62 (1963), 327–334.

———. ' "Attention Must Be Paid . . ." ' *College Engish*, 23 (April, 1962), 574–578.

Jackson, Esther M. '*Death of a Salesman*: Tragic Myth in the Modern Theatre'. *College Language Association Journal*, 7 (Sept., 1963), 63–76.

Kalven, Harry, Jr. 'A View from the Law'. *New Republic*, 136 (May 27, 1957), 8–13.

Kernodle, George R. 'The Death of the Little Man'. *Tulane Drama Review,* 1 (Jan., 1956), 47–60.

Krutch, Joseph Wood. '*Modernism*' in Modern Drama. Ithaca, New York: Cornell University Press, 1953.

———. *The American Drama Since 1918.* New York: Braziller, 1957.

Leaska, Mitchell A. *The Voice of Tragedy.* New York: Speller, 1963.

Lewis, Allan. *The Contemporary Theatre.* New York: Crown, 1962.

Lewis, Allan. *American Plays and Playwrights of the Contemporary Theatre*. Folkestone: Bailey and Swinfen, 1965.

Lumley, Frederick. *Trends in 20th Century Drama*. New York: Oxford University Press, 1960. London: Barrie & Rockcliff, 1960.

McCarthy, Mary. 'Naming Names: The Arthur Miller Case'. *Encounter*, 8 (May, 1957), 23–25.

――――. ' "Realism" in the American Theatre'. *Harper's*, 223 (July, 1961), 45–52.

――――. *Sights and Spectacles*. New York: Farrar, Straus, & Cudahy, 1956. London: Heinemann, 1959.

McCollom, William. *Tragedy*. New York and London: Macmillan, 1957.

Moss, Leonard. *Arthur Miller*. New York: Twayne, 1967.

Muller, Herbert J. *The Spirit of Tragedy*. New York: Knopf, 1956.

Nannes, Caspar H. *Politics in the American Drama*. Washington, D.C.: Catholic University of America Press, 1960.

Nathan, George Jean. *The Theatre in the Fifties*. New York: Knopf, 1953.

O'Connor, Frank. 'The Most American Playwright'. *Holiday*, 19 (Feb., 1956), 65, 68–70.

Popkin, Henry. 'Arthur Miller Out West'. *Commentary*, 31 (May, 1961), 433–436.

――――. 'Arthur Miller: The Strange Encounter'. *Sewanee Review*, 68 (Winter, 1960), 34–60.

――――. 'Arthur Miller's "The Crucible" '. *College English*, 26 (Nov., 1964), 139–146.

Prudhoe, John. 'Arthur Miller and the Tradition of Tragedy'. *English Studies*, 43 (Oct., 1962), 430–439.

Roberts, James L. '*Death of a Salesman*' Notes. Lincoln, Nebraska: Cliff's Notes, 1964.

Ross, George. ' "Death of a Salesman" in the Original'. *Commentary*, 11 (Feb., 1951), 184–186.

Rothe, Anna, ed. *Current Biography*. New York: Wilson, 1947. Pp.438–440.

Rovere, Richard H. 'Arthur Miller's Conscience'. *New Republic*, 136 (June 17, 1957), 13–15.

Schneider, Daniel E. 'Play of Dreams'. *Theatre Arts*, 33 (Oct., 1949), 18–21.

Seager, Allan. 'The Creative Agony of Arthur Miller'. *Esquire*, 52 (Oct., 1959), 123–126.

Siegel, Paul N. 'Willy Loman and King Lear'. *College English*, 17 (March, 1956), 341–345.

Sievers, W. David. *Freud on Broadway: A History of Psychoanalysis and the Modern Drama*. New York: Hermitage, 1955.

Steinbeck, John. 'The Trial of Arthur Miller'. *Esquire*, 47 (June, 1957), 86.

Steinberg, M. W. 'Arthur Miller and the Idea of Modern Tragedy'. *Dalhousie Review*, 40 (Autumn, 1960), 329–340.

Sylvester, Robert. 'Brooklyn Boy Makes Good'. *Saturday Evening Post*, 222 (July, 16, 1949). 26–27, 97–100.

Thompson, Alan. 'Professor's Debauch'. *Theatre Arts*, 35 (March, 1951), 25–27.

Tynan, Kenneth. *Curtains.* New York: Atheneum, 1961. London: Long-mans, 1961.

Warshow, Robert. 'The Liberal Conscience in "The Crucible" '. *Commentary*, 15 (March, 1953), 265–271.

Weales, Gerald. 'Arthur Miller: Man and His Image'. *Tulane Drama Review*, 7 (Sept., 1962), 165–180. Reprinted in Weales, *American Drama Since World War II.* New York: Harcourt, 1962.

————. 'Plays and Analysis'. *The Commonweal*, 66 (July 12, 1957), 382–383.

Welland, Dennis. *Arthur Miller.* New York: Grove, 1961. Edinburgh: Oliver & Boyd, 1961.

Wiegand, William. 'Arthur Miller and the Man Who Knows'. *The Western Review*, 21 (Winter, 1957), 85–103.

Williams, Raymond. *Modern Tragedy.* Stanford, Calif.: Stanford University Press, 1966. London: Chatto & Windus, 1966.

————. 'The Realism of Arthur Miller'. *Critical Quarterly*, 1 (Summer, 1959), 140–149.

Worsley, T. C. 'American Tragedy'. *New Statesman*, 56 (Aug. 23, 1958), 220.

Yorks, Samuel A. 'Joe Keller and His Sons'. *Western Humanities Review*, 13 (Autumn, 1959), 401–407.

Zolotow, Maurice. *Marilyn Monroe.* New York: Bantam, 1961. London: W. H. Allen, 1961.

INDEX